The MILITANT SUFFRAGE MOVEMENT

The MILITANT SUFFRAGE MOVEMENT

Citizenship and Resistance in Britain, 1860–1930

Laura E. Nym Mayhall

OXFORD

UNIVERSITY PRESS

2003

OXFORD
UNIVERSITY PRESS

Oxford   New York
Auckland   Bangkok   Buenos Aires   Cape Town   Chennai
Dar es Salaam   Delhi   Hong Kong   Istanbul   Karachi   Kolkata
Kuala Lumpur   Madrid   Melbourne   Mexico City   Mumbai   Nairobi
São Paulo   Shanghai   Taipei   Tokyo   Toronto

Copyright © 2003 by Oxford University Press, Inc.

Published by Oxford University Press, Inc.
198 Madison Avenue, New York, New York, 10016

www.oup.com

Oxford is a registered trademark of Oxford University Press

Library of Congress Cataloging-in-Publication Data
Mayhall, Laura E. Nym, 1963–
The militant suffrage movement : citizenship and resistance in Britain,
1860–1930 / Laura E. Nym Mayhall.
p. cm.
Includes bibliographical references and index.
ISBN 0-19-515993-4
1. Women—Suffrage—Great Britain—History.   2. Women's rights—
Great Britain—History.   3. Great Britain—Politics and government—1837–1901.
4. Great Britain—Politics and government—1901–1936.   5. Great Britain—History
—Victoria, 1837–1901.   6. Great Britain—History—Edward VII, 1901–1910.   7. Great Britain—
History—George V, 1910–1936.   8. South African War, 1899–1902.   9. Transvaal (South Africa)—
History—War of 1880–1881.   I. Title.
JN979.M395 2003
324.6'2'0941—dc21   2002192670

9   8   7   6   5   4   3   2   1

Printed in the United States of America
on acid-free paper

For Michael and Isabel

Acknowledgments

ecause this project is in part about the process of commemoration, I approach these acknowledgments with the fear that I cannot possibly do justice to the many individuals who have contributed so generously to whatever clarity and force the present argument may possess. From its inception in my research and writing as a graduate student (and earlier), the work presented here has grown substantially in scope and ambition. In the process, I have accumulated many scholarly and personal debts.

At Stanford University, Jim Knox provided invaluable assistance in locating materials, sometimes from a great distance. Paul Seaver and Estelle Freedman, members of my dissertation committee, read and commented on every chapter of the project that led to this one and more than once set me back on course. For her intellectual nurture, encouragement, and friendship, I especially thank Susan Groag Bell. My particular gratitude is reserved for Peter Stansky, humanist and mentor, without whose solicitude and encouragements the present work would not have been possible.

Funding for revision has come from a number of sources. My thanks to Catholic University's Faculty Grant-in-Aid Committee and Dean L. R. Poos for financial assistance with photo permissions; the National Endowment for the Humanities, for the means with which to work in the Charlotte Despard papers at the Public Record Office of Northern Ireland; and to the Obert C. and Grace A. Tanner Humanities Center, University of Utah, for the pivotal year spent reading and rethinking this project. I must thank especially the late Lowell Durham, whose warmth and hospitality made Salt Lake City feel like home.

Parts of this book have been presented in seminars at the George Washington University, Princeton University, and Catholic University and at meetings of the North American Conference on British Studies and the American Historical Association. I thank Dane Kennedy, Frank Trentmann, and my colleagues at Catholic University and in the NACBS and AHA for those opportunities, so helpful to me in revising my work.

Research for this book has drawn upon the resources of a number of libraries and archives. For this, I would like to thank David Doughan and Susan Cross, both formerly of the Fawcett Library (now the Women's Library); Sheridan Harvey, Pablo Calvan, and Dave Kelly, of the Library of Congress; the librarians and staff of the British Library; the Public Record Office at Kew (London); the Public Record Office of Northern Ireland (Belfast); Cambridge University Library; the BBC Written Archives at Caversham; and the circulation and interlibrary loan departments of Marriott Library at the University of Utah and Mullen Library at the Catholic University of America. Daniela Rizzi and Beverley Cook at the Museum of London were most helpful as we worked together to find illustrations for this book, as were Catherine Flood and Mark Vivian at the Mary Evans Picture Library. I thank them for all their help.

A number of scholars have contributed to this work by reading and commenting on it in progress, and I hope that I have thanked them all. For their help over the years, I thank Deborah Cohen, Alice Conklin, Susan R. Grayzel, Nicoletta Gullace, Carol Harrison, Susan Kingsley Kent, Jim Lehning, Philippa Levine, Robyn Muncy, Maura O'Connor, Pamela Walker, Chris Waters, and Angela Woollacott. For taking on the herculean task of reading and commenting on the entire manuscript, my deepest thanks go to Martha Sledge, Ian Christopher Fletcher, Michael Dunn, Colleen Hobbs, and the two anonymous readers for the press. My editor, Susan Ferber, has exceeded all expectations in her attention to this project.

The personal debts I must acknowledge are many. One of the most pleasurable aspects of this project has been getting to know the family of former suffragette Eunice Murray Guthrie. Patricia Cowan and Frances Murray have most graciously provided invaluable assistance and hospitality over the years, and for that I thank them. The late Leah Leneman was a model of collegial support, and I am not alone in feeling a great absence after her death. My teachers, both in public high school in El Paso, Texas, and in the history and English departments of the University of Texas at Austin, cannot possibly know how much they influenced this book and its author. My thanks to Herbert Warren, Janet Musgrave, and Jane Marcus. Special thanks to Brian Levack and Standish Meacham, whose undergraduate lectures on British history sparked my keen interest in subject, and whose subsequent support made possible my career in the field. For personal and intellectual sustenance through adversity, I thank Padma Anagol, Patrick McGinn, Marguerite Mayhall, Bryan Murdock, Richard Wetzell, Larry Joseph, Michael Saler, and Antoinette Burton. I also thank my parents, Wilma Walley Mayhall and R. F. Mayhall, and my mother-in-law, Carolyn Dunn, whose love and support have taken many forms throughout the years. Finally, to Michael and Isabel, the former who knew me well before this project, and the latter who has only known this project, my love and gratitude.

For permission to quote from archival materials, I thank Richard Pankhurst for permission to quote from E. Sylvia Pankhurst's papers; Patricia Cowan for permission to quote from Eunice Guthrie Murray's unpublished journals; the Suffragette Fellowship Archive at the Museum of London for permission to quote from materials in that collection; the Women's Library, London, for permission to quote from the Josephine Butler Autograph Letter Collection, the Teresa Billington Greig Collection, and the Fawcett Autograph Collection.

Parts of this book have been published previously. Chapter 2 draws upon portions of "The South African War and the Origins of Suffrage Militancy in Britain, 1899–1902," in *Women's Suffrage in the British Empire: Citizenship, Nation, and Race,* ed. Ian Christopher Fletcher, Laura E. Nym Mayhall, and Philippa Levine (London: Routledge Research, 2000), 3–17. Chapter 3 draws upon "Defining Militancy: Radical Protest, the Constitutional Idiom, and Women's Suffrage in Britain, 1908–1909," *Journal of British Studies* 39, no. 3, pp. 340–71 (©2000 by the North American Conference on British Studies. All rights reserved).

Contents

Abbreviations

ELFS	East London Federation of Suffragettes
ILP	Independent Labour Party
IWSPU	Independent Women's Social and Political Union
NSWS	National Society for Women's Suffrage
NUWSS	National Union of Women's Suffrage Societies
SDF	Social Democratic Federation
SWSPU	Suffragettes of the Women's Social and Political Union
UDC	Union for Democratic Control
US	United Suffragists
WCG	Women's Cooperative Guild
WEU	Women's Emancipation Union
WFL	Women's Freedom League
WFLNSO	Women's Freedom League National Service Organization
WPV	Women's Police Volunteers
WSNAC	Women's Suffrage National Aid Corps
WSPU	Women's Social and Political Union

The MILITANT SUFFRAGE MOVEMENT

Introduction

Rethinking Suffrage

On 25 June 1909, Marion Wallace Dunlop, member of the British militant suffrage organization, the Women's Social and Political Union (WSPU), stenciled the following words from the Bill of Rights (1689) on a wall in the outer precincts of the House of Commons: "It is the right of the subject to petition the King, and all commitments and prosecutions for such petitioning are illegal."[1] Wallace Dunlop was arrested and incarcerated, whereupon she refused to eat in protest against the court's adjudication of her actions as having criminal rather than political motivations. Her hunger strike, in fact, is the reason Wallace Dunlop remains one of the most well-known suffrage activists of the Edwardian period. Like Emily Wilding Davison, who died after hurling herself at the king's horse at the Derby in 1913 in protest against the government's treatment of suffragettes in prison, Wallace Dunlop, the "first hunger striker," emerges in histories of the militant suffrage movement as an exemplar of some British women's willingness to sacrifice their bodies for the achievement of political rights.

Suppose, however, that Wallace Dunlop's act itself—the stenciling of a portion of the Bill of Rights on a wall within the environs of Parliament—becomes the object of scrutiny, rather than her hunger strike once she was imprisoned. The original act and its central claim—that the subject has the right to petition the king for alleviation of grievances—says much about militancy in the campaign for women's suffrage in Britain. Wallace Dunlop's deed connects the Edwardian suffrage movement to a long tradition of radical protest and highlights suffragettes' use of the constitutional idiom, which they deployed to great effect while asserting their rights as citizens and resisting the government they had played no role in choosing (see figure I.1).

This book seeks to shed light on the rationale at the heart of Marion Wallace Dunlop's protest by exploring suffrage militancy as a political idea and a range of practices. It arises out of two parallel historiographies of the late-Victorian and Edwardian periods—British political culture and the women's

FIGURE I.1
WSPU member Marion Wallace Dunlop, June 1909, looking at stenciled words
from the Bill of Rights (1689). Museum of London.

suffrage movement. The Edwardian campaign for women's suffrage is frequently cast as part of the "crisis of the British state," in a very limited sense,
through discussion of some suffragists' use of militancy to press their claim.
Yet the Edwardian campaign should be seen as the culmination of a much
greater process culminating in the first years of the twentieth century whereby individuals negotiated with the state to redefine citizenship. For suffragists, Irish and Indian nationalists, and workers, repeated and unsuccessful
attempts to achieve inclusion in the political nation resulted in dramatic
changes in how they approached the state; between 1865 and 1910, all of
these groups moved at varying points from dialogue to confrontation. The
organized campaign for women's parliamentary enfranchisement moved in
these years from a liberal legislative battle into one that challenged the legislature, judiciary, press, public opinion, and government.

Any examination of suffrage militancy in Britain has to start in the nineteenth century, since much of what was argued then prepared the way rhetorically for the emergence of the twentieth-century campaign.[2] Militancy
had been staked out rhetorically as early as the 1880s.[3] Twentieth-century
suffragists knew of, read about, or had been involved in nineteenth-century
struggles for political rights. Political contingencies of the Edwardian campaign made possible the utilization of certain strategies that had not been vi-

able earlier, although they had been discussed. Nevertheless, the twentieth-century women's suffrage movement was perceived by contemporaries as different from the nineteenth-century movement, and it was distinctive in critical ways.

And so this book is necessarily concerned with dialogues between the present and the past, between Edwardian suffragism and its Victorian origins. Tracing connections between the nineteenth- and twentieth-century suffrage movements is not a linear process, nor is it a matter of mapping cause and effect. Various scholars have illuminated aspects of the languages within which suffragists couched their demands.[4] The process of unraveling suffragists' various identities and alignments has begun.[5] But the dialogue that took place within Edwardian suffragism has long been neglected. Suffragists engaged with their contemporaries outside the movement, and with each other, not only about strategy or tactics but also about models for women's citizenship. No consensus existed on what citizenship for women entailed. Even after women were included in the franchise, their exclusion from the realm of the political continued, and citizenship remained a masculine identity until the late 1920s.[6] In struggling to feminize citizenship, suffragists continually confronted previous understandings of it. Engaging imaginatively with the past, they sought to define a role for women in the future polity.

Campaigns for women's parliamentary enfranchisement in Britain provided a focal point for debates over citizenship and resistance in Britain in the years between 1860 and 1930. This period, bounded roughly in world history by the American Civil War and the Russian Revolution, witnessed unprecedented expansion of the electorate in Britain.[7] Historians traditionally have cast that expansion as a glorious and inevitable progression, as men of the working classes and women of all classes attained the parliamentary franchise through the Reform Acts of 1867, 1884, 1918, and 1928.[8] More recently, however, some scholars have come to question this triumphal narrative, sounding the resonance of imperial issues for domestic franchise questions and examining the actual impact of mass enfranchisement upon British politics.[9] Others have argued that attention to the parliamentary enfranchisement of women has overshadowed middle-class women's significant contributions to municipal politics, social reform, and philanthropy.[10] Feminist historians frequently cast the enfranchisement of women as a starting point for the progression of women's rights, a process some see culminating in the 1960s and 1970s with the women's liberation movement.[11] Ironically, this triumphal whig narrative, substituting women for working-class men after 1884, undermines attempts to explain the wider significance of women's suffrage, for recovering women's agency as an end unto itself ultimately marginalizes women's political activity. Further, to see the enfranchisement of women as the climax of liberal democracy is to accept the terms of the victorious progressive discourse. Such an account gauges political struggles solely by their outcomes, in this case, the acquisition of the vote, rather than analyzing the struggle itself to see what forces, ideas, and events shaped citizenship.[12] Finally, casting women's suffrage as the inevitable outcome of an evolutionary process, whereby all groups eventually attain citizenship, overlooks the extent to which women's exclusion from citizenship was an integral part of liberal democratic citizenship at the outset.[13]

Yet the struggle for women's parliamentary enfranchisement remains significant to any discussion of the constitution of liberal democratic citizenship in Britain.[14] The campaign for women's suffrage emerged in the 1860s as a radical liberal initiative seeking to extend the parliamentary vote to women of the propertied classes. From the beginning, suffragists engaged in a critical dialogue with liberalism. They sought to reinfuse the concept of civic virtue, or acting on behalf of the public good—a notion effectively domesticated or feminized in the early decades of the nineteenth century— into then-predominant liberal definitions of citizenship, which suffragists saw as artificially divided between public and private spheres.[15]

The struggle for women's suffrage played a key role in formulating liberal citizenship not only because it united home and politics but also because suffragists were only one group among many in late-Victorian Britain attempting to rethink the individual's relationship to the state. A growing body of scholarship suggests that after 1860 a variety of communities in Britain began to reevaluate the state's role in national life.[16] As historian Marian Sawer explains, liberal conceptions of the state as "night watchman," Ferdinand Lassalle's well-known phrase of 1862, came "under sustained criticism from within the liberal tradition." This critique took the form of what Sawer calls "social liberalism," a "belief in the positive duty of the state to provide a nurturing environment for individuals to develop to their fullest potential." Sawer recognizes this as an addition of "'feminine' functions to the more clearly masculine protector role" of the state.[17] Significantly, this paradigm shift in the conception of the state intersected with the campaign for women's parliamentary enfranchisement. At the same time the state took on the attributes of femininity, such as caring for the dispossessed, the elderly, and the unemployed, women claimed the vote as a means by which they could feminize politics.[18] Feminizing politics, however, did not mean only that women would bring their concern with social reform into public life. Central to suffragists' conception of women's contribution to the state was their belief in the ennobling effects of public life. An emphasis upon morality lay at the core of this argument. Morality meant not just that women would impart their values to political life but also that women were obligated to serve even if their nation's laws prohibited them from doing so fully. For suffragists between 1860 and 1930, citizenship was not an abstract status. Rather, they viewed citizenship as an active practice, an engagement with family, local community, state, and empire.

This book weaves together the concerns of three distinct literatures: women's suffrage; late-Victorian and Edwardian British political culture; and renewed interest in citizenship among political theorists. Women's suffrage as an area of historical study remains bifurcated, hinging on opposition between "constitutional" suffragists and "militant" suffragettes. "Constitutional" suffragists traced their lineage to the nineteenth-century campaigns, emphasizing women's methodical attempts to persuade members of Parliament through the use of petition, lobbying, and peaceful demonstration that women were worthy of voting in national elections. "Militant" suffragettes critiqued the "constitutional" approach as ladylike and unexciting and attributed invention of militant tactics to Christabel and Emmeline Pankhurst, whose WSPU organization they saw as responsible for achieving the parliamentary vote for women (age thirty and above) in 1918. One would imagine that these bifurcations would not hold anymore, especially with publication of Sandra Stanley Holton's *Feminism and Democracy* (1986), which argued eloquently for a kind of fluidity between militants and nonmilitants, at least in the Edwardian movement's early days. Yet the "constitutional" versus "militant" opposition still holds sway. For some historians, militancy remains an aberration, a period of excess in women's political activism, and one not particularly productive; for others, militancy represents both a culmination and a transcendence of late-Victorian women's political activism.[19] In this way historians are split along much the same lines they identify as having split the movement in the early twentieth century.

Much scholarship on the Edwardian movement tends to discuss militancy exclusively in terms of WSPU practices, taking that organization's use of spectacle as the definitive component of militancy.[20] Historians have divided their attention between the collective suffrage demonstration and procession, and the individual exhibition of women's bodies in pain, through the hunger strike and forcible feeding.[21] Art historian Lisa Tickner has examined suffragette spectacle as part "of a broader debate about definitions of femininity and women's place in public life."[22] Literary critic Barbara Green has posed the WSPU's agitation as exemplary of "performative activism" and "visibility politics" in early-twentieth-century feminist practice, creating "almost entirely feminine communities where women celebrated, suffered, spoke with, and wrote for other women," and which "allowed women to put themselves on display for other women."[23] These analyses seek to restore agency to women, a laudable goal given traditional historical treatments of women's political activism that portray militancy as the behavior of irrational actors.[24]

But to represent the hunger-striking, or even the demonstrating, suffragette as the primary corporeal representation suffragists used to construct a political identity is to oversimplify a complex and dynamic movement in which the meanings of womanhood, citizenship, and militancy were continually debated. Rather than focusing on the passionate bodies of suffragettes in protest, this book insists that at the heart of militant protest lay a rational political calculus. To understand militancy as being primarily about the deployment of women's bodies in public space is to accept one extreme end of the campaign as the whole campaign and to miss the continuum along which suffragettes practiced militancy. Militants attempted to reconfigure citizenship through a critique of the law; their struggles to do so in the courtroom, on the street, and through legislation exhibited a belief in their own reasoning capacities as female citizens. Understanding their movement as concerned primarily with staging public spectacles of womanliness overlooks the point that Edwardian women sought to represent themselves politically, not merely visually. To say that the two forms of representation are the same is to conflate two related but distinct processes.

A major goal of this book is to reintegrate women's suffrage into broader treatments of British political culture by making visible the tangle of connections between radicalism and women's political activism in the late-Victorian and Edwardian eras. Drawing from a rich and varied set of recent works tracing the persistence of the radical political tradition in the nineteenth century, this book places the militant campaign for women's suffrage squarely within that tradition. Much recent scholarship has expanded our notions of what constituted radicalism in the nineteenth century. At least three different strands can be discerned; each has its champions and points of emphasis. Gareth Stedman Jones, James Vernon, Patrick Joyce, James Epstein, and Anna Clark have done much to rethink the relationship between popular politics and radicalism in the early to middle nineteenth century. Eugenio Biagini and the "currents of radicalism" school see radical liberalism of the latter part of the century as a middle- and working-class movement concerned with the expansion of democracy. Stefan Collini has studied the liberal intellectual traditions that intersect with radicalism.[25] While these strands diverge at certain points, they also collectively contribute to an overall picture of a late-nineteenth-century radical political culture rooted in historical precedent and deriving legitimacy from its use of the constitutional idiom. The strategies, tactics, and arguments used by those suffragists who would become militant suffragettes drew upon radicalism's vocabulary of protest and its emphasis on British liberty, the rule of law, and notions of fair play, in the attempt to reinscribe women's virtue in citizenship.

Suffragettes' published writings on their struggle for parliamentary enfranchisement reveal that these activists participated vigorously in late-Victorian debates about the role of the state in individuals' lives. Of primary concern to suffragettes was the basis from which the state governed. Like many of their contemporaries, they rejected the idea that the state's authority rested in its monopoly on force and insisted that individuals exist in a consensual relationship to the state. Suffragettes were all too aware that their sex impinged on their ability to act as citizens. Feminist political theory of the past two decades, as well as citizenship theory, has been helpful here in connecting suffragists' concerns to wider political debates. Political theorist Ruth Lister reminds us that citizenship, an "ostensibly gender-neutral concept, is, in fact, deeply gendered."[26] The work of political scientists Carole Pateman, Nancy Fraser, and Chantal Mouffe points to ways of thinking about gender and its relationship to the state that have illuminated suffragettes' strategies. Especially important has been their attention to how the gendering of political subjects both enables and frustrates women's attempts to engage actively as citizens.[27]

Two definitions dominate recent writings on citizenship. The civic republican tradition, originating in ancient Greece, defines citizenship as an obligation in that political participation constitutes civic duty. It understands citizenship as a dynamic identity, subject to both internal and external pressures, but one that ultimately inheres within the individual. The liberal tradition, emerging in the late eighteenth century, posits the citizen as an individual possessing civil and political rights as a hedge against the encroachments of the state. It defines citizenship as a status, that is, as a static and potentially fixed identity imposed by the state.[28] Late-nineteenth- and early-twentieth-century suffragettes grappled with the legacy of both traditions, embracing aspects of each but ultimately rejecting liberalism's desire to fix citizenship as status. Contemporary scholars have elaborated on this critique. Political theorist Mary Dietz has argued that under liberalism, "citizenship becomes less a collective, political activity than an individual, economic activity — the right to pursue one's own interests, without hindrance, in the marketplace."[29] Historian Mary Shanley has observed that liberalism's conception of the citizen is inadequate because it does not provide the language for human interdependence, neglecting the centrality of families for human communities.[30] Susan James notes further that democratic liberalism excludes women from full citizenship both "by denying women the full complement of rights and privileges accorded to men, and, more insidiously, by taking for granted a conception of citizenship which excludes all that is traditionally female."[31]

Informed by these debates, this book examines suffrage militancy on its own terms, with emphasis on suffragettes' language and practices. Militant suffragism should be seen not only for its implications for the social history of gender but also in relation to British political and intellectual traditions of the eighteenth and nineteenth centuries. Chapter 1, "Gender, Citizenship, and the Liberal State, 1860–1899," argues that the organized campaign for women's suffrage emerged in the 1860s as a radical liberal initiative seeking to extend the freedoms of citizenship to women of the propertied classes. In the 1880s, suffragists began to diverge according to radical or liberal political affiliations. By the 1890s, new ways of thinking about citizenship engagement were becoming visible.

Chapter 2, "The South African War and After, 1899–1906," pursues that line of argumentation during British military engagement with the South African republics. The war, it is argued, solidified division of suffragists into two camps, the liberal and the radical independent. Liberal suffragists embraced a model of citizenship valuing service to the nation, whereas radical independent suffragists adopted a model encouraging women's resistance to authority as long as their right to vote was not acknowledged by the state.

Chapter 3, "Staging Exclusion, 1906–1909," explores the cluster of organizations that emerged in the years following the South African War, including the Women's Social and Political Union (1903), the Women's Freedom League (1907), the Men's Political Union (1910), and the Women's Tax Resistance League (1909). These groups constituted overlapping points on a continuum along which militants enacted resistance through various practices of militancy. Deploying an idiom of constitutionalism, suffragettes staged protests illustrating their exclusion from the political nation. Suffragettes utilized a range of strategies designed to highlight what they saw as the arbitrary and historically anomalous exclusion of women from the constitution. Staging exclusion from the constitution articulated women's suffrage as an explicitly political struggle in which suffragettes fought with the government and among themselves over the elasticity of the British constitution.

Chapter 4, "Resistance on Trial, 1906–1912," argues that suffragettes expanded the scope of militancy from the realm of extraparliamentary agitation to a challenge of the authority of the law. Suffragettes began by attempting to force the judiciary to interpret existing law as already enfranchising women. When the judiciary held fast to interpretations of the law excluding women from the parliamentary franchise, suffragettes interrogated the law's authority. The courtroom became a key site of protest as militants used it as a public forum for articulating their grievances with the state. Suffragettes diverged yet further from suffragists as the former no longer accepted the authority of the law unquestioningly but instead attempted to separate the law's morality from its basis in state power.

Suffragettes' struggle with the legitimacy of the British state necessitated engagement with an important political legacy of liberal political revolutions of the eighteenth and nineteenth centuries: the embodiment of the citizen as white, male, and middle-class. Chapter 5, "Embodying Citizenship, 1908–1914," explores femininity and freedom, two primary idioms adopted by suffragettes in their attempt to claim citizenship for women. The creation of a feminine embodiment of citizenship took two forms—Joan of Arc and Florence Nightingale. Freedom was explored to greatest effect through its opposite, slavery, which stood as a metaphor for the condition of voteless British women. Recasting citizenship's embodiment through femininity and freedom brought suffragettes into dialogue with each other and the wider political culture.

Chapter 6, "The Ethics of Resistance, 1910–1914," charts continuing dialogue and innovation within the militant suffrage movement as suffragettes struggled among themselves to define the scope of resistance. A minority escalated violence into forms of terrorism, including window smashing, arson, and bombing, but the vast majority rejected the use of violence. In the attempt to recast militancy away from the use of violence, militants both worked across organizational lines and created new groupings. Militant resistance remained an active, if contested, component of suffragettes' conception of citizenship well into the Great War.

Suffragettes' belief in resistance as an important component of engaged citizenship faced important challenges during the First World War as the British government redefined any opposition to the war as treason. Chapter 7, "At War with and for the State, 1914–1918," argues that all militants embraced the service model of citizenship while the nation was at war. At one extreme was the WSPU, which espoused an understanding of service to the nation that could only be characterized as militaristic. Other militants were active in the peace movement, seeking speedy resolution to the war. Still others, less willing to oppose the war outright, took refuge in a modified service model of citizenship, one redirecting their service away from the nation's war effort and support for combatants and toward those noncombatants neglected at home, poor women and children. Yet the principle of resistance animating prewar militancy remained an important feature of certain militants' conception of citizenship during the war. Resistance simply took other forms, including opposition to the state's erosion of women's civil liberties and continuation of the struggle for women's suffrage at a time when political battles for rights were seen as selfish and divisive.

The conclusion, "Fetishizing Militancy, 1918–1930," posits the 1920s as a key decade in the reformulation of the meaning of citizenship. In the years immediately following the war, the act of militancy and its motivation as resistance became separated. Subsequent discussions of the prewar suffrage movement valorized one version of militancy at the expense of the political rationale underlying individual acts of resistance. The consequence of this was twofold: suffragettes were made out to be irrational political actors, and militancy's emphasis on citizenship as engagement with the state was lost. This shift in the meaning of citizenship occurred at a time when the meaning of the vote was itself diminishing. Women's enfranchisement in 1918 came at a point when many historians believe that party organization and the manipulation of public opinion had come to matter far more than did individual voters.

In the final analysis, the militant suffrage movement constituted a key arena of struggle in women's achievement of political rights in Britain. It played an essential role in Britain's movement toward democracy in the late nineteenth and early twentieth centuries. Suffrage militancy in all its manifestations produced an engagement with the state that closely approximated the civic republican ideal of the citizen in action. Militant suffragists' activism and their goals of a society regenerated through feminine virtue thus form a vital chapter in the growth of liberal democracy in Britain.

Chapter 1

Gender, Citizenship, and the Liberal State, 1860–1899

Historians typically discuss the organized campaigns for women's suffrage within three explanatory frameworks. The first is as a single-issue campaign, beginning with women's parliamentary engagement with the Second Reform Bill in 1867 that extended the vote to urban working men, continuing through disappointments in 1867 and 1884, and culminating in the emergence of militancy during the Edwardian period. These accounts approach women's suffrage either in terms of the parliamentary context and the political calculus involved or as social movements led by feminists.[1] The second approach taken by historians is to treat the campaigns as engagements with party politics, particularly with the Liberal Party and emerging Labour Party.[2] A third approach is to see women's suffrage, particularly the campaigns waged in the twentieth century, as part of the "crisis of the British state," the fragmentation of the liberal consensus of the nineteenth century that ultimately resulted in replacement of laissez-faire state government with collectivist forms in the twentieth century.[3]

This chapter and, indeed, this book suggest another approach to understanding organized campaigns for women's parliamentary voting rights between 1867 and 1928, situating them as part of the consolidation of liberal democratic citizenship. Twenty-first-century liberal democracy understands political citizenship to be a status extended to those individuals born within the geographic boundaries of a particular nation-state who have attained majority. Citizenship under liberal democracy consists of representative government and the right to vote. But contemporary British liberal democratic citizenship is the outcome of a long process that began after the French Revolution and developed over the nineteenth and twentieth centuries. For most of the nineteenth century, and a good deal of the twentieth, the British state was liberal but not liberal democratic. It was liberal because it was committed to individual liberty and a form of representative government, but not democratic because voting rights were restricted to those who were understood to have a stake in the polity: white property-owning or white laboring men. Including in the electorate anyone outside of those categories raised fears among political elites that the lowest common denominator would unduly influence political decision making.[4]

To argue that Britain possessed a liberal state by the late nineteenth century is not to argue for ascendancy of the Liberal Party and its values. It is useful, however, to distinguish between Liberalism and liberalism, one being a political party, the other a system of political thought. As historian Jonathan Parry has written, the Liberal Party between the 1850s and 1880s was a coalition incorporating "an astonishing range of classes and groups, from aristocrats to artisans, industrial magnates to labour activists, and zealous Anglican high churchmen to nonconformists and aggressive free-thinkers." It incorporated small businessmen in urban centers in the midlands and the north as well as Dissenters, trade unionists, intellectuals, and aristocrats in the south of England.[5] Historian Jon Lawrence reiterates this point, observing that Liberalism was "at heart a national political movement—a broad and heterogeneous coalition of 'reformers.'"[6] Many of the assumptions of liberalism as a system of thought, including beliefs in parliamentary sovereignty and the rule of law as well as a faith in freedom and the "absorbing qualities of the state," were, by the late nineteenth century, becoming a kind of common sense among the educated middle class in Britain.[7] Liberalism as a system of thought posited the rational individual as the unit of society; but this individual was always posited as a rational *male* individual who assumed responsibility for his wife and children and represented them in the public sphere.[8]

Nineteenth-century liberalism proceeded cautiously when considering the relationship of voting to citizenship. Throughout much of the nineteenth century, citizenship itself was a contested identity as liberal discourse favored "subject" over "citizen."[9] Implicit in the former was a set of duties and obligations to the state; "citizen" carried with it a whiff of the French Revolution's dramatic social leveling, something feared by British politicians and, indeed, the great majority of the British middle classes.[10] Nevertheless, franchise reforms made from 1832 until 1884 increasingly conveyed assumptions about the changing nature of citizenship. If citizenship is thought of as a process whereby some groups are brought into the decision-making apparatuses of the state while others are explicitly excluded, then the franchise reforms of the nineteenth century provide insight into which groups were considered to be capable of governing themselves and others, and which groups (and on what basis) they were to govern.[11]

The process of defining liberal citizenship in Britain can be said to have begun with repeal of the Test and Corporation Acts in 1828, passage of the Catholic Emancipation Act in 1829, and public discussion of the slave rebellion in Jamaica in December 1831. By removing restrictions on participation in public office from Roman Catholics and Protestant Nonconformists, legislation began to incorporate religious minorities into the body politic. Simultaneously, attempts by slaves to overthrow planter rule in Jamaica mobilized abolitionist sentiment in Parliament. While slavery officially ended in the British Empire in August 1834, those newly freed men did not acquire the status of citizens but instead became subjects of the empire.[12] The Reform Act of 1832, generally acknowledged by historians to be fairly conservative in its effects, nevertheless set a precedent for a process of electoral and parliamentary reform. It not only increased the electorate but also introduced important reforms in Parliament, including redistribution of seats, elimination of rotten boroughs, and increased representation of industrial towns. Franchise provisions of the act extended the borough vote to adult males on a uniform ten-pound household qualification in England, Wales, Scotland, and Ireland. In England and Wales, the county vote was extended to forty-shilling freeholders and men leasing land for at least fifty pounds a year, while in Scotland and Ireland the county vote included ten-pound freeholders and some categories of tenants and men leasing land. Overall, the percentage of male adult voters in England and Wales increased from about 13 to 18 percent. In Scotland, the number of adult male voters rose to about 12 percent, while in Ireland that number hovered around 5 percent. Overall, the number of adult male voters in the United Kingdom totaled approximately eight hundred thousand (in a population of about sixteen million).[13]

Perhaps the most significant aspect of the 1832 Reform Act was its basis in what historian Catherine Hall has called "the rule of difference." The act's wording explicitly excluded women. Simultaneously, debates within Parliament about slavery and Catholic emancipation drew distinctions between citizens and subjects, those who were empowered to participate in the operation of government through exercise of the parliamentary franchise and those without formal political power who nevertheless could claim legal protection under the British Crown.[14] The former included property-owning white men; the latter, British women and male and female imperial subjects. The explicit exclusion of women from the 1832 Reform Act made women's demand for inclusion inevitable; identifying women as a group without franchise rights created a political identity and a cause.[15] In the decades following passage of the Reform Act, women's suffrage was an active question, debated among those committed to challenging the status quo. Unitarian and socialist feminists debated the merits of women's suffrage in the 1830s and 1840s, laying the groundwork for radical liberal feminists' adoption of women's suffrage as a cause in the 1860s.[16]

Expansion of the electorate reemerged as an important political question in the mid-1860s when pressure from working men's organizations and growing public interest in democracy combined to bring franchise reform to the attention of members of Parliament. Debate surrounding passage of the 1867 Reform Act emphasized voting rights as a privilege conferred upon those who possessed adequate virtue by nature to be citizens.[17] In this sense, midcentury understandings of citizenship borrowed from the ancient Greek civic republican tradition that emphasized the virtues of participation in the public sphere.[18] But citizenship in the mid-nineteenth-century British polity was conferred only upon certain kinds of virtue: rational masculinity; property ownership; white skin.[19] This became evident as the Reform Act of 1867 gave the vote in boroughs to adult male owners and ten-pound lodgers (men who paid at least £10 per year for lodgings), with twelve months' residence required. The electorate in England and Wales increased from 20 to 36 percent, leaving roughly two-thirds of the adult male population and all women unenfranchised.[20] Political theorists Stuart Hall and Bill Schwarz thus conclude that the reforms of 1867 "clearly demonstrated that the liberal state was organized to counter mass democracy and universal suffrage. The masses were to be incorporated in the nation, but indirectly, on the basis of a limited suffrage."[21]

Women's suffrage emerged on the public agenda in the context of debate over passage of the Second Reform Act. During 1866 and 1867, feminists gathered signatures on multiple petitions as evidence of women's desire to be included in the proposed electoral reforms.[22] In May 1867, John Stuart Mill, Radical Liberal M.P. for Westminster, introduced an amendment to the bill under consideration that would omit the word "man" and substitute the word "person." Mill was supported in Parliament by a loose coalition of Liberals and Radicals, but his amendment was defeated by a vote of 196 to 73.[23] Out of the failure of Mill's amendment came the organized campaign for women's suffrage (see figure 1.1). By 1868, women's suffrage organizations in Manchester, Edinburgh, London, Bristol, and Birmingham had federated to form the National Society for Women's Suffrage.[24] The first organized campaigns for women's suffrage culminated in support of a bill expressly concerned with women's parliamentary enfranchisement, the Women's Disabilities Bill, introduced in the House of Commons in May 1870 by Jacob Bright (Radical Liberal, Manchester). The bill proposed to extend the parliamentary franchise to women ratepayers throughout the entire United Kingdom.[25] Its failure motivated women to continue lobbying for their rights over succeeding decades.

Those women activists engaged in supporting a bill enfranchising women in the years between 1866 and 1873 drew upon the language of liberalism to make their case. A primary strand of liberal suffragists' argumentation was the assertion of women's right to vote on the grounds of property ownership. Feminist Helen Taylor expounded upon this rationale in the liberal periodical the *Westminster Review* in 1867. Taylor supported women's claim to parliamentary representation on grounds that "property represented by an individual is the true political unit among us." Citizenship, she urged, rested on a legal right, not a natural one.[26] In so doing, she adopted a strategy prevalent among British liberals since the French Revolution of eschewing the notion that individuals held rights under natural law. Millicent Garrett Fawcett echoed this view some fifteen years later when she rejected the notion that women's right to citizenship was "inalienable." Suffragists' emphasis on

FIGURE 1.1
John Stuart Mill,
Radical Liberal M.P.,
depicted in May 1867
as championing the
rights of women.
Mary Evans Picture
Library.

"expediency," she argued, meant they sought the vote only for those women "who fulfill all the qualifications which the law demands of the male elector; that is for householders in boroughs, the owners of freeholds, and the renters of land and houses, above a certain value, in counties." Liberal suffragists viewed women's exclusion from the right of voting, given the duties they performed for the state—the payment of taxes, their eligibility for some public offices—as "an anomaly which seems to require some explanation."[27]

While some liberal suffragists initially highlighted the constitution's extension of citizenship to property owners, other mid-nineteenth-century liberal suffragists emphasized the moral dimension of women's participation in politics. Barbara Bodichon argued in 1866 that women should be given the parliamentary franchise because doing so would increase "public spirit." She urged that middle-class women's concerns dwelt too much on their own homes and families. "Give some women votes," she wrote, "and it will tend to make all women think seriously of the concerns of the nation at large."[28] Bodichon's argument made no attempt to link women's natures to the constitution or their exercise of the franchise. Like other midcentury liberal feminists, Bodichon aimed at integrating into the political life of the nation only those women who would meet existing property qualifications. Liberal feminists' early arguments were based on the assumption that middle-class women would eventually be enfranchised and that their political gains were an inevitable part of the evolution of the liberal state. Just as the reforms of 1832 and 1867 gradually included working-class males in the franchise, suffragists assumed that women's inclusion would begin with middle-class women and eventually be extended to women of the working class. Suffragists therefore sought to define middle-class women as potential electors on the basis of class rather than sex. In this respect, nineteenth-century liberal suffragists agreed with their male counterparts, who sought to maintain a middle-class standard of respectability for determining who possessed the parliamentary franchise and, hence, political citizenship. Nineteenth-century liberal suffragists were not democrats—they did not seek the creation of a political system in which every adult man and woman held the parliamentary vote as a matter of course.

There were, however, radical or "advanced" liberals whose arguments in the 1860s promoted a more democratic vision of citizenship. Richard Marsden Pankhurst, Radical Liberal solicitor and future husband of Emmeline Pankhurst, née Goulden, argued in 1868 in the liberal *Fortnightly Review* that the 1867 Reform Act should be interpreted as enfranchising women. He advanced three reasons for this analysis. First, he cited the etymological origins of the word "homo," which in classical jurisprudence and juridical science, as well as English common and statute law, included both men and women. "Women," he urged, "are within the intention of the Act, because they are within the meaning of the language by which the intention is expressed." Second, he argued that franchises were extended by description; an individual's competency to exercise that franchise was not at issue. Barring women from the exercise of the franchise merely because they were women rendered them "subjects of absolute and incurable mental defect." Third, he asserted that "any individual who enjoys the electoral right is not, in the eye of the Constitution, invested with it in virtue of being of a certain rank, station, or sex. Each individual receives the right to vote in the character of a human being, possessing intelligence and adequate reasoning power." He concluded, "To give to 'The Representation of the People Act, 1867,' such a true legal interpretation would be to make it a new Great Charter."[29] Pankhurst thus raised in the late 1860s an argument for women's suffrage with enormously radical implications, for it proposed extending the suffrage well beyond middle-class women to working-class men and women. In short, Pankhurst proposed adult suffrage, the extension of the parliamentary franchise to all men and women who had attained majority. Liberal suffragists would not embrace this position until the twentieth century.

The nineteenth-century women's suffrage movement was characterized by loose groupings of suffragists working together under the aegis of national umbrella organizations. No single organization or individual dominated the nineteenth-century movement, and a series of organizational splits littered the movement's topography with a confusing array of groupings. The National Society for Women's Suffrage (NSWS), which had originated in the 1868 unification of regional suffrage committees of London, Birmingham, Bristol, Manchester, and Edinburgh, split into two organizations between 1872 and 1877 over disagreement about whether members ought to participate in the international campaign to repeal the Contagious Diseases Acts, legislation empowering police to incarcerate and examine women suspected of engaging in prostitution. The two organizations reunited in 1877 as the Central Committee of the NSWS. A further schism occurred in 1888 when members disagreed over whether to allow the women's sections of political parties to participate in the committee's organization. Despite these differences, the nineteenth-century movement possessed a remarkable degree of agreement on the strategies to be employed in agitation for the vote. These included lobbying members of Parliament and the presentation of petitions to Parliament or deputations of ministers. The primary area of disagreement was over whether their campaign should focus on single women or should include married women as well (see figure 1.2).[30]

The 1870s and 1880s were crucial to shaping women's demand for the parliamentary franchise. Three developments in particular must be highlighted. Although unable to pass a measure for women's parliamentary enfranchisement, in 1869 Radical Liberal M.P. Jacob Bright managed to pass a bill giving women ratepayers in England and Wales the borough franchise, allowing women to vote in local government elections; Scottish women received this right in 1882. Further franchise extensions came with the Education Act of 1870, which allowed women possessing the municipal vote in England and Wales to vote in and stand for school board elections. Single or widowed women ratepayers in England and Wales could vote for and stand as poor law guardians, while qualified Irish women could vote for, but not stand as, poor law guardians. Women ratepayers were empowered to vote for county councils in England and Wales in 1888, and in Scotland the following year.[31] Simultaneously, a growing number of middle-class women undertook settlement work, living among the working poor in industrial areas with the aim of improving workers' lives through personal interaction and the introduction of culture and hygiene. Settlement work politicized many middle-class women, who came to see that real change could be effected only by women's possession of the parliamentary vote.[32] Finally, passage in 1883 of the Corrupt Practices Act, which outlawed payment of party canvassers, led to the creation of women's auxiliaries to the main political parties which came to serve as reservoirs of volunteer election workers. Conservative women formed the Primrose League in 1884, and Liberal women formed the Women's Liberal Federation in 1887 (with groups splitting off as the Women's Liberal Unionist Association in 1888 and the Women's National Liberal Association in 1892).[33]

Participation in local government, settlement work, and party canvassing gave women practical experience of citizenship and inevitably raised ques-

FIGURE 1.2
Women lobbying a member of Parliament on women's
rights during the general election. Engraving by Fred
Barnard in *Illustrated London News,* 27 March 1880.
Mary Evans Picture Library.

tions about their continued exclusion from the parliamentary franchise. As
W. S. B. McLaren, Liberal M.P., observed in the late 1880s, "The fact is, 'the
game is up.' It is useless any longer to contend against woman entering political life. She is in it already."[34] Historian David Rubinstein has argued that
women's political organizations in the 1890s, by giving women power to can-
vass for politicians and to speak on platforms on their behalf, raised contradictions about women in politics: women were needed and utilized by politicians during elections, but those same politicians remained uninterested in
giving women parliamentary votes.[35] Yet, as historian Jonathan Schneer has
shown in the troubled candidacies of Jane Cobden and Lady Sandhurst to the
London County Council in 1889, it would be easy to overestimate the significance of these new municipal roles for women, given entrenched opposition to women exercising real political power once elected. Subsequent challenges to women's voting rights on the London County Council ensured that
while women could be elected to county councils from 1889, they could not
cast votes in those positions until 1907.[36] Perhaps most significant, however,
changes in women's practical experience of citizenship were not viewed by
members of Parliament as evidence of women's fitness for the parliamentary
franchise. That franchise was understood as an explicitly political responsibility, while local government was seen as a social and economic one.[37]

The distinction between the local and the national prevailed when electoral reform came up again in 1884. Discussion surrounding passage of the Third Reform Act emphasized the importance of equalizing men's votes in counties with those in the boroughs. After the passage of the act, one reform act applied to the whole United Kingdom for the first time, as it extended the parliamentary franchise to all adult male householders and lodgers paying ten pounds a year in rent, in both the counties and the boroughs. Electoral qualifications were standardized in the counties and the boroughs, enfranchising roughly 60 percent of adult men, leaving about 70 percent of all adults in the United Kingdom without the parliamentary vote.[38] By expanding the electorate to include larger numbers of working men, the 1884 act effectively silenced demand for further reform, thereby hampering women suffragists' efforts for a generation.[39] The 1884 act thus established the parameters of Edwardian citizenship; voting rights were dictated less by class than by age and marital status.[40]

By the 1880s, suffragists' arguments had expanded to include gender-specific attributes of citizenship. Women, they argued, were necessary in a wholly new way to the function and operation of the state, given their "natural" abilities within the domestic realm. Millicent Garrett Fawcett spoke directly to this point before an audience at Toynbee Hall in 1889. Observing that English public opinion was moving in the direction of the parliamentary enfranchisement of women, Fawcett argued that the "difference between men and women, instead of being a reason against their enfranchisement, seems . . . the strongest possible reason in favour of it; we want the home and the domestic side of things to count for more in politics and in the administration of public affairs than they do at present." She went on to assert that the very survival of the nation rested upon the institution of the home; anything endangering the home endangered the nation.[41]

This speech and its venue, a settlement house in London's East End, underscore a wider change occurring in the 1880s: feminist criticism of liberalism's exclusion of women on the grounds of their sex. In preceding decades, as growing numbers of liberal feminists began to question the political, economic, and social restrictions placed upon middle-class women, liberalism itself came under attack. Feminists' criticism focused on two aspects of liberalism: its inability to deal with women's sexual oppression, and its refusal to incorporate women into the political realm.[42] Fawcett's talk, "Home and Politics," spoke to both of those concerns as it presented a critique of liberalism's separation of the public and private. Fawcett and other liberal feminists argued that women's natures made their full participation as citizens necessary, increasingly urging that women be enfranchised on the grounds of the contributions they would make to the polity. Suffragists put forth women's successes in local government, municipal government, boards of education, settlement houses, and poor law boards as examples of how and where women acted as citizens.[43]

Suffragists' new emphasis in the 1880s and 1890s upon the distinctively feminine contributions women would make to the polity must be seen as part of a wider reconceptualization under way in late-Victorian Britain of the relationship between citizens and the state. New groupings among liberals, so-called social or "new" liberals, sought to break down distinctions between the family and the broader political community by extending an "ethical duty of care into the public sphere."[44] Suffragists embraced the radical liberal belief that participation in the public sphere had ennobling effects and combined that belief with one in women's inherent morality. Women voters would both improve politics and be improved by participation in public life.[45] Viewed this way, women's public spirit could be seen as an extension of women's sphere of private duty rather than as a threatening expansion of their roles into the masculine public realm. Women's enfranchisement, by this definition, was not necessarily a radical or revolutionary demand; duty or service was its emphasis.

Of course, a contradiction existed at the heart of this stance because all parties interested in fact were clear that parliamentary enfranchisement of women would transform British political life. From its inception, the campaign for women's parliamentary enfranchisement was understood to portend enormous change. Josephine Butler noted in 1869 "the secret dread" most Englishmen held that women's enfranchisement "should revolutionize society."[46] Well into the Edwardian period, contemporaries viewed women's parliamentary enfranchisement as a radical demand. The jurist A. V. Dicey urged in 1909 that "the concession of parliamentary votes to women must be, in Great Britain, either for good or bad, a revolution," because "woman suffrage must lead to adult suffrage."[47] Indeed, much of the opposition to women's suffrage centered on the real and imagined consequences for domestic life of women's participation in public. Contemporaries feared that women's demand for parliamentary enfranchisement pushed at the boundaries of women's social citizenship. Yet suffragists found themselves awkwardly positioned within liberal discourse. If it was becoming the business of the state to promote moral goodness, then surely women, the exemplars of that goodness, should have the vote.[48]

But to see the struggle for women's parliamentary enfranchisement merely as a liberal franchise reform is to neglect another, equally important, dimension of those campaigns, the challenge women suffragists posed to the authority of the state. While women's movement into local politics provided them with the practical experience of citizenship, further making the case for their parliamentary enfranchisement, the practice of citizenship radicalized suffrage activists by highlighting the discrepancy between their status as subjects and their lived experience of citizenship. And while Victorian suffragists shared with fellow Britons a belief in the rule of law and parliamentary government, their inability to write women and their contributions into the constitution would of necessity challenge those two precepts. Increasingly, the nineteenth-century women's movement concerned itself with the underlying conceptual basis on which the state rested, asking from whence the authority of the state originated. What, feminists asked, was the relationship between the rule of law, parliamentary sovereignty, and the authority of the state?

Suffragists came at these questions from a historical perspective. Their own understanding of the history of women's activism over the previous fifty years emphasized the importance of challenging the state's authority. The major battles of the nineteenth-century women's movement illustrate the extent to which nineteenth-century feminist movements questioned the authority of the law in establishing women's status.[49] Late-Victorian feminists dated the first of these challenges to the struggle Caroline Norton mounted in the press and Parliament in the 1830s and 1840s as she fought to maintain custody of her children and gain independence from an abusive spouse.[50] Feminists waged subsequent battles over married women's property, access to divorce, and marital rape.[51] These issues all raised questions about the state's ability to legislate fairly where women were concerned.

New rhetoric and new organizations in the late 1880s and early 1890s suggest that something significant was happening to late-Victorian suffragists' definitions of citizenship. Historians point to a number of factors influencing these changes. Olive Banks sees a decline in the number of feminists of liberal political orientation and a corresponding increase in the number of feminists among socialist women.[52] Other historians trace feminists' growing critique of women's sexual subordination in marriage.[53] Another development of the late 1880s and 1890s was the emergence of loose coalitions on the Left bringing together radical liberals, socialists, and other progressives. New groupings among suffragists should be seen in the broader political context of splits between radicals and liberals in nineteenth-century British politics. The same forces generating a fragmentation of consensus within the Liberal Party resulted in shifts among suffragists.[54] The exact timing of the deterioration of consensus within the Liberal Party is less important here than its consequences for the late-Victorian political Left.[55] Historian Jon Lawrence urges that the demise of the Liberal Party "did most to shape the character of Edwardian 'Progressivism.' Many on the left came to believe that a progressive popular politics needed to be anchored in the organizational strength and rational aspirations of the labour movement."[56] Rodney Barker suggests that the term "progressivism" better describes the broader context of social radicalism and new liberalism characteristic of the 1890s, noting that "progressive Liberalism and socialism were not at the time separated from one another with the simplicity and clarity with which they have retrospectively been segregated," a point Duncan Tanner has reiterated.[57]

By the 1890s, support for women's suffrage had shifted from being primarily a concern of liberals (and some conservative feminists, like Frances Power Cobbe and Emily Davies) to preoccupying growing numbers of progressives, a group I will call radical independents.[58] Radical independents borrowed from mid-nineteenth-century radical liberalism a hostility to aristocratic privilege and corruption, but they inflected that hostility with a principled belief that, eventually, justice would prevail.[59] As suffragist Elizabeth Wolstenholme Elmy claimed, "However power and privilege may rage, justice is stronger than either, and justice is the very basis of the woman's claim."[60] Radical independents were also influenced by new liberals and socialists who sought collectivist solutions and supported the emancipation of women.[61] They constituted a growing group of people aligned on the Left who agreed on issues across party lines, including opposition to Britain's participation in the South African War, support for women's suffrage, and a desire to see more state intervention at both central and local levels.

Three organizations in particular—the Women's Emancipation Union (WEU), the Women's Franchise League, and the Union of Practical Suffragists within the Women's Liberal Federation— illustrate splits between radical independent and liberal strands of suffragism. All three drew upon a body of activists whose political allegiances could be loosely termed "liberal," although the outer extremes of the first two organizations more closely approached forms of socialism. The Women's Franchise League, founded in 1889, adhered to an "ultraist" policy of embracing the principle of women's suffrage over any attempt at political compromise.[62] The Women's Emancipation Union, created in 1891, emphasized justice for women in its arguments for voting rights. The WEU raised the specter of physical force in women's struggle for the parliamentary franchise. In November 1892, WEU member Miss Cozens received a stern rebuke in the liberal *Woman's Herald* for her public "outburst about dynamite," leading the paper to categorically deny any connection between the WEU and Liberal women's and suffragist organizations.[63] The Union of Practical Suffragists within the Women's Liberal Federation, formed in 1893, stressed that women's Liberal associations ought to work only for those political candidates who would support women's suffrage in the House of Commons.[64] In their emphasis on justice, and their willingness to break ranks with party to secure women's political rights, these new organizations demonstrated suffragists' unwillingness to accept liberal definitions of women's complementarity and their eagerness to expand the practice of citizenship.

Resistance and rebellion figured prominently in this new conception of citizenship. Radical independents never abandoned liberal feminism's belief in the centrality of service to citizenship, but they redefined service in critical ways. A new assertiveness emerged in these suffragists' pronouncements in the 1890s. The WEU's program claimed "equality of right and duty with men in all matters affecting the service of the community and of the State." Nor was the WEU's agenda focused solely on the acquisition of voting rights. It also claimed equality for women in the areas of education, industry, the professions, marriage, and parental rights.[65] In a paper given at the WEU's London conference in 1896, feminist Charlotte Carmichael Stopes likened the women's suffrage movement to *Novum Organum,* Francis Bacon's sixteenth-century screed against custom, authority, and tradition. Stopes urged women to "protest against the teachings of the Courts of Law."[66] And suffragists privately adopted Lord Byron's admonition that "who would be free must themselves strike the blow."[67] The political languages used by radical independent suffragists radicalized their movement, making the moral dimension of politics essential. Radical independents refused the liberal notion that citizenship was a status bestowed on deserving individuals; rather, they viewed citizenship as an active engagement with their communities. Eventually, these women would endorse active resistance as a means of claiming the vote and acting as citizens.

The WEU and Women's Franchise League both folded in the 1890s, and the ideas they espoused about how political change would come about seemingly disappeared. Before its demise, however, the Women's Franchise League played a critical role in removing the primary obstacle to unity among liberal suffragists with its successful agitation for an amendment to the 1894 Local Government Act that provided qualified single and married women with the local government franchise.[68] As a consequence of the precedent established by this legislation, inclusion of married women in future parliamentary reform no longer divided liberal suffragists. In 1897, the National Union of Women's Suffrage Societies (NUWSS) brought together previously antagonistic groups, serving as an umbrella organization for the majority of regional women's suffrage organizations. Its goal, to work for women's suffrage on a nonpartisan basis, fulfilled part of the radical independent agenda by removing women's suffrage activism from party politics. The NUWSS, however, eschewed any discussion of challenging the state's authority in pursuit of rights for women.[69] Yet the legacy of the WEU and the Women's Franchise League for twentieth-century suffragism would be significant. As historian Sandra Stanley Holton has argued, the WEU and the Women's Franchise League suggested new ways of thinking about women's citizenship and brought together new constituencies for women's suffrage activism.[70] And members of these organizations continued their involvement in national political issues, most notably, opposition to Britain's prosecution of war in South Africa. Radical independents' interest in women's suffrage did not abate; many of these activists merely regrouped in organizations that would become known in the early twentieth century for practicing suffrage militancy.

Chapter 2

The South African War and After, 1899–1906

British involvement in the military conflict known to contemporaries alternately as the South African War and the Boer War seemingly brought the activities of organized suffragists to a halt. By and large, historians have accepted liberal suffragist Millicent Garrett Fawcett's 1925 recollection that "the war naturally caused an almost complete suspension of work for Women's Suffrage."[1] Yet evidence contemporary to the conflict in South Africa suggests that the great majority of women active in the organized suffrage movement believed in the necessity of continuing to press their claim. Delegates to the conference held in 1900 by the National Union of Women's Suffrage Societies voted unanimously to continue its work to keep women's suffrage before the legislature during the war. Other evidence suggests that activity on behalf of women's suffrage actually increased during the war, as when, in December 1899, the North of England Society began to circulate a petition for women's suffrage among women textile workers in Lancashire, expanding the suffrage organizing among working women that had begun in the early 1890s.[2] And while both the Women's Emancipation Union and the Women's Franchise League folded in 1899, many of their members remained active in progressive politics in the early years of the new century, including women's suffrage, social reform, and agitation against the pending war in South Africa.[3]

Perhaps most significantly, however, the war motivated male and female activists involved in a range of progressive causes other than suffrage to consider critically how they might reconcile their opposition to the war with support for Britain and its empire. Opponents of the war, derisively termed "pro-Boer" by the contemporary press, included pacifists, anti-imperialists, isolationists, and internationalists. The pro-Boers were united by a belief that the British government was not justified in pursuing a war with the South African republics, and once the war began, they insisted that it be stopped.[4]

Mobilizing through the Stop the War Committee and the South Africa Reconciliation Committee, opponents of the war collected signatures for petitions against it, published pamphlets excoriating it, and organized mass meetings to present their views to the public.[5] Joining the ranks of the pro-Boers were a number of women activists in the Independent Labour Party, Social Democratic Federation, and Women's Liberal Federation. In linking their own struggle for political rights at home to their opposition to the war, these women joined others on the left whose activism during the war radicalized prevailing discourses on citizenship.[6] The South African War thus marked a significant turning point in the struggle for women's parliamentary enfranchisement in Britain. Much as the 1865 Morant Bay Rebellion in Jamaica and the Fenian rising in Ireland had constituted the backdrop for public and parliamentary discussion of the 1867 Reform Act, Britain's prosecution of war against the South African Republic (Transvaal) and the Orange Free State would provide context for further franchise reform in Britain until the First World War.[7]

Division among progressives over British justification for the war brought into high contrast two understandings of citizenship circulating at the turn of the century. At the time the conflict began, women suffragists were ostensibly in agreement with a model of citizenship exemplified by prominent liberal feminists such as Millicent Garrett Fawcett and Josephine Butler, who urged the expansion of voting rights to women who met existing property qualifications on grounds of the services those women could render the nation and empire.[8] Yet the range of opposition to the war among suffragists and other progressives pushed into being a nascent analysis of citizenship and its obligations, one in development during the 1890s but given full articulation during the war. This model drew upon a legacy of masculine radical argumentation for the people's moral right to participate in the nation's political life and refined an evolving understanding of the relationship between citizens' consent and legitimate government. For a number of suffragists, the war provided a compelling example of where and when resistance to "constituted authority" had become necessary. The war in South Africa brought these two models of citizenship, the social-service and the radical-independent, into conflict and pushed the campaign for women's parliamentary enfranchisement in new directions, highlighting women's demand for self-representation.

As late as 1890, South Africa existed primarily as "a geographical expression," composed of two British colonies (Natal and the Cape Colony), two independent republics (the Transvaal and the Orange Free State), and numerous autonomous African polities, including Zulu, Xhosa, and Bosotho Kingdoms. Power in South Africa since the 1880s, however, resided in British merchant capitalism and imperialism. Discovery of diamonds in Kimberley in 1868 and gold on the Witwatersrand in 1886 accelerated the processes by which indigenous groups were brought under the control of European industrial ventures.[9] South African political events assumed new importance in British domestic politics in 1881, when Britain was forced as a consequence of its humiliating military defeat at the Battle of Majuba Hill to grant the Transvaal "'complete self-government, subject to the Suzerainty of Her Majesty.'"[10] The newly restored Transvaal Republic then established an elective Volksraad and president, limiting the franchise to those white men resident in the republic for fourteen years or more. This legislation enfranchised Afrikaner (Boer) men, descendants of the Dutch settlers who had been moving inland to evade British control since the early nineteenth century, and left without voting rights those white men characterized as alien, known as Uitlanders, who had come to South Africa in pursuit of gold and diamonds. The Uitlanders were a motley crew. Originating in England, Scotland, Ireland, continental Europe, Australia, and North America, most spoke English, and few were vocal about their political status in South Africa during the 1880s. Most saw their residence in South Africa as a temporary expedient for commercial gain, and their grievances reflected that outlook, focusing on inflation, high taxation, and corruption in the Transvaal government. For their part, the Afrikaners feared Uitlander influence in the Transvaal and sought to limit that group's political power.

The Uitlanders' grievances did not carry great importance in British domestic politics until after 1895, when the Transvaal entered diplomatic relations with Germany, Britain's main imperial rival in the region. Over the next four years, a strategic campaign, combining pressure from British mining interests and British officials in South Africa, gave the appearance that Uitlander grievances underlay the conflict in the Transvaal. In March 1899, Alfred Milner, British high commissioner, orchestrated events in the region to highlight the political disabilities of British subjects. Milner arranged for presentation to the British Parliament of a petition, signed by over twenty-one thousand British Uitlanders, requesting British intervention on behalf of their franchise rights, to coincide with delivery of an official report from the British mining community in South Africa, indicating it would not be separated from the Uitlanders' cause. Uitlander enfranchisement thus presented itself as a logical solution to the unfolding crisis.[11]

Britain entered into formal negotiations with the Transvaal over the citizenship rights of its subjects in South Africa during the summer of 1899. Milner met with Paul Kruger, four-time elected president of the Republic, in conference at Bloemfontein, in the Orange Free State, between 31 May and 5 June 1899. The two men debated terms for the enfranchisement and naturalization of British subjects in the Transvaal, setting into motion a public debate in Britain over the possibility of war. Milner refused to accept any residence requirement above five years, but when Kruger eventually succeeded in persuading the Volksraad to reduce the residence requirement for Uitlanders from fourteen to seven years, Milner abruptly began to argue that the real issue at stake was British paramountcy in South Africa. Public sentiment in Britain in favor of British intervention in the region increased with the publication of Milner's "helots" dispatch in June 1899. In private correspondence with Colonial Secretary Joseph Chamberlain, Milner had urged that action be taken to redress "'the spectacle of thousands of British subjects kept permanently in the position of helots, constantly chafing under undoubted grievances, and calling vainly to Her Majesty's Government.'"[12] Despite the emotive appeal of the "helots" dispatch, contemporary opponents of British intervention in the Transvaal interpreted Milner's change of position as evidence that the franchise controversy merely provided the means to an end: British supremacy in South Africa. Historians largely concur with this assessment.[13]

The issue here, however, is less with the causes of the war than with the rhetorical purposes to which the Uitlander franchise was put by the British government, and how that rhetoric resonated in late-Victorian political culture. From April through October 1899, the war was rationalized in the press and in Parliament in the language of liberal political rights.[14] Public discussion of the possibility of war highlighted issues central to the construction of Britain as a liberal imperial power: freedom versus slavery; the franchise rights of white men; the inevitability of progress; and the legitimacy of using force in obtaining freedom. Freedom and its opposites, slavery and tyranny, were mobilized in support of Britain's war effort. For supporters of the war, the importance of the Uitlander franchise paralleled the necessity of protecting indigenous Africans from enslavement by the Afrikaners.[15] Tyrannous Boers, enslaved Africans, and British helots all required liberating, by force if necessary.

Within months of the commencement of hostilities in South Africa, Millicent Fawcett and Josephine Butler, two leading liberal feminists, emerged together as important voices on the relationship of organized women to the war. The irony of their unity on this question was lost on few. Fawcett had distanced herself from Butler in preceding decades over the question of feminist involvement in the campaign to repeal the Contagious Diseases Acts, which empowered local authorities to arrest and incarcerate suspected prostitutes.[16] For her part, Butler's involvement in the international repeal movement left her little time for more traditionally conceived political struggles such as the parliamentary franchise.[17] In 1899, the two leaders found themselves on the same side of one issue—support for British prosecution of the war in South Africa—that would shape debate on citizenship for the next decade.

Fawcett and Butler knew that they held a minority position among suffragists in their support for the British war effort. Ray Strachey, Fawcett's earliest biographer, noted that "among the pro-Boers were many of Mrs. Fawcett's old friends, many of her fellow workers in the women's cause and some of her husband's old colleagues," and that her support for the government's position on the war led many to attack her as a jingo.[18] And while Josephine Butler privately expressed reservations about the war, she ultimately saw it as a moral test of Britain's imperial resolve. To her son, Butler wrote in December 1899: "If there is blame it seems to me to lie further back—with

Rhodes' ambitions to wealth . . . and also perhaps with the want of knowledge of South African facts, history and character on the part of Chamberlain and the government. . . . However this is not the moment for criticism. It is too grave a moment, and those who fight and those who stay at home must stand shoulder to shoulder." A few days later, she revealed the biblical framework within which she placed the war: "I have often asked myself if this may be the beginning of 'the great Tribulation' of the latter days."[19]

In 1900, Butler published *Native Races and the War,* for which she would receive much criticism. She defended Britain's participation in the war on the grounds that victory would allow the British to save the native peoples of South Africa from the depredations of the Boers. As long as British laws and social mores had been enforced in South Africa, she asserted, "its native populations [had been saved] from bondage or annihilation."[20] Butler clearly viewed publication of her book as a bridge across which she and Fawcett could meet. In June 1900, she sent a copy to Fawcett, with a note explaining:

> I am not sure if you will care for the whole of the book. I was impelled to address the latter part a little to my "Abolitionist" friends who have gone so woefully astray. I can count on the fingers of one hand those few in England (of our Abolitionist Federation) who are not strong pro-Boers; and our Continental allies of course are largely the same. And the Women's Liberal Federation grieves me much. Mrs. Leonard Courtney says the Boers "only ask to be let alone"—a modest request. Thieves and burglars also ask only to be let alone.[21]

Both Butler and Fawcett believed women could be instrumental in the British mission to save blacks from the Boers. Women would present the human face of the imperial mission, providing education, domestic arts, and civilization. Historian Antoinette Burton has argued that "English women from Elizabeth Heyrick to Josephine Butler to Millicent Garrett Fawcett argued that British women deserved the vote—or at the very least, representation in the public sphere—because of their capacity to sympathize with and represent the interests of Afro-Caribbean slaves, Indian prostitutes, and non-western women more generally."[22] The health and well-being of dependent Afrikaner women and children were Fawcett's contribution to this list during the war.

For Fawcett, the war represented an opportunity for British women to demonstrate their fitness for citizenship by their willingness to perform services for the nation and empire in its hour of need. Fawcett's support of the war took two forms. Early in the conflict, she worked with other members of the Women's Liberal Unionist Association to create pamphlets outlining the British position on the war and disseminate them among British subjects in southern Africa, including doctors, clergymen, consuls, and businessmen.[23] Fawcett's most controversial service, however, came following Emily Hobhouse's 1901 report on her investigation of the concentration camps created by the British government to intern Afrikaner, and sometimes English, women and children in the Transvaal, Natal, and the Orange Free State during the guerrilla stage of hostilities.[24] Hobhouse's discovery of appalling living conditions and high mortality rates among those incarcerated prompted Sir Henry Campbell-Bannerman, leader of the Liberal opposition in Parliament, to denounce British "methods of barbarism" and eventually led to the creation of a seven-member women's committee to investigate the camps on behalf of the British government.[25] Fawcett, who chaired the committee, concluded from her tour of thirty-three of the thirty-four camps that their governors did the best they could considering the Afrikaners' primitive hygienic habits. By drawing attention to the deplorable conditions in which Afrikaner women chose to raise their children in the British camps, Fawcett hoped both to make visible the inadequacies of the Afrikaners' hygienic practices, and hence level of civilization, and to suggest ways of improving their cleanliness and, by extension, their fitness for self-governance.[26] One unintended consequence of bringing together in the camps a previously geographically scattered population, she claimed, was implementation of systematic education of Afrikaner children for the first time. Fawcett's report, written on behalf of the Concentration Camps Commission, was issued as a government blue book in 1902. It argued in dispassionate, administrative language for the necessity of the camps and for a continuing British predominance in the region after the cessation of hostilities.[27]

For many liberal suffragists, their war service underscored the disparity between their own rights and those of the imperial subjects on whose behalf they were working. Liberal feminists in general noted the discrepancy between their own status as permanent Uitlanders in Britain—as they possessed no parliamentary votes and under current law never would—and the temporary disqualification from voting of five to seven years that British men in the Transvaal would experience if Britain were to win the war.[28] Fawcett laid out the parallels succinctly:

> The actual origin and cause of the war were on lines that very strongly emphasized the reasonable and irrefutable nature of the claim of British women to a share in the government of their country. For in the first instance the war in South Africa was caused by President Kruger's persistent refusal to admit Englishmen and other "Uitlanders" long settled in the Transvaal to any share in its citizenship. They and their industries were heavily taxed; a very large proportion of the whole revenue of the State was derived from them, but they were denied the vote and therefore had no share in controlling the expenditure or the policy of the State in which they lived. They not unnaturally raised the cry, "No taxation without representation," and in other respects almost inevitably took up and repeated the arguments and protests which for many years we had urged on behalf of the unenfranchised women of Great Britain.[29]

Fawcett's analogy, between white middle-class British women in Britain and those white British men living in South Africa while extracting value from the land invoked a kind of argumentation familiar to British suffragism since the 1870s. Frances Power Cobbe's influential essay of 1869, "Criminals, Idiots, Women, and Minors," held as self-evident the logic of certain British women's right to the parliamentary franchise, in contrast to what she cast as the more dubious claims of other groups. As her title suggests, Cobbe found it ridiculous that women should be disqualified from voting along with men who had broken the law, persons held to be mentally incompetent, and individuals who had not attained majority.[30] A Liberal Imperialist, Fawcett nevertheless endorsed enfranchising British property-owning women in Britain before expending effort on behalf of the political rights of those British men who had left home to search for gold and diamonds on another continent. Fawcett thus endorsed the Liberal argument that property ownership should supersede other criteria for determining citizenship; property should trump sex.

Yet liberal feminists' understanding of the war's relationship to citizenship had further implications. The model of citizenship to which Fawcett and Butler appealed held service—and service specifically gendered feminine, such as "support"—as its highest value. The liberal feminist periodical the *Englishwoman's Review* repeatedly emphasized this aspect of citizenship and documented the "steadfast and loyal" work of women on behalf of the war effort, from Queen Victoria and the princesses to ordinary women up and down the social scale. Wealthy women funded hospital ships, officers' wives amassed clothing for the soldiers, and women living in "houses whose very outside speaks of narrow means" were able somehow to send "cases of books, papers, [and other] soldiers' comforts." Of equal importance, the paper suggested, were nurses tending the injured at the front and members of the Women's Liberal Unionist Association explaining the origins of the war to Britons at home.[31] Implied throughout was that the duties women performed for the nation and empire during the war established their fitness for citizenship. In the value they placed on service, Butler and Fawcett thus conformed to much mainstream fin de siècle thinking on citizenship, as well as to suffragists' own argumentation in the decades since passage of the Second Reform Act.[32]

This understanding of social service rested upon clearly demarcated racial hierarchies. Both Fawcett and Butler believed that the end of the war would provide an opportunity to renegotiate political relationships between Britons and Afrikaners in South Africa. Fawcett observed in December 1899: "'I don't think much of the suggestion to disfranchise the Boers of Cape Colony. I expect the settlement after the war, even if everything goes on as we most wish, will offer tremendous difficulties, but I hope we are too deeply pledged to the principle of equal political privileges for all white races to abandon it.'"[33] And while Butler despaired of what she deemed the Afrikaners' retrograde Calvinist theological beliefs, she nevertheless placed Afrikaners closer to Britons on the evolutionary scale than to "the native races." She opined that *"equality of all before the Law; not by any means social equality,"* should be the goal of British rule in South Africa.[34] The editors of the

Englishwoman's Review articulated what this would mean in practice. A column from October 1900 expressed the hope that all who had struggled on behalf of the British war effort would "live to see a united South Africa, wherein, under the British flag, the two dominant races live together in peace and amity, because in secure freedom."[35] Whiteness and the necessity for cheap labor would reunite Afrikaner and Briton after the war. The peace settlement of May 1902 known as the Treaty of Vereeniging explicitly excluded blacks and people of color from political rights in an attempt to create a settlement both the British and South African governments could accept.

Another model of citizenship emerged during the war that emphasized consent rather than service. Many activists opposed to Britain's war in South Africa used their position to fuel arguments for a different kind of relationship between subjects (in this case, women) and the state. These pro-Boer suffragists did not use the condition of the Uitlanders or indigenous Africans as arguments for the war, as had Millicent Fawcett and Josephine Butler. Rather, they used the willingness of the British government to go to war over the question of Uitlander rights as justification for intensifying the campaign for women's parliamentary vote in Britain. That the British state was willing to use force to enfranchise its subjects abroad suggested simultaneously that force expended in such a service was legitimate and that subjects themselves had the right to resist a government refusing to acknowledge them as citizens. Pro-Boer suffragists refuted the claim that the indigenous population of South Africa was better served under British rule and pointed to the British government's hypocrisy in defending territorial and mineral claims in the name of franchise rights.[36]

This analysis of the war and of its implications for women's attempts to gain full voting rights would affect the development of new strategies, idioms, and organizations in the decade following the war. Many of those women and men who would become prominent suffragettes in the years after 1905 came to political consciousness during the South African War. Pro-Boer activists included Emmeline Pankhurst, Emmeline and Frederick Pethick Lawrence, Charlotte Despard, and Dora Montefiore, to name only those whose militant suffragism would make them famous. Most were active at the time of the war in radical circles, which encompassed a range of political positions, from socialism, broadly defined, to new liberalism. All shared a desire to fuse politics and religion.[37] These men and women, only some of whom had publicly committed themselves to women's suffrage in 1899, examined critically every argument made in defense of Britain's prosecution of the war, eventually putting their analyses to use on behalf of British women's franchise rights. Part of a broader community of progressives at the fin de siècle, radical independents argued that enfranchising women simultaneously addressed women's rights and the nation's needs.

Scrutiny of the fin de siècle radical press yields traces of a very public debate over the meanings of citizenship. Two London publications, in particular, reveal the impact of opposition to the war on radical suffragists' thinking. An evening newspaper, the *Echo,* purchased early in 1899 by Frederick Pethick Lawrence, barrister and radical, after a visit to South Africa persuaded him that the British government was inciting unrest among its subjects in the Transvaal, provided daily coverage and assessments of the growing crisis. The *New Age,* subtitled "A Weekly Record of Christian Culture, Social Service, and Literary Life," offered a range of progressive opinion on the implications of the war for Britons, Afrikaners, Africans, and other people of color in South Africa.[38]

These publications not only produced a critique of the war and of the cynicism of the British government's exploitation of the franchise issue but also expanded prevailing understandings of citizenship and voting rights. War would be desirable, the *Echo* argued in September 1899, if the British only sought to avenge earlier military defeats at the hands of the Afrikaners. A government serious about gaining political rights for British working men in the Cape Colony would use arbitration rather than military force.[39] In June 1899, the *New Age* asserted that "democracy demands enfranchisement everywhere" and suggested that any attempt to enfranchise the Uitlanders be met with a struggle on behalf of those Indians in the Cape Colony who had lost their rights in 1886.[40] By August, the journal admonished that democracy meant "the rule of all the people, by all the people, for all the people, regardless of race, of colour, of sex, or any of those distinctions which have heretofore prevailed, and served to divide the people, and render the many subordinate to the few."[41] A subsequent editorial urged enfranchised white men in South Africa—Afrikaner and Briton—to extend the franchise to indigenous Africans, thus demonstrating that Britons "interpret civilisation as the art of living together."[42]

These newspapers took up the question of women's enfranchisement with a new urgency, foreshadowing the tenor and rhetoric of much early militant suffragism. As early as July 1899, an article on "The Woman Question" in the *New Age* made an analogy between the condition of British women and the Uitlanders. The following week, the same column suggested that women form a "'deeds not words' secret society," and vow "to do justice, love, and mercy."[43] In September 1899, the column "Woman's World" suggested that British women watched not only the Uitlanders but also their own leaders for political guidance: "Our statesmen [are] showing us that they consider the question of the political enfranchisement of the Outlander a matter of supreme importance. They tell us that the unenfranchised must inevitably be wronged or stultified." Regardless of the war's outcome, the article urged, this example "should cause [women] to rise in mass and claim their own rights."[44]

Indeed, opposition to the war among radical suffragists would provide impetus for militant action. Dora Montefiore, a onetime Liberal turned socialist activist, developed an analysis of women's relationship to the state during the war that would have significant consequences for the future of the suffrage movement.[45] Early in the conflict, Montefiore published an influential essay in the *Ethical World*, a weekly paper edited jointly by Stanton Coit, minister of the South Place Ethical Society, and J. A. Hobson, known for his vigorous denunciation of capitalist interests in South Africa as the instigators of war.[46] Montefiore drew an analogy between the voteless women in Britain and the Uitlanders, the difference between their subjection being one of duration. She conceded that the five- to seven-year waiting period negotiated for the Uitlanders was politically unacceptable to the British government; nevertheless, she reminded her readers, British women who acted as citizens would never attain citizen rights at home. How, then, were women to acquire political rights? Montefiore's solution linked the evolving strategies of the nineteenth-century suffrage movement and an expanded vocabulary of political resistance in the twentieth-century campaign. "If nothing but war will meet the situation," she urged, "then war must be declared by women at all Parliamentary elections, by making woman's suffrage a Test Question." Eschewing the violence of war, she predicted that "woman's influence in political and social questions . . . shall in the end prove as powerful as an appeal to arms."[47] The significance of this argument lies not in its urging of a new strategy, for the Union of Practical Suffragists had been formed within the Women's Liberal Federation in the 1890s largely because a group of women Liberals wanted to make women's suffrage a test question at elections.[48] What is significant is the escalation of rhetoric—a declaration of war—and the connection of women's right to the parliamentary franchise with women's resistance to existing political institutions.

Montefiore argued that because women had no representation, they could not make their positions known to members of Parliament; therefore, women lacked representation and had recourse only to passive resistance.[49] She had outlined a variation on this policy to readers of the feminist paper the *Woman's Signal* in June 1897, suggesting that should the third reading of the women's enfranchisement bill then before the House of Commons fail, then those women "who believe in the justice of our demands should form a league, binding ourselves to resist passively the payment of taxes until such taxation be followed by representation."[50] She implemented this position in her own refusal to pay imperial taxes during the war. Montefiore was prosecuted for her wartime tax resistance in 1904, and she went on to recommend the tactic in 1906 to a controversial new suffrage organization, the Women's Social and Political Union, as a means of drawing attention to the campaign for women's parliamentary enfranchisement. She implemented the protest again, to spectacular effect, during the "Siege of Montefiore," at her Hammersmith, London, villa in May and June 1906. The house, surrounded by a wall, could be reached only through an arched doorway, which Montefiore and her maid barred against the bailiffs. For six weeks, Montefiore resisted payment of her taxes, addressing the frequent crowds through the upper windows of the house. WSPU meetings were held in front of the house daily, and resolutions were taken "'that taxation without representation is tyranny.'" After six weeks, the Crown was legally authorized to break down the door in order to seize property in lieu of taxes, a process to which Montefiore submitted, saying, "It was useless to resist *force majeure* when it came to technical violence on the part of the authorities."[51] Montefiore made her case in the local *Kensington News* that her refusal to pay imperial tax was linked to her exclusion from the parliamentary franchise. She was quoted in the paper as saying, "'I pay my rates willingly and cheerfully, because I possess my municipal vote. I can vote for the Borough and County Councils, and on the election of Guardians.'" Montefiore's success at mobilizing interest in the women's cause, and her clear articulation of her protest as one aimed at remedying her exclusion from the parliamentary franchise, popularized the concept of resisting the government as a new approach to campaigning for women's suffrage.[52]

The connection between Montefiore's opposition to the war and her lack of representation raised a question central to the formulation of militancy as political strategy: To what extent were women governed by laws they played no role in formulating? What obligations did women owe a state governing without their consent? For a growing number of British men and women at the turn of the century, "consent" replaced "service" as the criterion by which responsible citizenship would be practiced.[53] After the South African War, suffragettes would come to use it as a kind of shorthand for the disjunction between the state's exercise of physical force in the service of male franchise rights abroad while middle-class white women languished without votes in Britain.[54]

The radical independent model of citizenship promoted by Montefiore and other suffragettes after 1900 animated militancy's emergence within the twentieth-century women's suffrage movement. It was a model of citizenship that offered consent as a primary obligation of citizenship, exposed the state's reliance upon the exercise of physical force, and offered a more democratic conception of the state.[55] This model of citizenship suggested to some suffragists a wider extension of enfranchisement than that envisioned by the mainstream movement. In the months leading up to the commencement of hostilities in South Africa, articles in the *New Age* urged that not only the Uitlanders but also indigeneous Africans should be enfranchised. An editorial from November 1899 stressed that "democracy does not permit of the control of one community by another. It does not contemplate an Imperialism with physical force as its fundamental principle, but it does contemplate the Brotherhood of Nations, the Empire of the principle of peace and goodwill among men."[56]

It is tempting to view radical suffragists' deployment of arguments against an imperial war as a strategic move, demonstrating principled solidarity with Africans and other disenfranchised people of South Africa. More likely, however, the rhetoric was employed tactically, with radical suffragists playing metropolitan concerns off a colonial crisis within the imperial state. Radical suffragists revealed their allegiances in their frequent comparisons between their situation and that of the Afrikaners; the state of disenfranchised Africans and Indians in South Africa featured infrequently in their rhetoric. The Afrikaners' fight for national self-determination was compared alternately with that of the Irish, the American colonists, and the Polish, Greek, and Italian independence movements, which suffragists made analogous with their own cause.[57] Their complaints were not with the Afrikaners. Rather, they criticized the British government, both for exerting force on behalf of the Uitlanders' franchise rights and for using that force illegitimately against a weaker state. While radical suffragists' understanding of democracy argued against an understanding of the state as based on force and suggested a range of possible outcomes, including the eventual end to British sovereignty, it did not challenge racialized conceptions of citizenship, nor ultimately white supremacy, in South Africa.[58]

British involvement in the South African War accelerated expansion of the powers and reach of the state.[59] Yet the war had further political significance, both for the organized campaign for women's suffrage and for the practice of citizenship in Britain at the turn of the century. The controversies surrounding this imperial war linked the changing consciousness of women suffragists in the 1890s to the new methods and tactics of the twentieth-century movement. Liberal suffragist Millicent Garrett Fawcett alluded to this when she wrote of the women's suffrage movement's increased vigor after the South African War. The war, she acknowledged in 1912, "ultimately strengthened the demand of women for citizenship, for it has been observed again and again that a war, or any other event which stimulates national vitality, and the consciousness of the value of citizenship is almost certain to be followed by increased vigour in the suffrage movement, and not infrequently by its success."[60]

The South African War provided a critical turning point in the development of new idioms and organizations in the ongoing campaign for women's parliamentary enfranchisement in Britain. It presaged many of the issues that preoccupied suffragists and the nation during the First World War, such as the vexed relationship of service to citizenship. Just what did citizens owe the state? This question became especially difficult when the state did not recognize certain groups as citizens, that is, when it did not acknowledge women's political rights but nevertheless expected them to fulfill duties to the state. More significantly, the war exposed to critical scrutiny what journalist and future supporter of suffrage militancy Henry Woodd Nevinson would call "one of the most perplexing of all human problems"—the rights of liberty and the limits of revolt, creating new modes of political engagement and discourse.[61] This is most apparent in the array of fin de siècle movements in which consent and resistance figured in citizen engagement with the state. In 1902, a leading figure of the ethical movement, Dr. John Clifford, invoked the rhetoric of passive resistance in a campaign against the Education Act. Clifford emphasized citizens' right to resist government operating without their consent, and the moral responsibility of citizens to resist laws contravening Christian conscience and divine command.[62] Four years later, in South Africa, Mohandas Gandhi assumed leadership of the first Indian passive resistance campaign against attempts to institute a system requiring Indian and Chinese laborers to register with the Transvaal government, forcing them to leave their fingerprints on file and carry passes when moving between home and work. Gandhi's leadership of the movement took him to London in October 1906 to present a deputation to Lord Elgin at the Colonial Office and to build up support among Britons for an end to the pass system. Gandhi's cause received much attention in the contemporary British press.[63] Much evidence points to widespread connections between a variety of progressive movements, not least of which was their tendency to base passive resistance to government authority in the moral authority of citizens and subjects.

Perhaps the most significant of these connections lay in the networks of activists constituting the labor movement, which appeared to many men and women of radical persuasion to be the place where women's political demands could best be met. Historian Andrew Chadwick has noted that "discussion over the varying definitions, perceived scope, and means of maintaining and extending, 'political freedom,' were crucial in defining the political identity of both the Labour Party and the broader left" in the first quarter of the twentieth century.[64] Trying to understand this movement primarily in terms of individuals' organizational affiliations misses the vitality and complexity of the labor subculture in the first years of the twentieth century. While many men and women in the labor movement belonged to socialist organizations like the Independent Labour Party (ILP) or the Social Democratic Federation (SDF), others crossed organizational lines to work for broader social and political transformations.[65] Radical printer Thomas Cobden Sanderson recorded attending an ILP meeting in January 1902 with his suffragist wife, Anne, at which the lecturer considered the topic "Why Socialists and Radicals Should Co-operate." Later that year, Cobden Sanderson enthusiastically endorsed the labor movement as "a movement for the transformation of the world in the spirit of the whole, and for justice as the law of man's spiritual well-being and for justice as man's supreme law," suggesting a far wider scope of political activism than offered by participation in traditional labor organizations.[66] Ethical socialists expressed similar beliefs. They were committed to what Sylvia Pankhurst would call "the beautiful life of Socialism," less economic screed than radical critique.[67] Stanton Coit, leader of the West London Ethical Society, understood the goal of politics to "make Society, in the church, in the school, in the playground, in the factory, in the legislative halls, a spiritual organism."[68] The dimensions of this labor movement were sketched annually in the *Reformers' Year Book* (formerly *Labour Annual*), edited by Frederick Pethick Lawrence and Joseph Edwards. Their broad sweep of the groups comprising the labor movement in Britain between 1903 and 1909 revealed a range of organizations devoted to temperance, labor, and women, interconnected by personal and ideological commitments.[69]

But rifts emerged within this labor subculture in the years between 1905 and 1907. While women suffragists pursued the question of women's enfranchisement within the ILP and the SDF, debate intensified over the specific measures labor organizations would pursue. In 1905, differences arose between those committed to a parliamentary measure for adult suffrage and a so-called limited parliamentary measure enfranchising women on the same terms as men. In conference in Liverpool in January 1905, members of the Adult Suffrage Society and the Labour Representation Committee confirmed their allegiance to the principle of adult suffrage, while delegates at the ILP conference in Manchester in April of the same year passed a resolution in favor of women's franchise as a preliminary step toward adult suffrage.[70] Radical independents found themselves awkwardly positioned. If they pursued a measure enfranchising women on current property qualifications, they were accused of elitism, of seeking what the SDF called "fine-lady suffrage."[71] If they chose adult suffrage, however, they feared that women's enfranchisement would be postponed indefinitely.[72] Radical independents' frustration with socialist men's lack of enthusiasm for women's suffrage was matched by their frustration with those who would tether their cause to party politics. Radical independent suffragists sought to create a new option, one giving priority to women's suffrage and eschewing equally Liberal and Labor political affiliations. Many radical independents remained committed to adult suffrage, believing that women's suffrage would be a temporary stopping point along the way.[73] For these suffragists, the future of democracy hinged on women's suffrage. As socialist Frederick John Shaw explained in 1907, "The denial of citizen rights to women is more than a mistake in detail; it is a blasphemy against the spirit of democracy, the unpardonable sin."[74]

While the evidence suggests that a good many suffragettes retained ties to socialist politics and organizations, after 1905 an increasing rhetorical separation of women's suffrage from labor issues characterized suffrage politics.[75] Radical independents also began to implement the policy for which they would be known in coming years, that of challenging the Liberal Party to fulfill the fundamental principle of Liberalism, which they defined as "government of the people by the people, even such of the people as happened to be women."[76] The WSPU chose the 13 October 1905 Liberal Party meeting, held at the Manchester Free Trade Hall, as the occasion for unveiling a new approach to pressing the women's cause. During the question period, two WSPU members, Christabel Pankhurst and Annie Kenney, repeatedly queried Liberal candidate Sir Edward Grey about his party's support for women's suffrage. Ejected from the meeting by stewards and determined to conclude her protest by being arrested, Pankhurst spat at a policeman who was restraining her arms.[77] Pankhurst's arrest and incarceration were covered by the mainstream press and became the means by which the organization was propelled to national attention. Historians tend to focus on this episode as the "first militant protest," but that is hardly its most salient feature. The protest inaugurated the WSPU's challenge to the Liberal Party, soon to be returned to power in the coming year. Working outside party politics and challenging the party in power to live up to its ideals would bring new focus to a movement that seemed to some at the turn of the century to have lost momentum. By early 1906, a new intensity in the campaign for women's parliamentary enfranchisement could be seen emerging from within the tangle of issues radical independents negotiated.

Chapter 3

Staging Exclusion, 1906–1909

In the years following the South African War, a cluster of organizations emerged, creating a continuum along which militants enacted resistance. By early 1906, these militants had become known as "suffragettes" after the halfpenny mass-circulation *Daily Mail* derisively substituted the diminutive "ette" for "ist."[1] Suffragettes formed a number of organizations, including the Women's Social and Political Union (1903), the Women's Freedom League (1907), the Men's Political Union (1910), and the Women's Tax Resistance League (1909). Significant splits and regroupings would result in creation of the United Suffragists (1914), the East London Federation of Suffragettes (1914), the Suffragettes of the Women's Social and Political Union (1915), and the Independent WSPU (1916).[2] Between 1906 and 1918, suffragettes refined the right of resistance to illegitimate government as a right grounded in British constitutional principles. In contrast, the National Union of Women's Suffrage Societies, which in 1897 had united warring factions of the nineteenth-century movement and would become the largest suffrage organization of the Edwardian period, continued largely to confine itself to the assertion of women's right to citizenship.[3] Suffragettes' assertion of resistance as a right drew upon the historically based right of the people to resist corrupt and tyrannical government and thus links the women's suffrage movement to a long tradition of radical protest.[4] Through the assertion of their right to resist constituted authority, suffragettes attempted to define citizenship as an active practice. Women, they urged, were fit for citizenship because they acted as citizens who would not be denied their place in the political nation.

Resistance emerged as a feature of suffragettes' engagement with liberal citizenship for a number of reasons. One possibility is that some suffragists tired of presenting their demands within the same narrowly defined constitutional framework that allowed for the mere assertion of right.[5] The presentation of endless petitions and incessant lobbying of members of Parliament for legislation that was inevitably defeated began to frustrate many women active in the movement.[6] Suffragettes were therefore believed to have been motivated to move from constitutionalism to various forms of anarchy because seemingly having exhausted the legislative possibilities for women's enfranchisement, they fully rejected government's authority.[7] An alternative explanation accepts the pervasiveness of accumulating frustration—forty years of political agitation with limited success could, and did, operate as a rallying cry—but qualifies it. Those women who became suffragettes had, in fact, come to believe that the legislative avenues available to them had been exhausted. Far from rejecting constitutionalism, however, suffragettes—at least until 1910, and many until 1914—pursued strategies of resistance that drew upon the constitutional idiom. As had liberals, radicals, and conservatives throughout the nineteenth century, suffragettes staked claim to inclusion in the political nation by insisting that the British constitution live up to its own ideals.

The general election of January 1906 played a decisive role in shaping suffragette political strategy for several years to come. The House of Commons acquired a new complexion in early 1906, with Liberals holding 401 seats, while the Labour Party (transformed from the Labour Representation Committee) won 29, the Unionists 157, and the Irish nationalists 83.[8] Labour members were by no means united in support for a measure enfranchising women, and, in any event, they held insufficient seats to have much impact on the overall success of the measure.[9] Liberals posed the most formidable dilemma for suffragists. A majority of Liberal members of Parliament consistently polled in favor of women's suffrage throughout the Edwardian period, but the party proved ultimately unable to pass a measure because its leadership opposed it.[10] Suffragist Mabel Atkinson described how this new parliamentary configuration shaped suffragettes' political strategies. Faced on one side by Labour members who were "so advanced that they will not even temporarily accept anything less than adult suffrage," and on the other by Liberals bewildered by suffragettes' anger at their party's inattention to women's political disfranchisement, suffragettes determined "to take their proper share in controlling the future course of that legislation which must profoundly modify the daily lives of all English people—men, women, and children alike."[11]

Suffragettes aimed to take "their proper share" by making the Liberal Party fulfill the promises of liberalism. As Atkinson explained, "The work of Liberalism is to provide fair and equal political machinery, to make the form of government democratic . . . to carry out this reform is consonant with the principles and traditions of Liberalism."[12] In 1905, the WSPU began to implement this analysis. Following the humiliating treatment of a private bill for women's enfranchisement introduced by Bamford Slack, M.P. (Liberal), in May 1905, wherein the bill was never allowed to come to a vote in parliament, the WSPU condemned the actions of the House of Commons and resolved to work thereafter toward passage of a government bill for women's suffrage. Only a measure sponsored and supported by the government, they had come to believe, would be enacted into law.[13] They also adopted the practice, introduced by the Women's Liberal Federation in 1902, of challenging candidates at by-elections to pledge support for women's suffrage.[14] And they began to work against Liberal candidates at by-elections, on grounds that the loss of individual members of Parliament would demonstrate to the government the extent of electors' support for women's suffrage. This policy was followed in the general elections of January and December 1910 as well.[15] While the Liberal Party received special condemnation from the suffragettes, there was an overall estrangement among militants from party affiliations in militancy's early years. This began with the 1906 Cockermouth by-election, where members of the WSPU expanded their opposition from Liberal to Labour candidates who did not support women's suffrage. After the election, suffragettes rejected organizational affiliation with political parties as a matter of strategy.[16] This policy was eventually abandoned by suffragists in 1912, when the NUWSS adopted its Election Fighting Fund as a means of supporting Labour candidates in by-elections, thereby creating viable opposition to Liberal candidates.[17]

Suffragette protests in the years between 1906 and 1909 brought new visibility to the question of women's parliamentary enfranchisement. These protests tended to coincide with important events on the parliamentary calendar, such as the introduction and discussion of private members' bills to enfranchise women, and the opening of Parliament in the fall and spring and presentation of the king's speech, in which the monarch lay out Parliament's legislative agenda for the coming session. Between March 1907 and March 1909, three private bills holding out the promise of some measure of women's parliamentary enfranchisement were introduced by members of Parliament. Each bill passed through some of the stages of the parliamentary process, but each was eventually blocked by the machinery of the House of Commons.[18] Suffragettes organized demonstrations around debate of each of these bills. Historians have tended to focus on the large-scale demonstrations mounted in London, and other major cities, that brought together impressive numbers of women in spectacles designed to exhibit women's civic virtue before the public. The effectiveness of these protests was greatly enhanced by media coverage, which spread textual and visual descriptions of their beauty and organization well beyond the immediate experience of spectators.[19] To focus exclusively upon these spectacles, however, risks losing an important dimension of militancy: its links to political radicalism. Examination of suffragette militancy between 1906 and 1909 reveals a remarkable consistency in analyses of and remedies for women's political condition.

Drawing upon the constitutional idiom, suffragettes reworked a critique of tyrannical authority borrowed from early-nineteenth-century radicalism.[20] Suffragettes' claim to inclusion in the political nation borrowed heavily from radicalism's lexicon. Suffragettes shared radicals' critique of privilege and monopoly and viewed the evils of "sex subjection" as no less insidious than those of "class subjection."[21] They fulminated against the "Aristocracy of Sex [a position] that, in more barbarous and less advanced social States, the masses of men have occupied towards Royal and Feudal classes."[22] Once citizens, women would eliminate the "artificial distinctions that give one person an unfair advantage over another."[23] Suffragettes aligned themselves on the side of the rights of the subject—free speech, association, and religion—protected under the British constitution.[24] And they protested what they saw as the suspension of the rules when women claimed the rights attending their political responsibilities. Like radicals before them, suffragettes appealed to a British sense of fair play, noting that they suffered under "penalties and duties, without the corresponding right: coercion & repression, without any corresponding remedy."[25]

Suffragettes created narratives rooted in a belief in a lost golden age, retrievable through resistance to existing structures. The parliamentary enfranchisement of women, they urged, represented not political innovation but "'the restitution of their ancient political rights.'"[26] They located Britain's golden age at various points in time. Its dawning could be traced to the "Parliament of Saxons," which "was a Parliament of women," or only as far back as Magna Carta's use of *homo* to mean both man and woman.[27] Women's loss of constitutional rights in the modern era corresponded to a curtailment of progress in civilization, and a shift from direct to virtual representation in government.[28] Militancy, they averred, was not designed to persuade Parliament of the justness of women's position; rather, it sought to reach the "real master," the "sovereign people" of the country, "to coerce the House of Commons to do their bidding."[29]

The critique of privilege and monopoly rested upon a belief in "the people," which had been cast by the middle-class radical John Bright in the 1860s as masculine, responsible, and decidedly unaristocratic.[30] Suffragettes challenged the exclusivity of this ideal, asserting that "the People is made up of men and women. Both sexes must be represented before the People can be represented. Neither men nor women alone make the nation."[31] Just as the House of Lords was not a representative institution because it represented an elite, the House of Commons represented only men. "No Government can be representative until it includes women."[32] As "the people," women asserted a moral right to participate in government.[33] And as "the people," women had participated historically in engendering public spirit by "strengthening the hands of their leaders in the struggle for constitutional government."[34]

Suffragettes self-consciously cast themselves as inheritors of the radical tradition, with the goal of restoring citizenship to its uncorrupted origins. They understood themselves as radicals in a line extending back to the seventeenth century and made frequent comparisons between their struggle and that of bourgeois men against the Crown.[35] They sought parallels between their activism and that of earlier political rebels, including John Wilkes,

John Hampden, Oliver Cromwell, and John Pym, who they saw as critical to democracy's development.[36] They likened their fight to great emancipation struggles of the past, including the abolition of slavery, repeal of the Corn Laws, and Chartist agitation.[37] Suffragettes borrowed from other national histories as well, citing Russian peasants' struggles to gain political liberties from the czar, and battles for Italian unification.[38] They criticized their contemporaries for stopping with "root" reforms and lopping off any growth from the roots their fathers planted.[39] And they saw their activism as upholding specifically British values. Suffragettes, Christabel Pankhurst asserted, had no criticism to make of men's political successes in other countries, "but they feel it hard, that being the rightful heirs to the constitutional liberty built up by their foremothers and forefathers, they should have that inheritance withheld, while men of other races are suddenly and almost without preparation leaping into possession of constitutional power."[40]

This radical narrative of loss, resistance, and recovery underwrote the practice of militancy throughout the prewar period. It was especially prevalent between 1906 and 1909, when the constitutional drama emerged as the predominant mode of militant protest. The constitutional drama consistently emphasized two principles adumbrated by Women's Freedom League (WFL) founding member Teresa Billington-Greig: the assertion of women's political rights and the repudiation of laws extending obligations to women but not rights.[41] Constitutional dramas articulated the belief that women's rights as citizens had been systematically stripped from them by legislative action since the early nineteenth century, and that through property ownership certain women met the criteria for citizenship as defined by the British constitution.[42] Despite this disenfranchisement, they had argued, women continued to exercise the obligations of citizenship through the payment of taxes and the discharge of other responsibilities, notably in the realm of municipal social reform.[43]

Historians' emphasis upon the "nonparty" aspect of women's suffrage organizations tends to obscure the extent to which militancy was the approach more likely adopted by women of radical persuasion. Suffragettes employed the constitutional idiom in service of their political goals, which emphasized not a gradual liberal progression to reform but the radical necessity of rebellion to force reform. While suffragettes' protests challenged the authority of British institutions of government, they did not seek to restructure British society fundamentally. Suffragettes were radical in two senses of the word: they drew upon a historical tradition of radicalism, with its own rich vocabulary and repertoire of protest, and they constituted part of a turn-of-the-century political movement attempting to create a political space to the left of both the Liberals and Labour.[44]

The rhetorical framework of radicalism offered suffragettes two alternatives: withholding consent from government and, in more extreme cases, actually resisting the operation of government. Suffragettes and suffragists alike repeatedly urged that government was run best with the consent of the governed. Chrystal MacMillan, a member of the NUWSS and a close personal friend of several militants, argued in 1909 that "the chief landmarks in the history of the development of a constitution are those times at which the governed have ceased to give their consent to the established government, and the result has been either alteration in the form of government or civil war."[45] Suffragettes took the question of consent further, however, arguing that "the consent of the people—men and women—is necessary to make any law binding upon the inhabitants of the country."[46] As "the Government refuses to recognise women, let women refuse to recognise the Government."[47] Suffragettes interpreted this in various ways between 1906 and 1914, the best-known examples of militancy being window breaking, arson, and hunger strikes by members of the WSPU. Other suffragettes, however, implemented less violent forms of protest. Members of a variety of organizations, including the WFL, WTRL, and numerous smaller groups, undertook tax resistance and other innovative forms of passive resistance.

Radical narration of the constitution differed from a liberal one in several particulars. Whereas liberal suffragists continued to embrace the notion of gradual and progressive improvement, suffragettes emphasized that because those on top would always violently resist change, those seeking change would have to do so forcefully. This was as true of suffragettes' struggle with the Liberals in the twentieth century as it had been of the barons' dispute with the king at Runnymeade in the thirteenth century and parliamentarians' war against the monarch in the seventeenth century. "Political liberty," one suffragette wrote, "has always had to be wrested from English lawmakers by threats, riots, or the sword."[48] Other suffragettes sought to establish "the militant methods of determined women" as a universal political principle, citing successful contemporary instances of militancy in Glasgow, Turkey, Persia, and India.[49] How, then, suffragettes asked, was change to be brought about? WSPU leader Christabel Pankhurst offered one answer, employing a metaphor linking home to the constitution. She urged that "those who are outside the Constitution have no ordinary means of securing admission; and therefore they must try extraordinary means." A person locked out of her house, she observed, would break the window in order to gain access. "Just in the same way British women, who find the doors of the Constitution barred against them, are prepared to force their way in as best they can."[50]

Militants sought not to restructure their society but to make profound changes in the meaning of citizenship. Robert Cholmeley urged in 1909 "that until it is recognised that a woman may be a citizen, citizenship will not mean what it ought to mean, and government will not be able to do what it ought to do."[51] Citizenship, suffragettes believed, was a process, not a status, and women's struggles for political rights themselves constituted citizen engagement. Laurence Housman explained that "the power to organise and the determination to agitate are in themselves the beginning of a qualification for political enfranchisement, for they are a proof of political vitality, and show that a fresh section of the community has awakened from sleep."[52]

Other suffragettes urged that women already practiced the duties of citizenship; possession of the vote would acknowledge that fact. As Charlotte Despard proclaimed before a crowd in Eastbourne in May 1909: "We are citizens. That is our inalienable right. We believe we form an integral part of the body politic; of that nothing can deprive us."[53] Parliamentary voting rights may have been suffragettes' ultimate goal, but the act of engaging in the political sphere was paramount. Great disagreement existed within the militant movement over the use of violence, on the relationship of the means to the ends, about how decisions should be made within suffrage organizations, and whether or not men should be allowed membership in suffrage organizations. But all suffragettes agreed that militants sought to redefine citizenship not as a privilege but as a right based on the constitution and women's contributions to the nation. Women had earned the designation "citizen," and the struggle suffragettes mounted to secure their right to it would make them appreciate having the vote all the more.[54]

Suffragette militancy enacted the radical idea that citizens had the right to resist tyrannical authority; militancy's implementation became a contest over the uses and utility of physical force in negotiating with the state. Thus, suffragette militancy was performative and spectacular but not only, or even primarily, because it exhibited women's bodies in public. Suffragettes utilized a range of strategies, gendered in complex and sometimes contradictory ways, designed to highlight what they saw as the arbitrary and historically anomalous exclusion of women from the constitution. Staging exclusion from the constitution articulated women's suffrage as an explicitly political struggle, a kind of spectacular politics, in which suffragettes fought with the government and among themselves over the elasticity of the British constitution. While all militants self-consciously cast themselves as political actors engaged in the act of interpreting the constitution, they by no means held only one understanding of British political tradition or of their relationship to it, nor did they protest their exclusion in a monolithic way.[55] Two militant protests held in October 1908, one staged by the WSPU, the other by the WFL, illustrate important differences and similarities among suffragettes. Both protests focused on the House of Commons, and both highlighted issues around spectacularity. Both drew upon the constitutional idiom in staging women's political exclusion, but they differed fundamentally on the role violence would play in militancy.

On 9 October 1908, the WSPU issued a handbill inviting Londoners to join the organization in a deputation to the House of Commons, setting off a chain of events that culminated in the arrests and public trial of three Union officials, Emmeline and Christabel Pankhurst and "General" Flora Drummond.[56] Within days of its release, the handbill's wording—"help the suffragettes to rush the House of Commons"—prompted the Home Office to initiate proceedings against the women on the grounds that they were inciting crowds to violence.[57] On the evening of 13 October, thousands of people and some five thousand police constables scuffled for hours in Parliament Square as groups of suffragettes attempted to make their way to the House of Commons. About three dozen men and women were arrested.[58] The trial of the women, held in the Bow Street Police Court, and Christabel Pankhurst's celebrated examination of two members of the cabinet present in Parliament Square that day, David Lloyd George, chancellor of the exchequer, and Herbert Gladstone, home secretary, brought the women's claim to public attention as never before. At the "suffrage meeting attended by millions," Emmeline Pethick Lawrence's apt description of this widely publicized trial, suffragettes persuasively reiterated women's claim to inclusion in the constitution.[59]

This protest, initiated by Emmeline and Christabel Pankhurst, has been seen as a turning point in the development of WSPU militant strategy, but it paled next to the dramatic courtroom scenes resulting from Christabel Pankhurst's cross-examination of Lloyd George and Gladstone.[60] In fact, neither woman had participated in the "Rush" on the House of Commons because both had been arrested and taken into police custody immediately prior to the demonstration. Christabel Pankhurst's rhetoric around this protest of 1908 not only provides insight into how Union officials defined militancy at that time but also illuminates the principles upon which the practice of militancy rested and points toward its future development.

The "Rush" was cast as a constitutional challenge. In her closing arguments before Bow Street Police Court magistrate Henry Curtis Bennett, Christabel Pankhurst reiterated the historical and legal precedents informing the protest, claiming "a perfectly constitutional right to go ourselves in person to lay our grievances before the House of Commons." Suffragettes, she noted, were "but pursuing a legitimate course which in the old days women pursued without the smallest interference by the authorities."[61] Where the protest may have slipped the bonds of constitutional sanction lay in its execution, a point missed by neither the government nor the suffragettes. While small groups of suffragettes attempted to make their way into the House of Commons, the size of the crowds assembled outside Parliament on 13 October 1908, estimated by historian Andrew Rosen at sixty thousand, far exceeded the number provided for by the statute of Charles II that suffragettes used as justification for their deputations. Statute 13, Charles II (1661) guaranteed the right of subjects "to present any public or private grievance or complaint to any member or members of Parliament after his election or to the King's Majesty for any remedy to be thereupon had," but it specified that deputations not have more than ten members.[62]

The constitutional principle at stake in the "Rush" case became the linchpin of Christabel Pankhurst's arguments before the magistrate in police court. The *Times* paraphrased Pankhurst's representation of the women's offense:

Read in a reasonable way, the handbill in question might possibly be said to be an invitation to persons to unlawful assembly. That was the charge upon which Mr. John Burns was tried in 1886, and upon which he was acquitted. If it was not unlawful assembly, it was nothing at all, but they were not charged with that offence, for the reasons that such a charge would give them the right to a trial by a jury and the right to appeal.[63]

In all her public statements surrounding the trial, Christabel Pankhurst assiduously linked the constitutionality of the women's protest to the means they employed. In a speech given at St. James's Hall, two days after her arrest, she argued that suffragettes were following the historical example set by the barons who forced King John to grant Magna Carta, the "title-deeds of British liberty." The king conceded, she contended, because he feared the barons; suffragettes, she urged, must similarly make the government fear them. Pankhurst's speech revised British constitutional history, interpreting the accounting of its development "from precedent to precedent" as meaning an evolution derived from the use—or threat of the use—of force. She asked, "The Reform Bills—how were they obtained? Were they obtained by milk-and-water methods? Were they obtained by coaxing the Government, by trying to win their sympathy? No. They were got by hard fighting, and they could have been got in no other way."[64] "Hard fighting," then, spurred political reform, and in her interpretation of British constitutional development, the use of violence was integral to promoting change, rather than antithetical to political reform.

For Pankhurst, justification for the use of violence lay not merely in its constitutional function but in other realms as well, including those of a "higher law." In that same speech given at St. James's Hall, Pankhurst provided important perspective on the future of WSPU strategy as she deftly moved from an interpretation of WSPU militancy as constitutional practice to one resting upon the higher principles justifying the use of violence. Pankhurst began her speech before the crowd with an appeal to historical precedent and the constitution as grounds for challenging current laws prohibiting women from voting, pointing to the "constitutional" practices then exercised by militants, such as contesting by-elections and presenting deputations to Parliament. But her next rhetorical move threatened to dislocate the constitution from the center of the WSPU's justification for militancy. "Friends, if we are found guilty by the law of this land, we shall hold ourselves to be innocent by a higher law."[65]

This speech, pointing as it does, both toward and away from the language of constitutionalism, made reference to the historical legacy upon which the practice of WSPU militancy drew in 1908 and suggested how that organization would come to justify future violent action. What is telling, and original, in Pankhurst's interpretation was the slippage between constitutional principle and historical precedent; for Pankhurst, trained as a lawyer, the two became one and the same. By renarrating the history of constitutional conflict to emphasize popular violence as a counter to official despotism, Pankhurst stretched constitutional principles to accommodate the inclusion of women. Her rhetoric points also to alternative sources of legitimacy for protest in popular-radical culture, such as Christian and ethical movements, and suggests a shift in emphasis between two interdependent sides of the notion of "lawful" agitation and resistance.[66]

Marking a turning point in the WSPU's articulation of the use of militancy, the trial provided the organization with a forum in which it could be established definitively both that women were denied the constitutional means of redressing their exclusion from the franchise and that the government would bring its full weight to bear upon those women who dared to claim their constitutional rights.[67] The WSPU's evocation of the specter of violence, despite Pankhurst's disingenuous disclaimers, thus could be simultaneously rooted in constitutional precedent and set above that precedent. Finally, this notorious trial of the WSPU leadership left a public statement against which all other militants had to assert their views.

The WFL marked that same October parliamentary session of 1908 with protests designed to put forth its own interpretation of the constitutionality of militancy. On 28 October 1908, at approximately 8:30 P.M., while a licensing bill was being discussed in committee, cries of "Votes for women!" were heard from the Ladies' Gallery above the House of Commons. Two members of the League, Helen Fox and Muriel Matters, had chained themselves to the metal screen in the Ladies' Gallery that obscured women observers from view in the House of Commons. Matters held forth on women's suffrage to the members below, while Violet Tillard, another member of the League, showered the floor of the Commons with leaflets advocating women's suffrage. Simultaneously, leaflets were thrown by male supporters of the League from the Strangers' Gallery, and WFL members protested outside the House— at the entrance to St. Stephen's Hall, in the hall itself, and outside on the statue of Richard the Lionheart. House officials found that they were unable to remove Matters and Fox without dismantling the Grille, as it had been constructed in sections, "each section being fixed to stone mullions by screws." The women were taken into a committee room and their chains filed off when they refused to produce a key for the locks. Fourteen members of the League were arrested that day, and the Speaker ordered that both the Ladies' Gallery and the Strangers' Gallery be closed indefinitely (see figure 3.1).[68]

The Grille Protest, like the WSPU's inaugural militant protest in the Manchester Free Trade Hall in November 1905, aimed at the "'interruption' of male political discourse."[69] The organization reveled in the decision it forced upon members of Parliament: "between the adjournment of business and the removal of the insulting grille."[70] The *Times* described events in the chamber: "It should be mentioned that the shrill vociferation of the women and the disturbance for which they were responsible did not interrupt the proceedings of the House. Throughout the scene first MR. REMNANT and then MR. RAWLINSON addressed the committee, and, but for the fact that they had to raise their voices to a high pitch, one might have thought that they were

FIGURE 3.1
The *Illustrated London News,* 7 November 1908,
depicting a suffragette chained to the grille in the
House of Commons. Mary Evans Picture Library.

unaware that anything unusual was taking place."[71] The predominant imagery of this press account evokes less the successful interruption of political
discourse, however, than an eerie *tableau vivant:* parliamentary activity pro-
ceeding while women mouth grievances from afar. The *Times*'s account of
the Grille Protest demonstrates the extent to which the battle for the parliamentary enfranchisement of women was a symbolic struggle over whose narrative of events would prevail. By implication, if the women had *not* succeeded in interrupting the committee meeting in progress, then they had
not been forceful enough in making their case.

The symbolism of the Grille Protest extended well beyond suffragettes' attempt to interrupt male political discourse and resonated metaphorically in
at least three other registers. First, the protest drew attention to the Grille—
which kept women apart from the House and invisible to it—as a symbol of

women's exclusion from political representation. The protest forced members of Parliament to choose between listening to women's claims for political representation and removing a symbol of their exclusion from that representation. Second, it dramatized further erosions of women's historic rights by invoking the rules regulating the admission of women into the House of Commons, which, until the late eighteenth century, had allowed women to sit anywhere in the chamber.[72] Women's twentieth-century exclusion from the House of Commons—where they were allowed to sit and observe, but only as an invisible and unacknowledged presence—thus suggested a strong analogy with women's status as citizens within the nation. Third, the language WFL members used to describe the Grille, as "that sign of sex-subjection," resonated with the orientalist imagery of the oppression of purdah and the harem so characteristic of Victorian feminism.[73]

While not raising the specter of violence as had the WSPU's "Rush" protest of the summer, the WFL's dramatization of women's exclusion from the political nation in the Grille Protest similarly contributed to the production of militancy as political spectacle designed to draw attention to their cause.[74] Yet it is important to note that the impact of protests like the ones undertaken by the WFL and the WSPU in October 1908 depended, for visual and political impact, as much upon radical narratives of resistance and recovery as upon the exhibition of women's bodies in public space. The transgression of male political space depended upon the redeployment of radical narratives in the service of women's emancipation. These narratives, and what they implied, as much as the scenes of chaos portrayed by the press, explain why the Grille Protest reinforced divisions within the women's suffrage movement on the utility of militancy to the women's cause. After the protest, the NUWSS executive distanced itself from the WFL's "disturbances," distinguishing between the WFL's spectacle and its own "steadfast adherence to lawful and constitutional methods of agitation."[75]

In October 1909, the liberal feminist paper the *Englishwoman's Review* characterized both the WSPU hunger strike and the WFL's "Siege" of Westminster as "sensational" methods.[76] But even while their liberal contemporaries understood militant protests to be of a piece, members of militant organizations themselves differed as to what constituted militancy. This diversity was erased by the contemporary mainstream press, which represented women's suffrage campaigners in oppositional terminology of "constitutional" versus "militant," a terminology appropriated by suffragists themselves in the attempt to valorize their own efforts at the expense of other organizations. The NUWSS frequently expressed the concern that suffrage protests be "constitutional" and "law-abiding," while the WSPU consistently claimed its practice as the most authentic expression of militancy.[77] Often described as "emulating" the WSPU, the WFL as an organization devoted much time to the question of defining militancy, some would argue at the expense of practicing it.[78] Militancy, however, existed along a continuum. Militants shared certain premises, notably the importance of resisting the state governing without their consent, but they implemented that belief in a variety of practices. A range of activities constituted militancy, which suffragettes interpreted as either actively opposing or passively resisting government's functioning. Two further types of protests adopted by suffragettes during these years drew from radical precedent and claimed to return the practice of citizenship to its uncorrupted origins: posting of proclamations and presentation of petitions to the House of Commons.

On the evening of 12 October 1908, members of the WFL posted a proclamation calling upon the government to remove the sex disability implicit in the existing parliamentary franchise and demanding the immediate enfranchisement of women. In London, members of the League successfully posted the proclamation in Westminster and the City, on the private residences of cabinet ministers, on public buildings, and on letter boxes. Also plastered were Cleopatra's Needle, Boadicea's statue, the law courts, Nelson's Column, and General Gordon's statue. Reports conflicted over the organization's success in placarding the houses of Parliament, the *Times* asserting that these were too well guarded to be reached by the women, the WFL claiming success at Parliament and at the gates of Holloway Prison, where suffragettes in London typically were incarcerated.[79] More notoriously, WSPU member Marion Wallace Dunlop attempted first on 22 June 1909 and then successfully on 25 June to stencil a portion of the Bill of Rights on the wall of St. Stephen's Hall in the House of Commons. Arrested with Wallace Dunlop was Men's Political Union member Victor Duval, who helped stencil the notice advertising the upcoming Women's Deputation on June 29: "It is the right of the subject to petition the King, and all commitments and prosecutions for such petitioning are illegal."[80] The arrest of Wallace Dunlop (later infamous for being the first member of the WSPU to undertake a hunger strike) for her act at Parliament was equally significant.[81] In her self-defense before the magistrate in police court she stated: "'I wrote these words because they were in danger of being forgotten by our legislators, and because I intended that they should be indelible.'"[82]

Presentation of petitions to the prime minister, and eventually to the king, was also a significant part of militancy from the beginning. These attempts were much more than annoyances to public order or even opportunities for suffragettes to stage extraparliamentary protests. The suffragettes' attempts to reach Parliament through the crowds assembled to watch them meant that their protests and their claims would be debated in the streets. Once arrested, suffragettes used police courts as a venue in which they could make their case before a wider public. The WSPU and WFL both attempted to present petitions to the prime minister in the summer of 1909; comparison of the two illustrates important differences in the two organizations' implementations of militancy. In late June, Mrs. Pankhurst wrote to Prime Minister H. H. Asquith requesting that he receive a deputation of women on the twenty-ninth of that month. She pointed out that in his recent speech to the Russian Duma, he had characterized "constitutional government as the greatest instrument of freedom which the genius of mankind has yet invented" and requested that he hear from a deputation of women's organizations on the exclusion of women from the parliamentary franchise.[83] On 24 June, Philip Snowden, Labour M.P. for Blackburn, asked the prime minister during parliamentary question time if he would accept the deputation of suffragists. Asquith indicated that he had already heard enough on the subject from women's organizations and that he had responded to the women in the negative.[84]

On the evening of 29 June 1909, suffragists assembled for the Woman's Parliament, a public meeting of WSPU members at Caxton Hall, just blocks from the houses of Parliament. Emmeline Pethick Lawrence presided over the meeting, which sent a deputation (the thirteenth since 1906) to the House of Commons. A letter was sent via special messenger to Asquith announcing the women's intention to present him with a petition; if he were to refuse them an interview, they would use "every possible effort to gain entrance to the House."[85] Meanwhile, thousands had congregated in the streets surrounding Parliament Square, and three thousand police guarded every approach to the House. The *Daily Chronicle* described the events as "a grim and rather terrible [drama], in spite of no actual tragedy of bloodshed." The protest began with the departure from Caxton Hall of Vera Holmes, on horseback, "a picturesque figure in her bowler hat and black riding habit." She rode as far as St. Stephen's Church, where she handed documents to a mounted police inspector, who threw them to the ground. Then she rode back to Caxton Hall.[86] A deputation of eight women followed Mrs. Pankhurst down Tothill Street into Victoria Street, where a squadron of mounted policemen cleared the path for them to reach the public entrance to the House of Commons (see figure 3.2). When they were refused entrance, Mrs. Pankhurst struck Inspector Jarvis in the face with her open hand, and she and her colleagues were arrested. At Emmeline Pethick Lawrence's command, hundreds of WSPU members attempted to approach the House of Commons from all directions, and a number of the organization's members broke windows at the government offices in Whitehall. Before midnight, the police had cleared the crowds from the immediate vicinity of Parliament, and 120 people had been arrested.[87]

The offenders were brought before Magistrate Albert de Rutzen in the Bow Street Police Court on 30 June 1909. Herbert Muskett, solicitor of the legal firm Wontner and Sons, appearing on behalf of the Metropolitan Police Commission, argued that police commissioner Sir Edward Henry's "actions had been dictated solely by the public duty cast upon him to maintain order and to keep the entrance to the House free from obstruction for members."[88] He indicated that he had been instructed to say that Inspector Jarvis's actions were inspired by Sir Edward Henry's duty to carry out the sessional order of the houses of Parliament to keep the streets surrounding Westminster free and open, which he was bound to do. Henry, Muskett asserted, had received no other government instructions.[89] Setting aside the question of access to Parliament, Muskett then focused upon the assault on

FIGURE 3.2
WSPU 29 June 1909 deputation to Prime Minister
H. H. Asquith at Westminster. The Women's Library/
Mary Evans Picture Library.

Inspector Jarvis and the window breaking in Whitehall, noting that "it became a matter for serious consideration when ladies who were carrying out
an agitation by what they said were constitutional means resorted to such
acts."[90] Upon cross-examination, it was determined that no one had, in fact,
complained that access to Parliament was obstructed by the women's protest.
On behalf of the defendants, Evelina Haverfield and Emmeline Pankhurst,
Mr. Henlé argued that the women had the right under Statute 13, Charles II,
to present a petition to the king through one of his ministers, provided not
more than ten persons were in deputation.[91] Addressing the magistrate,
Henlé contended that the police had not been obstructed from performing
their duties. The women had a right to present the prime minister with their
petition. The prime minister was wrong in denying the petition, "and the
police, in assisting him to resist it, were guilty of a wrong which would prevent them from relying upon the statute." De Rutzen then asked for time to
consider the points made. The defendants were remanded until 9 July, and

Mrs. Pankhurst promised that the WSPU would not repeat disturbances of this nature during the legal proceedings.[92]

In early July, the WFL undertook its own petitioning campaign, known as the "Siege of Westminster." In an ongoing effort to meet with Asquith, the League had requested on 14 June 1909 that he receive a deputation of members to discuss their demand for a government bill enfranchising women. Asquith's response, that his "statements on the subject [were] on the record," led the WFL to announce that it would send a deputation to the House of Commons "in order to obtain an audience in accordance with their right, as expressed in the 13th Statute of Charles II," to present a petition. At a meeting at Chandos Hall on 5 July, the League chose eight women to present its demand.[93] Later that same day, when the Commons began its evening sitting, the WFL's "Siege of Westminster" began. Its eight volunteers stood at public entrances to the Commons, awaiting the arrival of the prime minister. Upon hearing that Asquith was not within the precincts of the palace of Westminster, Amy Hicks, leader of the deputation, inquired of Inspector Scantlebury at quarter-hour intervals as to whether the prime minister had arrived. The women remained outside the Commons that evening until the House rose at 3:55 A.M. The WFL announced its intention to maintain the picket outside Parliament until a deputation from the League was accepted by the prime minister.[94] After two nights on the pavement, the WFL requested a meeting with the home secretary, Herbert Gladstone. Following standard constitutional procedure, the WFL wanted Gladstone to transmit a petition to Edward VII, whom they hoped then would prevail upon the prime minister to agree to see their deputation. The League followed this letter with a deputation to the Home Office on 8 July, during which Gladstone agreed to convey their petition to the king.[95] When the WFL received no further word regarding the petition, the picket was moved from the House of Commons to the prime minister's residence.

On the afternoon of 9 July, four members of the WFL arrived at 10, Downing Street and presented Asquith's doorkeeper with a copy of the petition, waiting for a reply. A crowd of approximately two hundred people had gathered by the time the police arrested the women for obstruction. The next night, and each night thereafter when the House was in session, a group of WFL members gathered at the entrances to St. Stephen's Hall, waiting to intercept Asquith. Further arrests were made at the prime minister's residence on following consecutive Mondays, 16 and 23 July.[96] The "Siege" continued throughout July, into August, September, and October, its drama heightened by its staging during the Commons' consideration of Lloyd George's "People's Budget" and the merits of a veto by the House of Lords.[97] Conservative opposition to the proposed budget, which increased taxes and provided for increased state expenditure on pensions for workers, inflamed discussion on the constitutional limits on the peers' powers.

As the "Siege of Westminster" unfolded, the police court case concerning the WSPU's 29 June attempt to present the prime minister with a petition resumed. On 9 July 1909, Albert de Rutzen determined that while the women had the right to present petitions to the House of Commons, they were wrong not to leave once they had heard that their request had been denied. Everyone held the right to petition members of Parliament, he argued, but "there was no right in a person desirous of petitioning the House to compel any member to present his petition, and that no action would lie against a member for refusing to do so."[98] The magistrate fined Emmeline Pankhurst and Evelina Haverfield five pounds under the Prevention of Crimes Amendment Act (1885) for resisting the police. After refusing to pay, they were sentenced to one month in the second division. The magistrate expressed the opinion that a conviction in this case would allow the defendants an opportunity to appeal; he noted further that if the high court would rule on the case, disturbances of this kind would cease. Emmeline Pankhurst promised that members of the WSPU would abstain from any more deputations at the House of Commons if a decision on the appeal would be heard before the end of the year.[99]

Both the WSPU and the WFL framed their attempts to present petitions to the prime minister within the context of early nineteenth-century radical protest, emphasizing in particular the people's right to petition Parliament.[100] Like their early nineteenth-century counterparts, they made explicit comparisons between their campaign and early modern struggles between king and Parliament, battling "despotism, constitutional infringements, and unjust taxation." Like their "Puritan forefathers," they were forced to draw upon the "instrument of remonstrance."[101] Yet suffragettes' deployment of the language and practice of constitutional struggle represented no mere reenactment of earlier struggles in the name of women's electoral rights; rather, the constitutional idiom they employed served to gender militancy in complex ways. The WFL consciously manipulated the image of women waiting patiently for their political rights, emphasizing the political maturity of those desiring enfranchisement. As the protests became a fixture in London that summer, the composition of deputations was formed more deliberately, with the WFL organizing groups of "representative" women at the House of Commons. This tactic was influenced by the massive suffrage processions in London of the two previous years and similarly contributed to the developing iconography of the suffrage movement.[102] The WFL drew attention to the more "womanly" women excluded from the franchise. These included "representatives of the working women of Britain . . . widows with little children dependent on their earnings, breadwinners and rent payers"; women prominent in social reform; women graduates in academic gowns; and nurses, whose uniforms, according to one WFL member, "caused great excitement in the crowd. Womanliness personified—and yet demanding their public rights! A woman graduate—that is understandable—but a nurse!"[103]

The imagery of the "womanliness" of the nurses, and of the character of the widows and their small children, drew a contrast between the WFL's

"Siege," where members patiently waited outside Parliament to claim their rights, and the WSPU's 29 June attempt to present a petition to the prime minister at the House of Commons. It also stood in marked contrast to the WSPU's window breaking at Whitehall. This contrast employed gendered notions of how women should seek political rights—quietly, passively, and with dignity—and challenged the idea that women would be less womanly if enfranchised. The WFL had long argued that women would be more womanly if granted the vote, since, once enfranchised, they could better care for their families and the nation.[104] The WFL's picket at Westminster in 1909 thus linked prevailing assumptions about womanliness to women's political participation and challenged the WSPU's representation of militancy as forcefulness and daring.[105] This contrast was not lost upon contemporary observers. Commenting on the picket, H. G. Wells "found that continual siege of the legislature extraordinarily impressive—infinitely more impressive than the feeble-forcible 'ragging' of the more militant section."[106]

Yet, if the WFL emphasized the "womanliness" of its demands and its methods, the "Siege of Westminster" also displayed women's capacity for self-governance and self-discipline, behaviors arguably rooted in older and notably masculine traditions.[107] The WFL's deployment of the language of constitutionalism in the summer of 1909 strove to appropriate the terminology of male radical protest. Repeatedly, the WFL rhetorically adopted a masculine political identity that served both to legitimate its own protest and to distance itself from the protests of the WSPU.[108] WFL commentators consistently compared the "Siege" with WSPU protests. Reporting on the first day of its protest at Westminster in the pages of *Women's Franchise*, the WFL noted the contrast between "dramatic embellishments" of prior deputations— "scenes of violence . . . cordon(s) of police . . . sensational arrests"—and the WFL's "peaceful band of women 'who only stand and wait.'" The WFL's assertion that "we have neither invited nor created disorder—we went less than ten in number—we have obeyed all the police regulations—yet still our members have been refused a hearing" simultaneously criticized the government and the WSPU.[109] By comparing the WFL's attempts to present Asquith with a petition with those of its rival, they made their point: even when women suffragists upheld the law, their petitions were denied.[110]

Throughout the summer and into the autumn of 1909, the WFL picketed the House of Commons, maintaining that Asquith needed to hear the views of a militant suffrage society on the issue of women's suffrage, since its approach was "entirely different" from that of organizations already heard by the government, including the Women's Liberal Federation and the NUWSS.[111] No further arrests of League members were made between 23 July and 18 August as the WFL prepared for an action designed to force a judgment on the constitutionality of its protest before the courts. The "Siege" entered a new phase on the afternoon of 18 August, when WFL members Charlotte Despard and Anne Cobden Sanderson appeared on the doorstep of Asquith's residence in Downing Street (see figure 3.3). Other members

VOTES FOR WOMEN.

MRS. DESPARD and MRS. COBDEN SANDERSON
Waiting for Mr. ASQUITH. Arrested August 19th, 1909.

FIGURE 3.3
WFL postcard depicting Charlotte Despard and
Anne Cobden Sanderson waiting outside Asquith's
door, 19 August 1909, to present him with a petition.
Museum of London.

of the organization soon joined them, and together the women waited almost twelve hours before they were arrested for obstruction. Their case came
before a magistrate the next day but was remanded until the twenty-seventh,
when it was heard before Henry Curtis Bennett at Bow Street.[112]

The prosecution pursued its case on two points. First, it emphasized that
the petition the women carried that day in Downing Street was not of the
proper form; it was, in fact, a remonstrance, that is, a presentation of grievances rather than of requests. Second, the prosecution asserted that, even as-
suming that the women had exercised a constitutional right to protest, they
were not exercising it responsibly at the time of their arrest.[113] The Irish M.P.
and barrister T. M. Healy, defending the women, disagreed. He contended
that the right of remonstrance—like that of petition—dated to the time of
Charles II. At that time, Healy urged, the "general body of the disenfranchised classes received a right . . . to put forward any remonstrance or any
private complaint," both to the king and to members of Parliament. That
right was reiterated by the First Statute of William and Mary—"that it is the

right of the subject to petition the King, and all commitments and prosecutions for such petitioning are illegal." Healy observed that the authorities'
attempt to control how the WFL presented its petition indicated that they
knew full well that the League had the right to do so. Nor could the women
be charged with obstruction, since "every one of them yielded like Lambs led
to the slaughter" when the police moved to arrest them.[114] When handing
down his decision, Magistrate Bennett carefully concurred with the League
that it held the right to petition the king, but he reiterated that the women
had not been reasonable in the execution of that right.[115] Despard and Cobden Sanderson were sentenced to pay forty shillings or spend seven days in
the second division of prison; they chose the latter.[116] Like the WSPU before
them, they appealed the magistrates' decision to a higher court.

The outcome of both cases proved highly unsatisfactory to suffragettes.
The WSPU case was heard in divisional court on 1 December 1909; the divisional court (King's Bench) dealt with the WFL's "Siege" on 14 January 1910.
The lord chief justice ruled that while members of the WSPU had a right to
present petitions to the prime minister, they could not force him to receive
their deputations. A similar decision was handed down regarding the WFL's
appeal. The women, the court contended, had alternative means of presenting petitions, and they had not used the public road lawfully. The charge
of obstruction was upheld.[117] Suffragettes reluctantly acknowledged that
their attempts to force the government to engage with the constitutional
principles underlying their actions had been unsuccessful.

In staging constitutional dramas, suffragettes drew upon a long tradition
of feminist challenges to law framed as appeals to precedent, of which suffragists' attempts to vote in the wake of the 1867 Reform Bill is just one example.[118] By repeatedly asserting their rights to organize deputations and
present petitions to the House of Commons and staging exclusion from Parliament and other public dimensions of citizenship, as a means of publicizing
women's exclusion from the political nation, they believed that women's exclusion would be remedied. The two adverse court decisions at the turn of the
year deepened suffragettes' conviction that the law would never treat them
fairly, that the government would hide behind legal technicalities to avoid
dealing with the more serious constitutional issues the women raised. Many
suffragettes came to believe that the constitution protected only men's rights.

Suffragettes did not merely stage their exclusion from the constitution;
they also repudiated the authority of the law. Rooting their rejection of the
law's authority in the principle that "government without the consent of the
governed is tyranny," they claimed the right to withhold consent until they
received representation in Parliament.[119] Withholding consent provided an
especially compelling argument where women could establish that they fulfilled the responsibilities of citizenship but lacked basic political rights. Tax
resistance formed an important part of suffragettes' overall strategy to reject
the legal obligations of women who lacked representation, drawing upon an
older tradition of tax resistance in England for its authority. WTRL member

Mrs. Darent Harrison invoked that history in her assertion of a "sense of intimacy and spiritual kinship which must exist between all who have ever defied the law of the day, in defence of eternal justice, and in obedience to the call of public duty."[120] The WSPU decided to resist payment of income taxes in November 1907.[121] The WFL urged "no vote—no tax" the following month.[122] Drawing once again on historical precedent, the suffragettes argued that in the seventeenth century, the king illegally levied taxes, whereas voteless women were illegally taxed by Parliament, an even more serious offense, since it occurred at a time of representative government.[123] Militants believed that, by refusing to pay taxes without representation, women would force Parliament to grant votes to women. Tax resistance was frequently presented as part of a larger strategy, as in January 1908 when Charlotte Despard defined WFL tax resistance as part of a larger general strike of women, which would extend to the refusal to bear children, to manage their homes, or to fulfill any of the citizen duties they currently performed.[124]

Tax resistance proved to be the longest-lived form of militancy, and the most difficult to prosecute. More than 220 women, mostly middle-class, participated in tax resistance between 1906 and 1918, some continuing to resist through the First World War, despite a general suspension of militancy. Suffragettes resisted payment of two general categories of tax: the first included property tax, inhabited house duty, and income tax; the second, taxes and licenses on dogs, carriages, motor cars, male servants, armorial bearings, guns, and game.[125] Contemporaries had several theories regarding tax resistance's appeal. Suffragette speaker and sympathizer Laurence Housman cited the clarity of tax resistance's logic as a primary reason for its popularity.[126] Suffragettes' tax resistance also cut across organizational lines. The formation of the Women's Tax Resistance League in 1909 brought women together from numerous organizations, including not only the WSPU, WFL, and NUWSS but also the London Society for Women's Suffrage, Conservative and Unionist Women's Franchise Association, Church League for Women's Suffrage, Free Church League, Catholic Women's Suffrage Society, Actresses' Franchise League, Artists' Franchise League, and the Women Writers' Suffrage League (see figure 3.4).[127]

Resisting the census provided a further opportunity to withhold consent through repudiating the law, one that brought militants together at a time when the WSPU's violence threated to alienate them from other groups.[128] The WFL initiated the protest in early February of the census year 1911, urging women to refuse to fill out census forms, thereby rendering the census "ineffective and unreliable for practical purposes."[129] The leadership of the WSPU had originally intended to abstain from the protest but was forced, according to Laurence Housman, by the "restiveness of its own rank and file to come in, give the protest its official blessing, and as a result make it doubly effective, and safe."[130] Indeed, the census protest proved successful. No arrests were made in connection with the protest, and only one prosecution was registered, against WSPU members who had spent census night on Wimbledon

FIGURE 3.4
Miss G. Eaton,
tax resister, with
goods seized by the
government for
payment of taxes.
Museum of London.

Common. Charges were brought against them not for resisting the census but for damaging the turf of the Commons.[131] Census resistance was popular among suffragettes for many reasons, not least because it involved less risk to participants than did tax resistance. A government prosecution for tax resistance could drag on for years, and the level of vigilance necessary to outwit the bailiffs may easily have proved too much for most women to maintain. The highly symbolic census resistance, though it required advanced planning, could be executed in one night, with minimal impact on participants' lives. WFL planning for the protest included the provision of detailed information on how to resist registration without incurring fines or imprisonment.[132] Census resistance brought the women's suffrage movement together to disrupt the machinery of the state, and not merely against the Liberal government, thereby enlarging the moral scope and enhancing the persuasiveness of the women's cause.

In the period between 1906 and 1909, suffragettes articulated resistance within the constitutional idiom, creating new identities and fields of struggle. Suffragette militancy confirmed the profound Victorian fear that women would slip the reins of domesticity, femininity, and constitutionality through their exercise of political rights. Through their creative dramas of exclusion and participation, militants demonstrated that women's citizenship was a process in the making. They showed also that their political participation and initiative could create a form of direct self-representation, unmediated by political parties, thereby reclaiming the populist heritage of two centuries and invoking a long tradition of popular mobilization against elites. In negotiating their political rights and their moral authority in the nation, suffragists were in dialogue not only with those opposing women's suffrage but also and always with supporters and fellow members.[133] Suffragists both challenged and reaffirmed culturally held assumptions about women in the public realm, replicating discourses of the wider culture. And until cessation of militancy during the First World War and the effective dismantling of resistance as a viable strategy, all discourse about women's suffrage and citizenship was shaped to a significant extent by the constitutional idiom.

Chapter 4

Resistance on Trial, 1906–1912

Attention to suffragettes' appropriation of the constitutional idiom highlights the legalistic dimension of suffrage politics. Throughout the Edwardian campaign for women's suffrage, suffragettes assiduously sought to legitimize their protests and their claim to citizenship by appealing to the law. In her contribution to Frederick John Shaw's edited collection *The Case for Women's Suffrage* (1907), Christabel Pankhurst argued that exclusion of women from the parliamentary franchise was at base a judicial decision. Elaborating upon arguments made by Charlotte Carmichael Stopes and others—that the 1832 Reform Act had introduced the limitation of sex into the parliamentary franchise—Pankhurst traced the judicial steps nineteenth-century women suffragists had taken to remedy their political exclusion. On passage of the 1867 Reform Act, she noted, suffragists in Lancashire had attempted to force the court of common pleas to rule on women's status as voters in light of Lord Brougham's Act of 1859, which had stipulated that "'in all Acts of Parliament, unless the contrary is expressly stated, words importing the masculine gender shall apply to women as well as men.'" Citing the court's ruling in *Chorlton v. Lings* (1868) that neither common law nor statute law enfranchised women, Pankhurst contended that the judiciary misinterpreted both so as to maintain women's exclusion from the parliamentary franchise.[1]

Pankhurst's argument regarding the judicial basis of women's exclusion from the franchise illuminates a long-neglected aspect of Edwardian campaigning for women's suffrage in Britain—suffragettes' engagement with the judicial apparatus of the state. Suffragettes and suffragists alike shared a conviction that judges had misinterpreted statute law when excluding women from the franchise in 1868.[2] Suffragettes inherited from the nineteenth-century feminist movement a set of strategies for challenging the law's exclusion of women from citizenship on grounds of their sex.[3] Suffragettes then developed a critique of the law—what it represented, whom it empowered, and how it was enforced—for use in resisting attempts by the judiciary to maintain women's status as political outsiders. These efforts to expand women's political access through the judiciary link suffrage agitation to other such protests of the early twentieth century, such as the wave of strikes undertaken by militant unionists in the summer of 1911. Like working men, suffragettes sought to reconfigure citizenship in order that those who fulfilled certain obligations to the state should have corresponding privileges.[4]

The judicial precedent set by *Chorlton v. Lings* began shortly after passage of the Second Reform Bill, with a mistake on the electoral register that allowed a woman, Lily Maxwell, to cast a parliamentary vote in a November 1867 Manchester by-election.[5] Maxwell's vote prompted suffragists in Manchester, Birmingham, Bristol, and elsewhere in Britain to mount petition campaigns to overseers and town clerks requesting that qualified women be put on the register. Overseers of twenty-four townships agreed to do so.[6] The campaign following netted some 3,924 women's claims in Manchester alone, some 92 percent of those canvassed. Results were mixed. Some revision courts removed women voters; twelve did not object to women voters, and four accepted women voters.[7] At its first annual meeting on 30 October 1868, members of the Manchester Suffrage Society determined to settle the matter definitively and chose four cases for appeal.[8] In November 1869, one of these four (*Chorlton v. Lings*) was argued before the court of common pleas. The court determined that the precedents for women's parliamentary voting were rare, concluding that "'in modern and more civilized times, out of respect for women and by way of decorum . . . [women] are excluded from taking any part in popular assemblies, or in the election of Members of Parliament.'"[9]

Chorlton v. Lings represented a pivotal point in Edwardian suffragists' understanding of the evolution of the campaign for women's parliamentary enfranchisement.[10] In her many publications, suffragist Charlotte Carmichael Stopes emphasized the importance of judicial interpretation in excluding women from citizenship. While acknowledging that the criteria of inheritance and matrimony historically had limited the number of women who could act as legal persons, Stopes insisted that no statute explicitly denied women the parliamentary vote. *Chorlton v. Lings* thus exemplified the judiciary's role in upholding masculine privilege by denying women what Stopes called "the natural and constitutional equivalent for a tax in a vote."[11] Lawyers, she contended, had decided "that the word 'man' always includes a 'woman' when there is a penalty to be incurred, and never includes 'woman' when there is a privilege to be conferred."[12] And judges, Stopes contended, concurred with this interpretation. Women's disabilities, then, she argued, "do not depend on Constitution or Statute, but on the limited vision of judges who did not know their Constitutional history in 1868."[13] Stopes's assessment would be repeated by suffragettes throughout the Edwardian campaign.[14]

The judicial decision in *Chorlton v. Lings* shaped suffragists' narration of their campaign long after militancy had ended. In 1931, more than a decade after the first women's suffrage victory in the United Kingdom, Sylvia Pankhurst presented the decision in *Chorlton v. Lings* as the precipitating event for forty years' agitation for the vote.[15] Pankhurst may have had a personal interest in framing it thus, since her father, Richard Marsden Pankhurst, had served as counsel for the appellants, but the pervasive references to the case in discussions of the struggle for the vote suggest that it continued to hold great significance for many suffragists. In *The Cause* (1928), Ray Strachey similarly portrayed the case as decisive in shaping the form taken by the women's movement after 1869. She quoted from a leading article in the *Times* on the outcome of the case:

> As we cannot affect a decent sorrow at the result, it might be thought more becoming that we should say nothing at all. But we are apprehensive that silence in this case might be considered more offensive even than a shout of victory. . . . The contention that women, being liable to taxation, must also be entitled to a share in representation, might justify women in a rebellion, but not a Court of Law in adjudging a privilege to them which no law, customary or statutory, can be shown to have conferred.

Even as the *Times*'s article was being written, Strachey observed, Manchester suffragist Lydia Becker, by bringing together women in a regional suffrage society, had begun to organize such a rebellion, albeit one on "peaceful, constitutional" lines.[16]

Chorlton v. Lings (1868) was upheld in *Beresford Hope v. Lady Sandhurst* (1889), in which women's incapacity for election as members of county councils rested upon the earlier decision.[17] Suffragists in the decades following understood the significance of these cases for their cause. In 1891, Harriet McIlquham singled out for criticism the judicial decisions rendering women's constitutional rights moot, derisively noting that the Master of the Rolls' declaration that neither common law nor the constitution allowed women to exercise public functions presumed "either gross ignorance of law and of fact, or inveterate masculine bias."[18]

Suffragists at the fin de siècle attempted again to use the courts to force acknowledgment of women's capacity as parliamentary voters, in legal proceedings that would become known as the Scottish Women Graduates' case.[19] In order to graduate from the Universities of St. Andrews, Aberdeen, Glasgow, and Edinburgh, all students were required to pay a fee. Their names were then placed on the Register of the General Council, which served as the statutory register of parliamentary voters in university constituencies in Scotland.[20] The Universities of St. Andrews and Edinburgh, and those of Glasgow and Aberdeen, each jointly returned one member to Parliament. One restriction was attached to the voting privilege: "'No person subject to any legal incapacity shall be entitled to vote at any Parliamentary Election or exercise any other privilege as a Member of the General Council of any University.'"[21]

The extent to which sex constituted legal incapacity became the focus of suffragist attention. In January 1906, the Committee of Women Graduates of Scottish Universities urged: "If it can be established that one group of women are competent to vote, it alters the whole aspect of the franchise for women." The committee set out to raise £1,000 to support a test case before the courts, sending out a printed appeal for funds.[22] The *Englishwoman's Review* publicized the case in April 1906, urging that since women had been admitted to graduation on the same terms as men, they held an incontestable right to vote on the grounds of their membership on general councils of Scottish universities. The graduates' claim, the journal urged, was exceptional in every way: "exceptional as to the nature of the representation, exceptional as to the Acts by which the election in question is regulated and the method in which it is conducted, exceptional, lastly, as to the position of the women who claim the right to vote."[23]

The case was heard in June 1906 before the Lord Ordinary, of the court of session, Scotland. Counsel for the prosecution noted that women had always been allowed to exercise all other privileges of membership in the general council aside from the parliamentary vote. The women asked the court to declare that once the women were on the register, they were entitled to receive voting papers, vote, and have their votes counted.[24] Lord Salvesen dismissed the case on 5 July, asserting that "person" meant male person, and that women were incapacitated from voting by law.[25] The women's appeal was heard in the extra division of the court of session, 16 November 1907, when the judge found that because there had been many different franchises in the United Kingdom, and all were exclusive to men, it must be concluded "that it was a principle of the unwritten constitutional law of the country that men only were entitled to take part in the election of representatives to Parliament."[26]

The women were represented by sympathetic male counsel in both 1906 and 1907. When the women brought the case before the House of Lords in its capacity as the final court of appeal, the appellants conducted the case themselves, with Chrystal MacMillan and Frances H. Simson presenting.[27] MacMillan prepared her arguments for appeal before the House of Lords in August 1908, when she and Eunice Murray, a Scottish member of the WFL, undertook a propaganda campaign outside Glasgow.[28] This collaboration between two women belonging to the NUWSS and the WFL, respectively, suggests the importance of legal strategies to militancy and highlights connections suffragists made between extraparliamentary pressure and interrogation of the judiciary.

The women chose their approach carefully. Their argument had to be that women already had the right to vote by virtue of existing laws; no discussion of the justice or expediency of women's suffrage would be considered.[29] Their appeal ultimately revolved around whether women were persons and whether, as persons, women were subject to any legal incapacity. They also emphasized that the franchise in question was a relatively new one, having been established in 1868, and therefore not subject to restrictions placed on earlier ones.[30] In arguments before the court, Chrystal MacMillan claimed that, according to the Representation of the People (Scotland) Act of 1868, women were defined as "persons," both according to the definition given (as anyone whose name was on the register) and in contrast with other uses within the act of "man" to designate voters in counties and boroughs.[31] Because the act did not define what was meant by legal incapacity, she looked at other statutes, beginning with the Act of Union (1707), and concluded from what she found in the legal record that sex was not a legal incapacity.[32] She also argued that "to speak of 'legal incapacity' at Common Law is an absurdity" because common law could not apply to a newly created franchise.[33]

MacMillan argued that the precedents set in *Chorlton v. Lings* and *Brown v. Ingram* did not apply to the Scottish Women Graduates' case for three reasons. First, appellants in the earlier cases were claiming the right to be put on a parliamentary register; the Scottish women graduates were already on the register. Second, the franchises dealt with in both other cases were older, property franchises; this one was a new, academic franchise. Third, in the other cases, the meaning of the word "man," not "person," was the issue in dispute. MacMillan argued that while the women were asking that the House of Lords "affirm that the statutes mean what they say," the respondents asked the Lords "to declare that, for a variety of reasons, the statutes do not mean what they say."[34] MacMillan concluded that if a contradiction existed between statute law and common law, the former should override the latter.[35] Simson added that "'men graduates vote not as being men, but as being graduates.'" Women were not allowed to vote, she argued, due not to the constitution's provisions but to custom's dictates.[36]

Among the critical components of the graduates' case were precedents for women's voting. Early in her preparation for the case, Chrystal MacMillan, honorary secretary for the Scottish Women Graduates, sought assistance from a veteran of the suffrage struggle, radical suffragist Elizabeth Wolstenholme Elmy. MacMillan wrote to Elmy in March 1906, requesting information on women who either had voted in recent years due to errors made on electoral registers or had voted in previous centuries as a matter of right.[37] Under questioning from the lord chancellor before the high court, MacMillan contended that women had been members of the old shire moots, or county courts, and that abbesses in Scotland and aristocratic women under the reigns of Henry III and Elizabeth I had voted for members of Parliament. The lord chancellor, however, declined to accept these few instances as proving the larger principle.[38]

The graduates' case was well publicized in the mainstream press. The *Times* reported the case in detail in its "Law Report."[39] The *Manchester Guardian* commented favorably on the impression that MacMillan made before the court, observing that "the Lord Chancellor followed her argument most carefully, and everyone present seemed to listen to every word of her lucid, if technical, plea. Her speech was mainly concerned with points dealing with the electoral law that governs Scottish university elections."[40] A large photograph of the Misses Melville, Simson, and MacMillan, taken outside the House of Lords, was printed in the *Manchester Guardian* on the day the report was published.[41]

The case was not successful in forcing a reinterpretation of existing law in favor of women's enfranchisement, however. In moving to dismiss the appeal, the lord chancellor asserted that no real legal precedents for women's parliamentary voting rights had been presented in the case. Those examples presented were exceptional, indeed, "irregular." He concluded:

> This disability of women has been taken for granted. It is incomprehensible to me that anyone acquainted with our laws or the methods by which they are ascertained can think, if, indeed, anyone does think, there is room for argument on such a point. It is notorious that this right of voting has, in fact, been confined to men. Not only has it been the constant tradition, alike of all the three kingdoms, but it has also been the constant practice, so far as we have knowledge of what has happened from the earliest times down to this day. Only the clearest proof that a different state of things prevailed in ancient times could be entertained by a court of law in probing the origin of so inveterate an usage. I need not remind your Lordships that numberless rights rest upon a similar basis. Indeed, the whole body of the common law has no other foundation. I will not linger upon this subject, which, indeed, was fully discussed in "Chorlton v. Lings."[42]

The judges argued that if such a change were in fact intended, the language would not be ambiguous, and the enfranchisement of women would be explicit.[43] They concluded, "If this legal disability is to be removed it must be done by an Act of Parliament."[44]

The Scottish Women Graduates' case has several implications for the campaign for women's parliamentary enfranchisement in Britain. Perhaps most significantly, and obviously, suffragists sought to attain the parliamentary franchise through means other than parliamentary lobbying and extraparliamentary pressure. In cases from *Chorlton v. Lings* (1868) to *Nairn v. Scottish Universities* (1908), suffragists attempted to force courts in England and Scotland to new interpretations of existing law, to use "judge-made law" to circumvent Parliament's unwillingness to extend the franchise to women.[45] The outcome of *Nairn v. Scottish Universities* had important implications for suffragettes' strategies because it forced suffragists and suffragettes to articulate distinctions in their understanding of the law. Critical legal theorist Robin West has argued that adjudication is in form interpretative, but in substance it is an exercise of power in a way that truly interpretative acts, such as literary interpretation are not. Adjudication has far more in common with legislation, executive orders, administrative decrees, and the whimsical commands of princes, kings, and tyrants than it has with other things we do with words, such as create or interpret novels. Like the commands of kings and the dictates of a majoritarian legislature, adjudication is imperative. It is a command backed by state power.[46]

Indeed, suffragettes came to see the act of judicial interpretation as an act of state power. Suffragettes shared the analysis of earlier radical critics of the law, including Jeremy Bentham, who saw in it "an elaborate protective screen to disguise the oppressive reality" of class privilege.[47] Suffragettes added the further privilege of sex, decrying what Florence Fenwick Miller called the "aristocracy of sex."[48] Bentham and other legal positivists had urged "that in order to facilitate legal criticism, legal critics and reformers should, as a conceptual or definitional act of will, separate law from morality." They led the way to "define legal authority as extensive only with its political authority— the authority over our actions that law wields by virtue of its use of force."[49] Suffragists, in contrast, shared J. S. Mill's belief that "the law was the most important instrument government could exercise directly for influencing both the actions and the character of its citizens."[50] They viewed the act of judicial interpretation as simply that: judicial interpretation of the law. They did not accuse the judiciary of overstepping its bounds, as did the suffragettes, who were incensed by the case.

As a consequence, militants, and even some nonmilitant suffragists like Chrystal MacMillan, produced a radical discourse about the clash between constitution and government, in this case including the judiciary. MacMillan characterized the judges' ruling as "the purely arbitrary setting aside of the obvious interpretation of the law."[51] Similarly, radical suffragist Elizabeth Wolstenholme Elmy urged that the case was "but the latest of several judicial decisions which, during the past half-century, have restricted or destroyed the earlier rights of women."[52] In *The Suffragette,* her 1910 account of the movement in progress, Sylvia Pankhurst noted that the Scottish Women Graduates' case not only had made evident yet further examples of British women's ancient rights and privileges but also had made visible the incommensurability of judicial decisions regarding men and women. She accused the judges of reading the provision of the Representation of the People (Scotland) Act of 1868 regarding the university franchise according to their interpretation of Parliament's intentions, rather than according to the actual wording of the act.[53] Liberal feminists, by contrast, saw the case merely as removing any alternative to a legislative solution. The *Englishwoman's Review* opined in January 1908 that the loss on appeal "ought to incite women to labour more earnestly for that Parliamentary recognition which will open to them the long-desired right to the franchise."[54] Liberal suffragist Millicent Garrett Fawcett glossed over the significance of the Scottish Women Graduates' case in her pamphlet "Women's Suffrage" (1912), in which she dismissed *Chorlton v. Lings* as the last time women could claim the vote "'by a sort of accident.'"[55]

Attempting to get the vote through judicial reinterpretation of statute law was problematic in several ways. Pursuing a legal case into the House of Lords was not a strategy available to all suffragists. Appellants in the November 1908 trial displayed a sophisticated understanding of the law, obtained through legal training, which was not easily accessible to most women. Further, it was expensive to try these cases, and appellants ran the risk of having to assume costs for both sides if they lost. More significantly, by the early twentieth century a strategy this complex could not compete with the publicity generated by more public displays of resistance: discussing the finer points of electoral law before a court failed to turn the issue into one ordinary Britons could care about. Even as the Scottish Women Graduates' case wound its way through the courts, suffragettes were turning from questioning the judiciary's role in maintaining women's political status, to forcing explicit confrontations between women and the legal system.

Concurrent with the appeal by the Scottish Women Graduates, suffragettes articulated new strategies for dealing with the law. Acknowledging their lack of success in attaining what Christabel Pankhurst in 1907 had termed "judge-made law" as a means of circumventing the House of Commons, they confronted more aggressively the judicial apparatus of the state. Suffragettes used pamphlets, columns in weekly suffrage papers, and courtrooms as sites for staging their exclusion from the political nation. In the 1950s, WFL member Teresa Billington Greig recalled their strategy: "We developed more rapidly the idea that every application of law could be made the cause of logical protest by persons shut out of citizenship—not only taxation but legislation in general is tyranny to them."[56] Suffragettes sought confrontation with the law in order to stage political agitation from within an institution of state power. There they challenged the state's belief in its fair and equitable application of justice, revealing inconsistencies in the application of law and forcing the government into dialogue on the legitimacy of women's demands as citizens. Their charge, that the power of the courts to adjudicate was less interpretive than it was an exercise of power, was an important part of a wider citizen engagement with the state in the Edwardian period, one challenging women and men to play a more active role in determining the functions of the state.[57]

Suffragettes inherited from nineteenth-century feminism a tradition of critiquing women's unequal status under the law. Battles over women's legal rights in the 1820s and 1830s, such as Caroline Norton's protracted struggle to gain custody of her small children, pointed to examples of the law's failure to protect women's rights. The primary point of feminist attack in the decades following was the common-law doctrine of coverture, which stipulated that upon marriage a woman's legal personality became subsumed in that of her husband.[58] Later arguments, by contrast, emphasized the necessity of women's enfranchisement in order for them to protect their own rights by having a say in choosing who would represent their interests in Parliament.[59] Elaborating earlier feminists' arguments, suffragettes rooted their demands for the parliamentary vote in their inability under existing law to protect themselves, their property, and their children. All Edwardian suffrage organizations, both militant and nonmilitant, produced and distributed numerous pamphlets denouncing women's legal status. With such titles as "Women Under the Law" and "Is the English Law Unjust to Women?" these pamphlets provided detailed examinations of women's current legal status and explored historical and philosophical development of that subordinate status in Western civilization.[60] Men with legal training, who constituted a disproportionate number of the members of the various men's societies for women's suffrage, wrote many of the pamphlets circulated by the Edwardian movement. Writing pamphlets for the cause may have seemed the most appropriate contribution they could make, given their professional expertise.[61]

Columns and articles in suffrage newspapers reiterated suffragist argumentation about the inadequacy of existing law and the bias with which it was administered.[62] They also dramatized women's exclusion from the constitution and from legal protections offered men. Suffrage newspapers and pamphlets circulated key ideas regarding women's position before the law.[63] Many of these writings explored the feudal principles underlying modern English law, with varying degrees of agreement on what this earlier political system meant for women.[64] Many put forth J. S. Mill's argument that women's current status was a remnant of earlier restrictions no longer applicable in modern society.[65] While these writings provided stark details of women's legal status, they served a practical purpose as well. Pamphlets and articles provided suffragists with the bare outlines of women's legal disabilities for use in making their case for the parliamentary enfranchisement of women. The opening lines of Henry H. Schloesser's pamphlet "The Legal Status of Women in England" state this quite explicitly: "It is the object of this little treatise to point out, as clearly and simply as possible, for the assistance of speakers and others, in what manner the legal rights and disabilities of women differ from those of men, in England at the present day."[66] Pamphlets provided suffragists with specific arguing points and detailed information regarding women's status at each stage in the life cycle (girl; single woman; married woman; mother; widow), shaping the arguments suffragists made before judges, to crowds, in drawing room meetings, and in conversations with friends and family members.

Antisuffragists countered with their own pamphlets, arguing that, given Parliament's passage of legislation on behalf of women, including the Married Women's Property Acts of 1870, 1874, and 1882, the Guardianship of Infants Act (1886), and the Summary Jurisdiction (Married Women) Act of 1895, women did not need the vote. Because women were maintained by their husbands, and their husbands were liable for their civil offenses, women had "the same capacity of acquisition, enjoyment, and disposition" of property as men. Married women enjoyed "a special advantage" because the law rendered portions of their property inalienable during marriage. Women could make contracts, even though they were not legally bound by them. In short, the "administration of the law is even more favourable to woman than is the letter of the law." Antisuffragists thus concluded that "Woman Suffrage [was] not necessary in order to procure Justice for Women."[67]

Suffragists repeatedly countered antisuffragists' claims that women were sufficiently empowered under existing law. In 1910, Margaret Wynne Nevinson, a member of the WFL and the Women Writers' Suffrage League, produced a short story in a series entitled "Woman—the Spoilt Child of the Law," in which she contrasted two women, the wife of a dissolute Lord, and an unmarried daughter of a carpenter, whose deaths were brought about by their despair upon giving birth to daughters. Despite vast differences in class, they were unable to control their own sexuality and reproduction, leading inevitably, Nevinson suggested, to their deaths. Nevinson's story, published in the WFL's paper, the *Vote,* made the point that women of all classes suffered equally from their disenfranchisement. Nevinson's juxtaposition of the story's moral and its title provided an ironic response to those who claimed women's rights were secured even without the franchise.[68] And even if women occasionally benefited from the law's protection, Cicely Hamilton, a member of the Women Writers' Suffrage League, the WFL, and the NUWSS, argued, those same laws contributed to the "intellectual pauperization" of women and should be eliminated.[69] Suffragists contended that even if all women's grievances were to be met with legal changes, women would still need the vote to protect their rights and to effect change in the area of social reform.[70]

If suffragettes shared with nineteenth-century feminists a critique of the tyranny of law, their innovation was to refuse the law's legitimacy. Using the courtroom as a key site of critique, suffragettes developed two primary strategies between 1906 and 1912: they refused to acknowledge the authority of the courts in trying them for offenses related to their political agitation, and they used the courtroom as a site for narrating militancy's defense.

Suffragettes implemented their attack on the law by refusing to acknowledge the law's authority. Upon arrest for obstruction or resisting arrest, some refused to defend themselves before magistrates in police court. The first of these protests followed the arrest of WSPU organizer Teresa Billington outside Asquith's private residence, Cavendish Square, on 21 June 1906. The case attracted public attention after Billington lodged a complaint of assault against the arresting officer.[71] Before magistrate Paul Taylor at the Marylebone Police Court, Billington refused to give her name or to ask the police any questions, stating, "I do not recognize the authority of the Police of this Court or any other Court of Law made by man. Neither do I accept your judgement until women have votes."[72] In October 1906, suffragettes implemented this principle again, following the arrests of WSPU members in the lobby of the House of Commons.[73] At Westminster Police Court the next day, the ten women were charged with speaking and behaving in a manner likely to lead to a breach of the peace.[74] All refused the right of the court to try their cases, and all were found guilty.[75] When offered the option of six months of keeping the peace (refraining from similar activism) or two months in the second division, they chose the latter. At the conclusion of the trial, the women refused to leave the courtroom, whereupon they were removed forcibly.[76]

After breaking with the WSPU in October 1907, the WFL continued the practice of police court protests. Like the staging of constitutional dramas, the protests made explicit women's status under the law. WFL propaganda emphasized the arbitrariness of the law, urging that "until Women are Voters, Law is but the Will of men. It is not human justice."[77] The law was little more than an external imposition: "Until women are voters, and therefore lawmakers, the Law Courts of this land have no just or moral jurisdiction over them; the only authority such Courts possess in the case of women is that of brute force."[78]

WFL members next implemented this critique from a different vantage point: as spectators in the courtroom. At Bow Street Police Court, on 14 November, 1907, Teresa Billington Greig and Irene Miller protested the judicial proceedings in progress, asserting from the public benches that the women on trial should not be subject to man-made laws.[79] On November 23, the WFL carried out protests against administration of "unjust man-made laws" in courtrooms across England and Scotland. Members were encouraged to attend the proceedings quietly, sitting in the public benches until a woman prisoner was brought into the courtroom. Only one member was to protest at a time; others were to wait for the second and third woman prisoner to be brought to trial. The official goal of these protests was not arrest; women were instructed to protest and then leave quietly.[80] To heighten their effect, simultaneous protests were carried out at the Guildhall, Marylebone, Marlborough Street, North London, Woolwich, and Southwestern Police Courts.[81] Similar outbursts were reported from Glasgow as well, at the Central, Northern, and Partick Police Courts.[82] One protest, uttered from the public benches at Greenwich, demanded: "Your Worship, . . . I must rise to protest against the administration by men only of laws made by men only, and enforced by men upon women and children. As long as women are denied the elementary rights of citizenship . . . this trial by force constitutes a very grave injustice."[83]

This new policy led suffragists to publicly articulate differences between the WFL and the WSPU. Christabel Pankhurst wrote to the *Manchester Guardian* criticizing the WFL's protests and asserting the "political" nature of all WSPU protests, which she characterized as aimed only at opposing the government. A letter by WFL secretary Edith How Martyn in the same column argued that members of the WFL would protest "application of man-made laws to women until women are given the Parliamentary vote."[84] At least in

1908 and 1909, the WSPU refused to use the courtroom as a venue for defying masculine legal authority, emphasizing that suffragette "prisoners took up an extremely dignified attitude in court, not disputing the evidence except to show the political character of their action."[85] Despite sharing a critique of the law as the exercise of arbitrary power, the WFL and the WSPU implemented that insight differently, with the WSPU simply using those proceedings to stage their exclusion from citizenship.

Suffragettes utilized the courtroom to great advantage in 1908. The WSPU scored politically in October of that year when Emmeline Pankhurst, Christabel Pankhurst, and Flora Drummond were tried in police court for inciting demonstrators to "rush" the House of Commons. The case offered the WSPU an opportunity to implement a new strategy: suffragettes moved from refusing to speak on their own behalf to using the courtroom as a platform from which they could both make a case for women's right to citizenship and critique the government's hypocrisy in excluding them. In his examination of state trials of early nineteenth-century radicals, historian James Epstein has argued that these trials enabled radicals to confront "the power and agency of the state" in the courtroom as both sides struggled for "power of and over language." Trials, he notes, shared a number of characteristics with the theater: "pomp and ritual spectacle, rich costumes, dramatic tension and pathos, fine rhetoric, and occasional humor." For male radicals, state trials provided unprecedented occasions for mediation "between elite power and plebeian opposition to that power."[86] The metaphor of court as theater is appropriately applied to suffragette trials, where the state's power was on display. Equally important, however, was the performance of resistance on the part of the defendants. Suffragettes viewed the outcome of these trials—the conviction and imprisonment of those resisting—as secondary to the opportunity provided to make a case for women's citizenship rights before the public. Public trials created unique opportunities to bring the women's case before the state, to demonstrate the unequal power of women, and to show to what extent they were "up against the law."[87]

Confronting the law on its own turf and on its own terms, suffragettes made a strong argument for women's rights as citizens. The press obligingly provided suffragettes with a national audience for their protest, extensively covering the trial and highlighting Christabel Pankhurst's assiduous arguments in the language of radical protest.[88] Emmeline Pethick Lawrence, treasurer of the WSPU, wrote of the trial in later years: "We could not but realize that the proceedings for two days in Bow Street Police Court had been like a suffrage meeting attended by millions. In fact, the whole newspaper-reading world had been presented with our case."[89] The major dailies published verbatim reports of the trial's proceedings, and the tabloids splashed photographs of the defendants across their pages, taking not only the issue of women's suffrage but also, in this case, Christabel Pankhurst's accusation of judicial prejudice into the homes of millions of Britons.[90] The crowds gathered in the streets outside the courtroom debated the merits of the women's case (see figure 4.1). Speaking from within an institution of state power, suffragists grasped the opportunity to present their arguments directly to the people. The major papers allowed individuals to read the proceedings and decide for themselves the merits of women's case. The trials themselves were events of high drama, pitting women against the state and drawing upon a rhetoric of radical protest.

Suffragists portrayed themselves as rational political actors, and their movement as orderly and respectable. In cross-examination, Emmeline Pankhurst asked Herbert Gladstone "whether he recognises this morning that this is a political agitation?" Gladstone replied, "Of course, there is a political agitation to get the franchise for women." Emmeline Pankhurst: "Do you think we should be likely to break the criminal law if we got the same means of representation as men?" Gladstone: "I am sure your motives are good. It is a hypothetical question which I cannot answer."[91] Christabel Pankhurst developed this line of argumentation further, asserting the political, and therefore not criminal, nature of their offenses. She claimed that the government deliberately avoided charging women with illegal assembly so that the matter would remain in police court; the government did not dare

FIGURE 4.1
Crowds gathered outside Bow Street Police Court
during the "Rush" trial, October 1908. Museum of
London.

take its evidence before a jury because women would be acquitted. Police court, she declared, was for drunks, not political offenders.[92] Witnesses for the WSPU attested "that there was never any intention to make use of violence, and that the demeanor of the crowds which collected was perfectly orderly." Witnesses also testified that most people in the crowd that day sympathized with suffragettes. The defendants called twenty-four witnesses in one day of testimony alone; fifty more were promised for the next session. Mrs. Pankhurst apologized to the court for using so much time, but, she asserted, "we are fighting for our liberty" (see figure 4.2).[93]

The press portrayed the women sympathetically, as in the opening lines of the *Daily Telegraph*'s coverage of the trial on the morning of the twenty-sixth. "No matter how little he might sympathise with female suffrage in principle, no matter if, believing in the inherent rightness of the cause, he were frankly opposed to the militant methods which have recently characterised the crusade, he must have been a callous and stony-hearted individual whom Saturday's proceedings at Bow-Street Police-court left wholly unmoved." Long after the sentence imposed had been forgotten, long after the "halo of martyrdom" conferred by sentencing was gone, the "powerful and impassioned speech by Mrs. Pankhurst will linger in the memory of all who listened to it."[94] Press accounts were clear that what happened in the courtroom had an impact on public opinion of the women's cause. The press evaluated courtroom protests on how they were managed, noting the small turnout of suffragettes at a trial at Rochester-Row Police Court following the Grille Protest in October 1908: "If the suffragists had hoped to secure a further advertisement for the proceedings there was bad stage management somewhere. But, doubtless, the organisers of the WFL felt that having made their protest in the most effective fashion to bring it before the public eye there was no occasion to get their supporters to demonstrate outside the court."[95]

Trials served as especially useful means of conveying the underlying rationale of women's protests. Observers of demonstrations might miss the rationale for protest, but trials gave suffragettes opportunities to articulate from within an institution of state power the meaning of what otherwise could be reduced to spectacle with unclear meanings. WSPU attempts to petition the prime minister provide a case in point. At the March 1909 trial at Bow Street Police Court, following WSPU attempts to petition Asquith and mass window breaking on 25 February, suffragettes used the courtroom as a venue for urging magistrates to refrain from enforcing unfair laws. Claiming the right of the subject to present petitions, Emmeline Pethick Lawrence described the charge the women faced—of obstructing the police—as "a breach of the technical law." She exhorted the magistrate that in his capacity of administering the law, he represented more than the mere technicalities of law: "I put it to you, sir, if I may, that you represent something deeper, something more abiding than the mere conventionalities of the law—I mean the great abiding principles of equity."[96] WSPU member Rose Lamartine Yates similarly told the magistrate that while she was charged with ob-

FIGURE 4.2
Christabel Pankhurst, Flora Drummond, and
Emmeline Pankhurst at Bow Street Police
Court during the "Rush" trial, 14 October 1908.
Mary Evans Picture Library.

structing police in execution of their duty, "she considered that the police had obstructed her in what she conceived as the discharge of a higher duty— the assertion of every subject's constitutional right to lay grievances before the Government."[97] The spectacle landing women in the courtroom thus was only part of the women's protest; the courtroom's provision of a public venue for staking claim to women's inclusion in the constitution was the other, equally significant, part.

Suffragettes' arguments, however, were less likely to be heard sympathetically if their actions involved the use of violence. In 1909, Alison Neilans and Alice Chapin of the Women's Freedom League were tried on charges of interfering with a by-election in the London constituency of Bermondsey and injuring an election official in the course of their protest. Due to the severity of the charges, the women were tried in the central criminal court before a jury.[98] The Bermondsey trial, however, held only mixed success for suffragettes, for if the two women won the right to trial by jury, they lost the right to a sympathetic audience in the public benches, as Mr. Justice Grantham ruled that all female spectators be removed from the courtroom.[99] Ironically, the organization with which the newspapers had the most sympathy, at least until 1909, was the WSPU. Despite attacks on property carried out by the WSPU, the courtroom demeanor of its members was womanly, patriotic, and not excessively passionate. The WFL's unfortunate Bermondsey episode made that organization susceptible to the charge of recklessness and irresponsibility, especially as accounts of injuries to the election official received widespread press coverage. The use of violence against property and harm done to individuals then created a problem for suffragettes in the courtroom. Women lost the moral high ground when their actions were perceived as harmful or destructive.

Perhaps the zenith of suffragette performance in the courtroom drama came with the May 1912 trial of WSPU leaders at the Old Bailey for conspiracy to incite violence.[100] The government charged Frederick Pethick Lawrence, Emmeline Pethick Lawrence, Emmeline Pankhurst, and Christabel Pankhurst with conspiring to organize the mass window-breaking protests on 21 November 1911 and 1 and 4 March 1912. The first three were arrested on 5 March 1912; Christabel Pankhurst escaped to Paris. The defendants were indicted on a total of fifty-four counts. The general indictment charged that the defendants had on various dates together and with Christabel Pankhurst and others conspired "to commit damage, injury, and spoil to the amount of £5 and upwards to certain glass windows." All three pleaded not guilty.[101]

Extensive newspaper coverage of the trial brought the public into the courtroom, where readers, including those distinctly at odds with the movement, could see for themselves the arguments made by both sides. Unlike suffrage newspapers, which tended to circulate among the faithful, or at least among those not unsympathetic to the cause, mainstream dailies reached militancy's intended audience: the wider public. The defendants took every opportunity offered by the papers to make their case through the use of great drama, humor, and historical precedent.

The press portrayed the women's deportment at the trial sympathetically. The liberal daily paper the *Daily Chronicle* likened the mood in the courtroom to that of a "drawing room entertainment," with none of the usual "grim and dreadful justice" of the place apparent. The paper noted that "women with flowers and feathers in their hats . . . smiled and made little signs of greeting to three people in the dock [who bore] no resemblance to other accused people who sometimes stand here in despair."[102] An "air of mutual courtesy and amiable discussion" characterized the proceedings. A certain amount of entertainment value was evident in the proceedings even though the courtroom acted as a theater for the dramatization of political grievances. The *Daily Chronicle* noted that "Lord Coleridge, ideal in courtesy and in patience, presided over this gathering, which to an outsider unfamiliar with the real issues might have seemed like an academic discussion on Women's Suffrage and the morality of stone-throwing as a political argument."[103] Occasional sparring between prosecution and defense was portrayed as amusing, and entertaining exchanges were highlighted.[104] Overall, the press portrayed the suffragettes as smart, capable, admirable women determined to have their say.

Suffragettes were also represented seriously, as political actors in pursuit of an ideal. The *Standard* characterized the trial as a political one and covered the entire six days' proceedings. The *Daily Chronicle* observed that "with a mass of documents 'put in' by the Crown, and with large numbers of police witnesses the trial of the Suffragette leaders resembles a State trial in its length and importance." Mrs. Pankhurst, the *Daily Chronicle* noted, cross-examined a number of the government's witnesses "very cleverly in order to draw admissions from them that the women who had broken their windows were not actuated by any personal malice, but had acted for their political principles."[105] The *Manchester Guardian* noted that Mrs. Pankhurst's opening speech "was a piece of eloquent pleading, delivered with charm of manner and full of literary grace, fit, indeed, to stand beside similar appeals in famous political cases."[106]

The trial provided the WSPU with a public forum in which it could portray itself as a large, successful, well-run organization representing the political aspirations of thousands of women all over the country. One correspondent for the *Manchester Guardian* noted that "the array of documents [seized by police in the raid on the offices of the union] formed a remarkable tribute to women's economy, foresight, and genius for organization."[107] The women on trial were demonstrably not hysterical or irrational; they were rational political actors behaving in the service of an ideal. In her cross-examination of Frank Glenister, manager of the London Pavilion, Emmeline Pankhurst established that members of the Union routinely held very large and very orderly meetings in the hall; attorney for the defense, T. M. Healy, forced Glenister to acknowledge that he was unaware that he was "letting the Pavilion as part of the machinery of a great conspiracy."[108] Frederick Pethick Lawrence similarly got Detective-Inspector Francis Powell of Scotland Yard to admit, based on his several months' attendance of WSPU meetings, that "the meetings have all been very well attended by an orderly class of people."[109] Not only did the women claim to be political actors, but they established that the government also saw them that way. Under cross-examination, Detective-Sergeant Charles Bagent admitted to Emmeline Pankhurst that the suffragettes were watched closely by a "special branch of the Criminal Investigation Division," one devoted to "political work."[110]

The greatest triumph for the WSPU, however, was that its members were given the opportunity to defend themselves in front of a jury. Before a panel of citizens, the WSPU made a public case before the nation for the political, rather than the criminal, nature of their actions. Despite the attorney general's insistence that women's entitlement to the parliamentary franchise was not at stake in the trial—the issue, he reminded the court, was the WSPU's "attack upon the private property of perfectly unoffending, innocent persons"—the defendants repeatedly urged that theirs was a political trial.[111] Invoking historical examples of other trials, such as that of the Chartist Ernest Jones, they attempted to claim the "criminal's dock [as] the finest of all platforms from which to utter a vindication of political liberty." Their testimony drew contrasts between criminal and political activity with Frederick Pethick Lawrence arguing that "the demand for the franchise differed fundamentally from the ordinary grievances of daily life." He urged that if tradesmen or landlords treated women poorly, the women could take custom elsewhere or use the law courts; but they did not have votes with which to turn out the government. Emmeline Pankhurst argued that "if we the accused people are not accused of a political offence, then I cannot see how we can be accused at all. Is it to be conceived for a moment that we three defendants and my daughter, who is not present, would ever take any part in this agitation at all for any reason or purpose other than a political one?" Again and again, the three differentiated between criminal activity undertaken in pursuit of private gain and political agitation undertaken on behalf of larger principles.[112]

The trial allowed the leaders of the WSPU to narrate militancy's defense. They demonstrated that the word "militancy" had been applied to their protests well before they had used violence against property; that well before they had used violence, they were arrested and incarcerated; and that they acted as they had because they had been driven to the use of violence by the government's intransigence and politicians' treachery. An amusing exchange occurred between T. M. Healy, counsel for the defense, and Archibald Bodkin, counsel for the prosecution, in which Healy presented Bodkin with an unattributed statement that could be read as incitement to violence: "Formerly, when the great mass of the people were voteless, they had to do something violent in order to show what they felt. Today the electors have the vote. Let no one be deceived, therefore, because in the present struggle everything is peaceful and orderly, in contrast to the disorderliness of very great struggle in the past." Bodkin declined to identify the speaker until the attorney general, Sir Rufus Isaacs, was present. Healy wryly concurred, saying "that would be very happy to me, because I am quoting from the speech of the Attorney-General."[113]

In opening and closing statements, as well as through examination of witnesses, the leaders of the WSPU presented a narrative of the struggle for women's suffrage that emphasized the nobility of women's motives. Frederick Pethick Lawrence took great pains to make a case for the character of the defendants, depicting his wife, Emmeline Pethick Lawrence, himself, and Emmeline Pankhurst as social reformers dedicated to improving the lives of the poor. The narrative of the women's suffrage campaign presented in the courtroom portrayed a lengthy process of women's attempts to acquire franchise rights peacefully and their betrayal by the government.[114]

Ultimately, the central dispute was over the incitement that led to disturbances, with the government blaming the defendants, and the suffragettes asserting "other and more powerfully provocative reasons in addition to the incitement." Indeed, Frederick Pethick Lawrence's opening statement had urged that the conspiracy was not on the part of the women but on the part of the government. Testimony during the trial revealed profound differences between suffragettes' definition of militancy and the government's; numerous witnesses attested that militancy meant police attacks on them while they were trying to approach Parliament.[115] Pethick Lawrence asserted that "hundreds of women had been sent to prison for merely going in procession to the House of Commons and asking to be admitted."[116] He also argued that the authorities treated suffragettes differently from other political offenders: the women were being tried for offenses for which they had already been imprisoned, and police accounts of the women's speeches deviated significantly from the speeches the women had made.[117] The Conspiracy Trial gave the WSPU a public forum in which to contrast punishments women received at the hands of government with those of male political offenders, and of sex offenders. Suffragettes successfully brought women's political status to international attention; appeals to the prime minister in support of the defendants' claim to be political prisoners were made by Jean Jaures, Romain Rolland, Madame Curie, Edward Bernstein, Victor Adler, Upton Sinclair, and more than one hundred British members of Parliament.[118]

The 1912 Conspiracy Trial was most effective in forcing the government into dialogue with the suffragettes. This was particularly apparent when Emmeline Pankhurst successfully interrupted the prosecution's closing statements multiple times, challenging the government's version of events. She turned the trial into a conversation, a dialogue between a woman and a representative of the law, who let his peevishness show. In his closing statements, Attorney General Sir Rufus Isaacs, conducting the prosecution on behalf of the director of public prosecutions, noted that he had with great difficulty restrained himself from airing his own views during the case, but he allowed himself the following: "I do ask you to remember that in these matters, and particularly in the moments of danger, the balance is not all on the side of the men. As we know from recent events [alluding to the sinking of the *Titanic*], when there is grave peril, when there is a question of only a limited safety being provided for those who are in peril, we know that the order which is given is 'Women and children first.'"[119] Playing the chivalry card made the women's point: they were not viewed as autonomous political actors.

Even the outcome of the trial vindicated the WSPU's position. Jurors found the defendants guilty but requested leniency on grounds of "the purity of motives underlying [their] agitation." In publicity following the trial, the WSPU made much of the fact that the jury returned a verdict "technically" guilty, but not morally guilty.[120] The trial turned out to be a high point in WSPU rhetoric, however, for the organization's escalation of violence in the spring of 1912 stripped from it any public sympathy gained from the Conspiracy Trial. As militancy escalated into 1913 and 1914, WSPU confrontations with the law became less about forcing public acknowledgment of women's status relative to men's and more about making life difficult for the government while women remained unenfranchised. Nevertheless, militants' legal challenges were as significant to their overall movement as was their mass mobilization of extraparliamentary pressure, for those challenges furthered suffragettes' claim to inclusion in the constitution.

Chapter 5

Embodying Citizenship, 1908–1914

In formulating resistance to constituted authority, suffragettes struggled with legacies of liberal political revolutions of the late eighteenth and nineteenth centuries. As historian Joan Scott has argued about the French Revolution, the "abstract gesture of embodiment—the attribution of citizenship to (white) male subjects—complicated enormously the project of claiming equal rights, for it suggested either that rights themselves, or at least how and where they were exercised, depended on the physical characteristics of human bodies."[1] Questions of embodiment lay at the very heart of the demands suffragettes made upon the state: sexed female, they demanded incorporation into a body politic conceptualized as male. Suffragettes repeatedly encountered resistance to their claims on the basis of their sex. At one open-air suffrage meeting in Campden Hill Square in February 1914, Emmeline Pankhurst compared the women's struggle to earlier male franchise campaigns. She reminded the crowd that "when your forefathers fought for their liberty they took lives," to which a voice in the crowd replied, "'You are only a woman.'"[2]

Scholarly examination of suffragettes' embodiment of resistance, that is, the corporeal form they attempted to give political agency, tends to focus on the suffragette hunger strike and forcible feeding.[3] Suffragettes undertook the hunger strike in protest against the government's refusal to recognize their protests as having political, rather than criminal, intent. WSPU member Marion Wallace Dunlop initiated the first such hunger strike in June 1909 after her arrest for stenciling a portion of the Bill of Rights on a wall inside the precincts of Parliament. She declined all food for ninety-one hours before she was released by prison authorities.[4] The hunger strike was adopted subsequently by numerous WSPU members following arrest for window breaking and other forms of militancy in the months of June and July 1909. The government's initial response was to allow suffragettes to refuse food for several days, but fearing for the women's health, officials then released them from prison. In August 1909, however, Herbert Gladstone, home secretary, made the controversial decision that suffragette hunger strikers should not be allowed to continue their protests without intervention. In September, the government's new policy was implemented when suffragette hunger strikers incarcerated in Winson Green Gaol, in Birmingham, were fed forcibly through a rubber tube inserted in the mouth or nose. The government continued to use this procedure until early 1913.[5] Suffragettes' accounts of these feedings make for horrifying reading. Many describe the terror they felt when restrained by wardresses and doctors, and some, the pain experienced when the tube forced liquid into their lungs rather than the stomach. Some suffered the physical consequences of having been forcibly fed for the rest of their lives.[6]

Historians and literary critics have focused on the hunger strike as exemplary of the protests suffragettes mounted in the Edwardian movement, constructing the hunger strike as a means of building community, denying masculine authority, and creating a feminist spectacle.[7] The embodiment of resistance, however, was both more complicated and more contentious than portrayals of heroic suffragettes undertaking the hunger strike would suggest. One example of this is suffragette representation of forcible feeding as sexual violation. The forcible feeding of suffragette hunger strikers was represented in both WSPU propaganda and the mainstream press as a kind of rape.[8] Yet those images were not interpreted in the same way by all viewers. Images of women ravished by the state certainly could outrage women and men alike; they could also appeal to a different sensibility, one convinced that women who transgressed gender prescriptions deserved whatever violence was meted out to them. A kind of voyeuristic pleasure could be had in imagining the suffragette body in pain; popular graphic representations of suffragettes being forcibly fed presented these women as young and attractive, perhaps eliciting quite different responses in viewers than would reading personal accounts of their experiences.

This chapter examines another aspect of suffragettes' attempts to give physical dimension to their political agency, taking as its focus the idioms through which suffragettes negotiated citizenship's embodiment, the most frequently deployed being femininity and freedom. Femininity embodied an ideal to which participants of the movement could refer for moral confirmation. The figures appealed to were numerous, but most frequently invoked were Joan of Arc and Florence Nightingale.[9] Freedom was invoked through recent historical examples of resistance in action. Favorites included agitation surrounding the 1832 Reform Bill and disenfranchised male Britons in South Africa prior to 1899.[10] The most significant historical example alluded to and enlarged metaphorically was that of slavery, referring both to the enslavement of Africans in the Americas and to the sexual enslavement of white British women up to the present. Both idioms—femininity and freedom—legitimated movement away from the constitutional idiom to other ways of conceptualizing women's resistance, as suffragettes represented their struggle to each other and the general public. Examination of the range of representations suffragettes used to represent the embodied nature of their struggle further confirms the existence of a continuum of militancy within the movement. Differences among suffragettes' use of the idioms of femininity and freedom are important precisely because those differences were of degree, not kind. Viewing those idioms as existing along a spectrum of belief places all militants in dialogue with one another while maintaining significant distinctions among them.

By now, it has become axiomatic that Joan of Arc served as standard-bearer for the meanings of womanhood for members of the WSPU. Numerous historians and literary critics have accepted and elaborated upon Christabel Pankhurst's description of Joan of Arc as the "patron saint" of the suffragette movement.[11] Perhaps the most succinct statement of the symbolic role historians ascribe to Joan of Arc comes from Sheila Stowell's description of the figure of Joan in the 1909 London production of Cicely Hamilton's *Pageant of Great Women:*

> And Joan of Arc, "patron saint" of the movement's most radical wing and equestrian leader of their processions, makes her appearance at the vanguard of the "Warriors." Her virginity and gender rendering her the ideal symbol of unsexualised womanliness at the same time that her militancy and transvestism precluded containment by conventional domesticity, Joan of Arc proved an enduring icon and a popular role [model].[12]

Representations of Joan of Arc were not limited to WSPU productions, however. Art historian Lisa Tickner observes traces of the iconography of Joan of Arc in NUWSS publications, a presence she describes as Joan "in her gentler capacities," where her "military accoutrements . . . are purely spiritual."[13]

If Joan of Arc existed in the iconography of the two organizations still generally understood to be the two poles of the Edwardian campaign—the WSPU and the NUWSS—then it is striking that she played a relatively insignificant role in the symbolic universe of the organization most frequently portrayed as the middle ground, the WFL. Joan of Arc was virtually absent from WFL representations of the feminine ideal, though individual members engaged privately with her. Charlotte Despard, president of the WFL, mused over possible meanings of Joan of Arc for suffragists in diary entries of January 1914, where she recorded reading a number of biographies of Joan.[14] Upon closer examination of the publications and practices of the NUWSS, the WFL, and the WSPU, it becomes clear that Joan of Arc was both more and less than what is claimed of her.

Joan of Arc emerged as one exemplar of the feminine for English suffragists at a particular moment in the history of her own popular cult. Numerous historians have traced the vicissitudes of Joan of Arc's career as symbol since her death at the stake in 1431.[15] All agree that English representations of

Joan of Arc in historical and literary accounts up until the eighteenth century portrayed her as "a witch and strumpet, justly condemned."[16] Joan of Arc appears to have entered English national consciousness in a positive light with Robert Southey's epic eponymous poem of 1793, in which he extolled her patriotic zeal and national spirit.[17] Throughout the nineteenth century, English interpreters understood Joan to be a "symbol of nationalism" and a "heroine of national liberation."[18] Lord Gower's 1893 biography begins with the assertion that "there is nothing in history more strange, and yet more true than the story which has been told so often, but which never palls in its interest—that life of the maiden through whose instrumentality France regained her place among the nations."[19] Joan of Arc's popularity in England was such that a shrine in Westminster Cathedral was proposed in 1909.[20]

In France at the same time, Joan's significance, as "phenomenon," to borrow Nadia Margolis's terminology, made impossible any attempt to define her simply, but Margolis and other historians have outlined a figure of Joan of Arc that conforms to the symbol of national integrity implicit in Lord Gower's tribute of 1893.[21] Margolis further points to the oppositions embodied within this figure in fin de siècle France: "Joan-as-Jesus," emphasizing "the cult of passive suffering and divine grandeur," and "Joan-as-Napoleon," coexisting "out of the need to commemorate earthly, military triumph." The ultimate appropriation of Joan by the forces arrayed against republicanism at the turn of the century, however, leads Margolis to assert that Joan had emerged in France by 1914 as a symbol of "an isolationist, racist, repressive form of patriotism."[22] Simultaneous with the appropriation of Joan of Arc by the French Right was the campaign for her canonization, initiated by the bishop of Orleans in May 1869. The years following were dedicated to the multistage process of making a saint: official documents attesting to the sanctity of her life were collected, and papal lawyers prepared her case for trial. Joan was declared "venerable" in 1894, beatified in 1909 (this penultimate stage making her available for limited public cult), and canonized in 1920, rendering her "worthy of universal public cult."[23] Kenneth Woodward has argued that "the lives of the saints constitute an important—some theologians would say the most important—medium for transmitting the meaning of the Christian faith." Through the Acts of the Apostles, he goes on to say, even Evangelical Protestants can be seen as following "core models of Christian behavior, experience, and identity."[24] If the veneration of saints is thus a liturgical act, what are we to make of these religious and nationalistic versions of Joan and their use by suffragists in Britain in the early part of this century?[25] Did suffragists make use of "Joan-as-Jesus" and "Joan-as-Napoleon"? Or did they distinguish between saint and patriot?

For the suffragettes, Joan seems to have held the status of "patron saint," but in a qualified fashion—qualified both by the relationship between religious sentiment and national feeling within the British women's suffrage movement and by the gendered character of suffragette appropriations of Joan. Members of the WSPU claimed her "godly and militant qualities," "placing special emphasis on the resoluteness Joan of Arc had demonstrated during her short life."[26] Christabel Pankhurst, especially, emphasized Joan of Arc's willingness to stand her ground, regardless of the bodily consequences. In her autobiography, Pankhurst asserted a spiritual kinship between Joan and the suffragettes, claiming the latter "would no more be negotiated into surrender and compromise than would she!"[27] For certain members of the WSPU, then, Joan stood as a symbol of womanly valor in the face of obdurate prejudice, her purity of motive and body confirming her righteousness. But Joan of Arc did not exist in suffrage iconography as an exemplar merely of a universal womanly valor, a warrior in the cause of women. Rather, she was adopted as a warrior in the cause of *British* women.[28] Suffragettes celebrated her explicitly martial qualities—"a woman as leader of men," to borrow from a recent article on the historical Joan—and her significance as icon of national unity.[29] These aspects of suffragettes' appropriation of Joan argue for continuity between WSPU militancy in the years leading to 1914 and its militarism in the years following. Joan of Arc, celebrated by Christabel Pankhurst as the "perfect woman" and the "perfect patriot," provided a logically consistent symbol to lead women in their appeal for formal admission into the councils of the nation.[30] Joan was granted just such leadership in the Women's Coronation Procession of 1911. With fellow WSPU members "General" Flora Drummond and Charlotte Marsh, color-bearer, Marjorie Annan Bryce led some forty thousand women from almost thirty suffrage organizations in a procession setting off from the Embankment and concluding in a mass meeting at the Albert Hall. The largest and most successful of the Edwardian suffrage processions, the Women's Coronation Procession skillfully orchestrated the unity, harmony, and cooperation of the women's movement in support of the British Empire (see figure 5.1).[31]

Joan's cult among suffragettes is further characterized by the place she occupied at the juncture between activity and passivity. Certainly, the succor provided to suffragettes by Joan's martyrdom points to some of the more complex purposes to which she was put. While on hunger strike in prison, WSPU member Mary Richardson wrote to Kitty Marion: "I have been thinking of Joan of Arc to-day—How marvellous she was all alone, with vile men night and day so tormented."[32] Some suffragettes, after all, offered themselves up for violation, and the passivity required for the hunger strike and inevitable forcible feeding was frequently portrayed as analogous to Joan's and, indeed, Christ's passion.[33] In the early Church, martyrdom and exceptional suffering were two of the most effective means by which sanctity could be achieved, a model many WSPU members embraced.[34] Christabel Pankhurst's celebration of Joan's martial qualities, in contrast, emphasized the masculine aspect of the venerated Joan at the expense of other characteristics gendered feminine, and suffragette iconography, particularly as the violence of WSPU protests escalated after 1912, mirrored this celebration.

The double nature of Joan—her manifestation of both the active and the passive—also found expression in nonmilitant suffragist Millicent Garrett

FIGURE 5.1
WSPU member Marjorie Annan Bryce as Joan of Arc
during the Women's Coronation Procession, 17 June
1911. Museum of London.

Fawcett's 1905 tribute to what Fawcett called the "special wonder of Joan"—
her "union of the man and of the woman, strength and tenderness."[35] This
formulation was not a celebration of androgyny, of the blending of masculine and feminine qualities. Fawcett's paean pointed to a gendering of resistance within the suffrage movement, more explicitly visible in her charac-
terization of Joan as possessing "the man's weapon, the sword, as well as the
woman's weapon, the tongue." According to Fawcett, Joan "loved her standard forty times better than her sword."[36] In Fawcett's formulation, the sign

or the word was equivalent to material acts, an argument other militants would come to share once militancy became violent.

The range in meaning attributed to Joan here points to the struggle among suffragettes to define the extent and limit of women's resistance. If by 1912 many suffragists agreed that some form of resistance was an ethical necessity, and some that it was an ethical imperative, all understood it as an embodied relation, one in which resistance took on gendered attributes. Along the continuum of resistance, from the NUWSS's "sword of the spirit" to Emmeline Pankhurst's "argument of the broken pane," the very definition of militancy was expressed in gendered language.[37] In a defense of WSPU tactics at the Old Bailey in 1912, Emmeline Pankhurst examined a number of contemporary definitions of militancy, all evoking opposition, combat, and warfare.[38] In contrast, a 1913 article in the *Vote* by Mrs. Saul Solomon entitled "Breaking to Mend" claimed Florence Nightingale as a model for militancy. For Solomon, it was Nightingale's "passion of Race-Motherhood which possessed the soul and nerved the arm of this remarkable" woman. "The same force of self-abnegating love," she continued, motivated suffragettes to undertake militancy.[39] These two articulations of militancy—"a state of warfare" and a "self-abnegating love"—present a gendered polarity within understandings of resistance not exclusively oppositional (some suffragists held both simultaneously), but certainly practiced as gradations between activity and passivity. The WSPU's motto, "Deeds, Not Words," carried an explicitly gendered meaning: "deeds" were active, "words" passive. The attributes of the former—valor, courage, and resoluteness—were masculine, with the passivity of words clearly linked with femininity. Within the WSPU's idiom of resistance, even the passivity necessary for submitting to forcible feeding was represented in masculine terms as active struggle. Mohandas Gandhi had recognized this in militancy's earliest incarnations. Watching suffragette deputations to Parliament in 1906 and 1907 from afar, he goaded Indians in the Transvaal to follow the example of suffragettes, asking, "While English women do manly deeds, shall we, though men, behave like women?"[40]

And despite the fact that womanliness was claimed as virtue by the WSPU, particularly as members represented themselves visually, it was also the case that femininities paraded by other suffragists celebrated passivity and service.[41] These alternative feminine ideals attempted to claim womanliness not only in defense against public opinion about the suffragettes but also as a hedge against what some suffragists saw as the masculine excesses of WSPU resistance.[42] This is seen most clearly in the WFL's self-conscious rejection of any identification with the separatist, martial aspects of Joan of Arc. The WFL embraced instead Florence Nightingale, "the lady with the lamp," a figure suffused with symbolism connoting the complementarity of men's and women's roles and the "womanliness" of suffragists' public demands.[43]

Literary critic Mary Poovey has observed that the figure of Nightingale "consolidated two narratives about patriotic service that were culturally available [in the mid–nineteenth century]—a domestic narrative of maternal nurturing and self-sacrifice and a military narrative of individual assertion and will."[44] Nightingale refuted women's "natural limitations," demonstrating that women could work in the public sphere without threatening the parameters of that sphere. WFL representations emphasized Florence Nightingale's skill as an administrator, especially her work to improve the conditions under which people lived.[45] Members compared Nightingale's motivations to the same "force of self-abnegating love" inspiring women to militancy. That force was "otherwise wholly contrary to the entire trend of her character and tastes. Hers, too, is a redemptive mission for fallen and suffering humanity."[46] Many WFL members worked as nurses or teachers; many believed in the essential complementarity of men and women, and the image of nurse as helpmeet fit that definition. An increasing number of suffragettes and those sympathetic to their cause rejected the martial qualities of Joan of Arc and embraced other femininities. The idioms through which the WFL spoke emphasized a profound belief in the essential "womanliness" of women—a belief in separate spheres, albeit overlapping and expanding ones, translated as a belief that men and women should work together, and that change should be gradual, not violent or revolutionary (see figure 5.2).

Suffragettes celebrated a wide variety of women whose attributes they characterized in similar terms. These included Josephine Butler, leader of the nineteenth-century international campaign to repeal the Contagious Diseases Acts; Lydia Becker, an earlier proponent of women's parliamentary enfranchisement; and Frances Mary Buss, a pioneer for women's education. These women's lives and accomplishments received attention in pamphlets, in articles in suffrage papers, and in suffrage processions, where they were represented as figures important to the history of women and of the nation.[47] Less glamorous than Joan of Arc, these representations of feminine civic valor circulated equally among militant and nonmilitant suffragists.[48]

Drawing attention to suffragettes' multiple embodiments of the feminine ideal suggests the complexity of their engagement with gender as a political identity. Suffragettes' ideals of femininity functioned in dialectic tension with each other, as much as, if not perhaps more so than, with images more generally available in British culture.[49] A good example of this tension lay in WFL member Margaret Wynne Nevinson's 1908 invocation of the "womanly woman," a figure she aligned with the goddess Minerva. Significantly, Nevinson's use of the figure of Minerva placed greater emphasis upon the goddess's support for the art of handicraft than the art of war.[50] A similar invocation of femininity can be seen in the photo series "Suffragettes at Home," published in the *Vote* in 1910. The announced purpose of the series was to present portraits of WFL members engaged in domestic pursuits to the "man-in-the-street," thus quelling anxieties about suffragettes' womanliness. The two prizewinning photographs, *Mrs. Joseph McCabe Bathing Her Baby*, and *Mrs. John Russell Tending Her Invalid Mother*, celebrated women's primary role

FLORENCE NIGHTINGALE MAKING HER NIGHT ROUNDS.
From " A History of Nursing," published by G. P. Putnam's Sons, London and New York.

FIGURE 5.2
Suffragette propaganda postcard depicting Florence
Nightingale: womanliness in its nurturing capacities.
Museum of London.

in the family as caregivers to the young and the elderly.[51] While the series certainly was conceived with the goal of silencing male critics of militancy by representing suffragettes as devoted to domestic pursuits, its appearance in the *Vote* makes it more likely that the photos were addressed to WFL members who sought reassurance that their own priorities were reflected in the organization.

If Joan of Arc and Florence Nightingale reveal the range of possibilities available to suffragettes for embodying women's citizenship, idioms of freedom and slavery assisted them in embodying resistance. Journalist and militant suffragist H. W. Nevinson commented in 1909 that he had "learnt the reality of the thing [freedom] only from the misery of its opposite."[52] He made the same point more explicitly regarding women suffragists in 1913, when he observed that women rebelled against the state only because they lacked the ability to vote for representation in the state their taxes underwrote. Nevinson articulated the complex set of feelings evoked by that imbalance: "Whence have originated, not only tangible and obvious hardships, but those feelings of degradation, as of beings excluded from privileges owing to some inferiority supposed inherent—those feelings of subjection, impotence, and degradation which, more even than actual hardships, kindle the spirit to the white-hot point of rebellion."[53] Nevinson thus identified as a central feature of suffragettes' understanding of freedom the tendency to define it more frequently in the negative than in the positive, largely through the idiom of slavery.[54]

A number of historians have recently established the tenacity of the language of slavery—and its metaphorical appeal—in Unitarian, feminist, and radical campaigns during the nineteenth century.[55] Certainly, the institutional and organizational connections between abolitionists and feminists in Great Britain contributed to the appeal of the language of slavery within suffragist discourse.[56] Yet the language of slavery underwent enormous transformation within British feminist discourse in the nineteenth and twentieth centuries. Events such as emancipation of slaves in the United States, passage of a set of Married Women's Property Acts in 1870, 1882, and later, and repeated use of the language of slavery in antiprostitution campaigns of the late nineteenth century imbued the analogy between women and slaves with a far different set of associations by 1910 than it held in 1861.[57]

Slavery remained for suffragettes an important metaphor for women's condition, an idiom through which they discussed women in the political sphere. In historian James Walvin's formulation, "slavery was seen to subsume many of the other political arguments about rights; it was, in fact, the most extreme form of a denial of rights."[58] Slavery was perhaps the central idiom for rationalizing resistance. If women were slaves, then metaphorically much followed: government was tyrannical; resistance was justified. Suffragettes thus had at their disposal great reservoirs of meaning. They could draw upon British feelings of superiority for having abolished the slave trade in the British colonies in 1834; by extension, those men who oppressed women by refusing them full political rights became associated with slavery and, hence, possessed less virtue. Slavery, however, proved to be a complicated idiom for twentieth-century suffragettes because its antithesis, freedom, had many tributaries, and suffragettes were divided about which to follow. Two primary understandings of freedom can be discerned among suffragettes, one drawing upon a classical republican tradition of citizenship, and one owing more to liberalism's conceptions.[59]

Nineteenth-century liberal commentators understood slavery's onus in terms of its limitations on an individual's ability to own property and to dispose of one's own labor. J. S. Mill made the analogy of women to slaves, the slave being "a person who could not own property, enter into contracts, or sue for injuries."[60] An important component of this definition of freedom was the necessity of removing impediments upon an individual's actions. This definition persisted into twentieth-century suffragette discourse. Frederick Pethick Lawrence urged that woman must become "possessor of her own soul, and cease to be held as property. She must govern herself and cease to be under the dominance of another. That is the meaning of this movement" (see figure 5.3).[61] Charlotte Carmichael Stopes observed in 1908 that patriots are never weary of singing "Britons never, never shall be slaves." Of course, they should not be so. But they forget that every Briton, who happens to be born a woman, is according to the definition, doomed to be a slave. "Slavery consists in having to obey laws in the making of which one has no voice." Therefore, all British women are slaves to-day. Their payments are not the taxes of a free people, but the tribute of a conquered and subject race. A sad, unconsidered result of this state of affairs is that no man born of a slave-woman can be really free himself until his mother is emancipated.[62]

Suffragist Chrystal MacMillan concurred, urging that "the phrase 'deriving their just powers from the consent of the governed' is merely expressing what we mean by 'liberty' in other words."[63]

An understanding of freedom as absence of restraint also underlay arguments made by liberal feminists in their agitation against the Contagious Diseases Acts in the 1860s and "white slavery" in the 1870s and 1880s. Public discussion of these controversial questions occasioned a shift in nineteenth-century liberal feminist understandings of slavery. Liberal feminists Josephine Butler and Annie Besant redefined personal liberty as bodily integrity of the individual, in women's case, sexual integrity. Besant articulated a liberal definition of freedom in her critique of the Contagious Diseases Acts,

FIGURE 5.3
Political cartoon depicting freedom as the absence of restraint. The Women's Library/Mary Evans Picture Library.

which empowered police to arrest and detain women suspected of solicitation. The acts, she charged, tore up the very "foundation stone" of the "citizen's personal liberty" by empowering the police to incarcerate women without providing proof of their guilt in court.[64] Butler's rhetoric was apocalyptic in its evocation of the spiritual and physical warfare needed to vanquish the forces of evil underwriting the Contagious Diseases Acts. Butler urged suffragists to pray for more "aggressive and militant virtue than we yet see among us. To live purely and blamelessly ourselves is not now enough; we must have the fibre of soldiers; the courage, if need be, of leaders of a forlorn hope, over whose dead bodies our fellow-soldiers will march to victory."[65]

Christabel Pankhurst furthered this line of argument in a series of articles in the *Suffragette* in 1913. Collected and published later that year as *The Great Scourge and How to End It,* the articles defined women's political disabilities in sexual terms. Pankhurst narrated *The Great Scourge* through the metaphor of slavery, making a sensationalist and separatist argument about the consequences of sexual slavery for women: "The opponents of votes for women know that women, when they are politically free and economically strong, will not be purchasable for the base uses of vice. Those who want to have women as slaves, obviously do not want women to become voters."[66] Pankhurst's emphasis on women's right to bodily integrity, the right to an absence of restraint from without, was rooted in a classically liberal definition of freedom. Rejecting women's connection to men, she posited a separatist polity for women. Men, she argued, saw women as

> created primarily for the sex gratification of men, and secondarily, for the bearing of children if he happens to want them, but of no more children than he wants. As the result of this belief the relation between man and woman has centred in the physical. What is more, the relation between man and woman has been that of an owner and his property—of a master and his slave—not the relation of two equals. From that evil has sprung another. The man is not satisfied to be in relation with only one slave; he must be in relation with many. That is to say, sex promiscuity has arisen, and from that has in its turn come disease.[67]

Until men adopted women's sexual standard of conduct, that is, until men embraced chastity and eschewed promiscuity, all women would remain in a state of slavery. Votes for women and chastity for men, then, were intertwined.[68]

The most controversial part of Pankhurst's argument, though, was its extension to married women. Hers was not exclusively a critique of prostitution but an application of prostitution to the marital relationship.[69] *The Great Scourge* asserted that "the system under which a married woman must derive her livelihood from her husband—must eat out of his hand, as it were—is a great bulwark of sex-subjection, and is a great reinforcement to prostitution. People are led to reason thus: a woman who is a wife is one who has made a permanent sex-bargain for her maintenance; the woman who is not married must therefore make a temporary bargain of the same kind."[70] Pankhurst included the government in her indictment of men's sexual enslavement of women, lambasting officials for implementing inadequate employment policies and for assisting in the procurement of female prostitutes for men serving in the British army and navy.[71] Agitation against white slavery became a major theme of WSPU efforts after 1912 and featured prominently in the rhetoric of both Christabel and Emmeline Pankhurst.[72]

Increasingly, the WSPU's emphasis on women as sexed bodies enslaved by men led suffragettes to leave the organization. Many saw Christabel Pankhurst's focus on women's bodily integrity as too limiting a definition of what their political activism sought. In 1914, former WSPU member Dora Marsden characterized Christabel Pankhurst as an "enigma": "no one knows what she is: she has lived in the public eye for eight years, she is setting well towards forty and has been known to express only two candid opinions: one on Mr. Asquith and one on the White Slave Trade. One watches with interest for the third."[73] Feminist Rebecca West confronted Christabel Pankhurst directly in a September 1913 essay in the *Clarion,* a socialist weekly. West summarized her position thus: "I say that her remarks on the subject [venereal disease] are utterly valueless and are likely to discredit the cause in which we believe."[74] Pankhurst's insistence that women segregate themselves from men was seen as too restrictive an understanding of feminism and was opposed by members of the United Suffragists, the WFL, and the East London Federation of Suffragettes. Pankhurst's emphasis on freedom's negative definition was one many suffragettes and feminists increasingly rejected, offering in its place a positive conception of freedom.

Organic freedom, the capacity to act as a citizen, came to define citizenship for an increasing number of suffragettes.[75] This definition was influenced by liberal conceptions of freedom insofar as all suffragettes agreed with J. S. Mill's assessment that slavery and tyranny were outmoded systems in need of overhaul.[76] But organic freedom owed more to radical conceptions of freedom from the late eighteenth and early nineteenth centuries that emphasized the freedom to act than it owed to liberal conceptions emphasizing freedom from restraint. Organic freedom emerged most clearly as a strand in suffragist rhetoric in the 1890s with renewed emphasis on the rights, duties, and responsibilities of citizenship.[77] Borrowing from the civic republican tradition and from Liberal and Idealist thinking on community, this conception of freedom emphasized that participation in the public sphere was an inherently ennobling activity. The citizen was made virtuous by and through participation in self-government.[78]

Slavery as metaphor remained important in this strand of thinking about freedom, although with a different emphasis. Charlotte Despard's essay, "The Ethics of Resistance" (1912), for example, invoked the relatively underused historical examples of Thoreau's opposition to slavery and Gandhi's passive resistance campaign to protect the political rights of Indians in South Africa. An important distinction had emerged in suffragette discourse between people's enslavement at the whim of tyrants and women's enslavement at the whim of men. Suffragettes were divided fundamentally in their analyses of women's oppression. While some, like Christabel Pankhurst, emphasized sexual integrity as fundamental to women's exercise of citizenship, others focused on the political structures enslaving men and women. Suffragettes invoked earlier struggles for national liberation to make their case; Giuseppe Mazzini's role in the unification of Italy was a favorite example.[79] Some suffragettes intertwined their work for women's suffrage with other liberation struggles. Dora Montefiore, for example, investigated serfdom in Russia as a problem, publishing a book on the topic in 1906.[80] Henry Woodd Nevinson's formulation, made some years after the campaign had ended, suggests the connection many made between women's suffrage and other campaigns for national self-determination. Of his activities in the spring and summer of 1907, he wrote: "I was occupied in contending, to the best of my influence, against the impending *entente* with the Russian Tsardom, and in my prolonged struggle to spread the knowledge of the Portuguese-slave system as I had seen it in Angola and the Islands. To these contests was now added the equally disturbing contest for Woman Suffrage."[81] For Montefiore, Nevinson, and numerous other suffragettes, the struggle for human freedom resonated across a spectrum of coercive relations.

Organic freedom was a fundamentally positive understanding of women's condition; it analyzed the source of oppression and offered the vote as solution. Characterizing the difference between voters and nonvoters as the "difference between bondage and freedom," WFL member Marion Holmes urged that "the right of voting confers upon the individual and the nation the dignity of self-government."[82] Rather than emphasize a constriction of women's opportunities, organic freedom emphasized the imperative of action. Charlotte Despard gave this conception of freedom an ethical thrust when she insisted that women's duty to resist those laws impeding their ability to provide for their children was a "sacrament setting upon them the seal of service, binding them together in a common hope and love."[83] Robert Cholmeley defined this type of freedom as "a cry not for relief from responsibility, but for a share in responsibility; not merely for an escape from tutelage, but for a recognition of guardianship."[84]

While all suffragettes agreed on the ethical imperative for resistance to authority in their struggle for political rights, a range of possibilities existed for representing resistance. Femininity and freedom, the two primary idioms through which suffragettes articulated beliefs about the emancipatory possibilities of women's enfranchisement, illuminate the struggle suffragettes fought over citizenship's embodiment. The WSPU's celebration of militarism and its emphasis on political activism as the removal of impediments constituted one end of the spectrum along which suffragettes debated citizenship's meanings. Certain consequences followed. For some members of the WSPU after 1911, resistance was no longer about convincing the government or the public that women ought to have the vote; rather, women's goal became to make political life so difficult that the government would be compelled to give women the vote. Meanwhile, other suffragettes, like those in the WFL, embodied citizenship as women's service to the nation, representing freedom as the ability to act, and they promoted an engagement with the state that both demanded and performed citizenship simultaneously. As with the practice of militancy, suffragettes' multiple representations of resistance created a continuum along which individuals and organizations articulated their understandings of the female citizen in relation to the state.

Chapter 6

The Ethics of Resistance, 1910–1914

The years between 1910 and 1914 were ones of dialogue and innovation within the militant suffrage movement as suffragettes struggled among themselves to define the extent and limits of resistance. Suffragettes continued to understand resistance as a component of active citizenship, but its means of implementation came under great scrutiny. A minority escalated violence into forms of terrorism including arson and bombing, but the vast majority rejected the use of violence. In the attempt to recast militancy away from the use of violence, militants worked across organizational lines and created new groupings. Read thematically, and not merely as a roster of organizations, it is clear that resistance remained an active, if contested, component of suffragettes' conception of citizenship well into the Great War.

All militants shared certain assumptions about the law and women's relationship to the state. First and foremost, they understood the law to be separated into spirit and letter, with written law an inadequate representation of higher truth. Suffragette rhetoric after 1910 emphasized suffragettes' duty to a higher morality, one beyond the laws of man and the scope of mere politics. Some suffragettes cast this authority as divine. WSPU leader Christabel Pankhurst claimed that militants upheld "the law of God" in challenging "the law of man."[1] "Law," she wrote, "is not morality and law is not justice." When the two conflict, "law must be broken, and the saviours of society are those who break it."[2] Others viewed the higher authority as "moral," rooting that authority in ethical, rather than strictly religious, principles. WFL president Charlotte Despard explained: "Laws—civil laws—we have been obliged to break. We recognise with many of the ancients, that there are times and seasons in human history when civil disobedience is the highest duty we can offer to our generation. Moral law we have not broken."[3]

Central to recognition of the split between letter and spirit was the role played by individual conscience. Emmeline Pethick Lawrence justified the use of militancy thus: "Do we by this defence endorse all anarchy? Certainly not! We are merely claiming that the final arbiter of right and wrong for the true Christian is not the decrees of the State, but the individual conscience."[4] On that conscience, according to Charlotte Despard, "the moral law [was] inscribed."[5] Militants understood that by obeying the dictates of conscience, they violated "the ordinary rules that govern the organisation of human society."[6] Suffragettes' supporters echoed this understanding. W. F. Cobb, rector at St. Ethelburga's, Bishopsgate, defended suffragette window breaking not as a politically astute action on the part of women but instead urged "that in an age of ease, cowardice and faithlessness, under a vote-catching, time-serving, place-hunting Government, one group and they women (not men, mind you) have dared to undergo torture for conscience sake."[7]

While all militants emphasized the importance of the individual conscience in mediating the split between the spirit and the letter of the law, they differed in how they understood law's underlying authority. This differentiation was not absolute as the categories suffragettes used often blurred. But emerging more clearly after 1910 was a distinction between human and divine authority. The British constitution remained an important source of human authority for militant action. Charlotte Carmichael Stopes articulated the authority of the constitution quite early in the militant phase of the movement. Her emphasis, tellingly, was on the "spirit" of the British constitution which, she urged, was "supposed to secure Liberty, Justice and Protection to all who live under its sway."[8] Tax resister Margaret Kineton Parkes concurred, reminding suffragists that since the British constitution was unwritten, it existed "not in the letter but in the spirit," defended by "lawbreakers rather than law-abiders." Parkes went on to say that "the Constitution being, on certain fundamental points an unstatutory one, it is quite possible for a statute to be passed which violates not its letter but its living spirit."[9] Other suffragettes rooted earthly authority in popular sovereignty. Laurence Housman characterized the "only source and sanction of Representative Government" as "the people themselves."[10] Charlotte Despard urged that militancy was breaking laws "in order to prove that they harked behind the conscience of the people."[11] Still other suffragettes located militancy's legitimacy in divine law. Rhetorician Cheryl Jorgensen-Earp has argued that after 1910 members of the WSPU came to see their actions as "ordained by God."[12] This does not suggest that other suffragists' understandings of their actions were not rooted in religious interpretations of social change. However, after 1910, an increasingly isolated group of militants in the WSPU articulated their political goals in millenarian language, while militants in other organizations moved away from those visions of change. In the final analysis, disentangling human from divine authority in suffragette discourse may be impossible. For many suffragettes, these two authorities were intertwined. Charlotte Despard invoked both forms of authority when she proclaimed that "'none of the very great reforms had been brought about without men and women having been ready to break the civil law. The civil law was not always the moral law, and was certainly not the Divine law.'"[13] Ultimately where suffragettes located authority for their actions differed in emphasis, with some suffragettes highlighting divine authority, and others, the constitution.

Suffragettes agreed also that the government used disproportionate force in its dealings with them. Of the arguments advanced against women's suffrage, the only one left standing by 1912 was the physical force argument, which held that men's physical superiority to women qualified men, and only men, to exercise political power at the national level.[14] As anti-suffragist A. MacCallum Scott put it, "It may be laid down as an absolute maxim of statesmanship that the only stable form of Government is one which secures that the balance of political power is in the same hands as the balance of physical force." He concluded: "In short, we count heads instead of breaking them."[15] Antisuffragist Heber Hart elaborated on this argument in his assertion that were women to have the parliamentary vote, "physical power and legal right would no longer be commensurate. . . . The vote would cease to be the last word in civil contention, because it would no longer reveal the ultimate truth of sovereignty, government, and law."[16] Suffragettes, however, consistently rejected this argument against their enfranchisement. Laurence Housman accused those advancing the physical force doctrine as "prejudiced against change" and of not believing in "the democratic principle."[17] Contemporary commentators ridiculed those subscribing to physical force on multiple grounds, not least the fact that men's parliamentary enfranchisement in Britain, unlike that of other European nations, was not contingent upon military service. Jurist Sidney Low urged in the pages of *Votes for Women* that "as long as Englishmen shirk the duty which men of most other civilised countries perform they have no right to exclude women from political equality on military grounds."[18] Interestingly, the premise that war service earned citizenship remained intact in Low's argument, the implication being that suffragettes did not object to the principle of equating physical power and legal right so long as the principle was applied consistently to men and women.

For most suffragettes, however, rejection of the physical force argument was at root an argument about the necessity of locating the state's legitimate authority in the consent of its citizens, not in the state's use of force. In the ongoing attempt to discredit the connection between physical force and state authority, suffragettes sought public exposure of the ways in which the government's legitimacy was maintained not by the rule of law but by law's violent enforcement. Indeed, suffragettes found in the law a double fiction: the violence necessary to uphold the law was denied officially yet exercised against them frequently, and the law, although allegedly gender-neutral, worked against them on the basis of their sex.[19] In exposing this double fiction, they sought to impeach the government's legitimacy. Much of the Edwardian campaign was concerned with revealing contradictions between the rule of law and its enforcement where women were concerned. Suffragettes pointed to the political nature of women's exclusion from participation in the nation, uncovering underlying tensions in liberalism.

Suffragettes challenged the state's use of force against them in two primary arenas: their treatment during arrest and while incarcerated. Throughout the Edwardian campaign suffragettes lodged numerous allegations of police brutality during protests and arrests. Most notorious were those of 18 November 1910, known to suffragettes as "Black Friday," when over 130 women filed complaints against the London metropolitan police for assaults committed upon them in the course of a WSPU attempt to take a deputation to the House of Commons. A significant number of those allegations included assaults not only violent but also sexual in nature.[20] Metropolitan police files reveal that while the severity of 18 November 1910 was unusual, complaints of assault by police were not infrequent.[21] Suffragette allegations of police brutality led to formation of an organization to monitor the treatment of women at the hands of the police. The Suffragists' Vigilance League announced its objective as being "to protest against the continuing arrests and prosecutions of Suffragists and their sympathizers. To hold watching briefs and be legally represented at all Police Court proceedings; to report upon sentences passed by Magistrates; to consider what steps may be necessary to take in all cases where Suffragists and their sympathisers are sentenced in the second and third divisions."[22]

Once arrested and sentenced, suffragettes criticized their treatment while incarcerated. Prior to January 1908, magistrates in police courts trying the suffragettes had sentenced them to imprisonment in the first division, which was interpreted by many suffragettes as the equivalent of being classified as political offenders. Suffragette prisoners' status became a point of contention between women and the Home Office after magistrates ceased sentencing them to imprisonment in the first division because suffragettes believed that "recognition of offending suffragists as political prisoners would amount to 'a tacit recognition of [their] citizenship.'"[23] The Prison Act of 1898, however, made no distinction between political prisoners and other kinds of offenders. The first division was reserved for misdemeanants; the second and third divisions provided for criminal offenders, the difference between the latter two being one of prior criminal record.[24] Prisoners in the first division were allowed a number of privileges, including wearing their own clothes, reading books and newspapers, and visiting with friends. In the second and third divisions, prisoners were required to wear prison uniforms, were kept in solitary confinement for all but one hour a day, and were allowed no letters or visitors.[25]

After members of the WSPU initiated hunger strikes in the summer of 1909 to protest incarceration in the second division, suffragettes and a number of doctors, journalists, and other public figures vociferously criticized the forcible feedings used by the Home Office to stop the practice. It soon became evident that public opinion went against feeding women against their wills.[26] Under initiative of the home secretary, Reginald McKenna, the Home Office pushed through a piece of legislation designed to break the hunger strike. In April 1913, the Prisoners (Temporary Discharge for Ill-Health) Bill, which suffragettes soon termed the "Cat and Mouse Act," passed into law. Under its provisions, hunger-striking suffragettes were released when prison authorities believed their health to be threatened; once recovered, however, the women were to be returned to jail. Suffragettes immediately seized upon the potential for propaganda detrimental to the government and expended great energy eluding capture and incarceration once released. They also attacked the government's efforts to curb militancy through this legislation, contending that government treatment of suffragette prisoners approached torture.[27] They cast their objections on constitutional grounds. A pamphlet, issued by the Repeal the Act Committee, urged that "the Cat and Mouse Act is unprecedented in the history of civilization and is contrary to the spirit of the British constitution, and the principles of British Law."[28] The WFL asked, "Is political agitation a crime?"— pointing to the "tyranny and unconstitutional action" of the Liberal government in "trying to crush a Political Agitation by methods of Imprisonment, Stomach Tube, The Gag, and Hose Pipe."[29] Violent and nonviolent alike, suffragettes were united during these years in criticism of authorities' use of violence against women.

Where militants ultimately parted ways was in the role they accorded to the use of violence in resisting the state. This issue erupted in public discourse in January 1911 when articles in anticipation of former WFL member Teresa Billington Greig's forthcoming book appeared in the progressive monthly, the *New Age*. *The Militant Suffrage Movement: Emancipation in a Hurry* followed in March. Read by some contemporaries as a critique of the WSPU, it was in fact a cogent meditation on the uses and meanings of violence in resisting the state.[30] Billington Greig engaged with a pressing question for all radicals in Britain since the 1880s, whether suffragette, Irish or Indian nationalist, or labor or socialist organizer—the role of force in dealing with the state. Militancy, she asserted, "interpreted itself to [suffragettes] not as the mere expression of an urgent desire for political rights, but as an aggressive proclamation of a deeper right—the right of insurrection."[31]

One way to read Billington Greig's critique of militancy is to place it within context of the evolving parliamentary situation. In 1910, parliamentary supporters of women's enfranchisement from all the parties came together in a committee with the goal of guiding a measure for women's suffrage through Parliament. This Conciliation Committee consisted of fifty-four members of Parliament: twenty-five Liberals, seventeen Unionists, six Irish Nationalists, and six members of the Labour Party. The committee sought to propose a bill that all parties and suffrage organizations would accept, and the situation looked hopeful when the government granted the committee's bill time for full debate and voting in June 1910. The bill introduced in the House of Commons by D. J. Shackleton (Labour) on 14 June passed its second reading on 11 July. Patterned after the Municipal Franchise Act of 1869, it granted the parliamentary franchise to those women possessing the household qualification and those women occupiers who met the ten-pound annual property qualification. It also enfranchised married women as long as the property on which they met the qualification was not the same property used to meet their husbands'. Estimates at the time suggested that one million women would be enfranchised by the bill. The bill passed its second reading with a majority in favor; once, however, it had passed to a committee of the whole, the government refused to allow further facilities for its discussion that session. Prime Minister Asquith then announced in late November that Parliament would be dissolved at the end of the month, but he promised that the government would grant facilities the following session for another such bill, although he refused to say whether the government would back it.[32] The WSPU responded by taking a resolution opposed to the government's action to the prime minister at Parliament on 22 and 23 November; the resulting demonstrations led to incidents of window breaking and numerous arrests. In the month following the WSPU's response, other suffragettes emphatically refrained from engaging in militant protests, and Billington Greig's articles in the *New Age* and her forthcoming book promised the first public engagement by a suffragette with the WSPU's increasingly violent protests. Billington Greig's timing seemed especially pointed, as many suffragists had viewed the Conciliation Bill as a promising development and the WSPU's renewal of militancy a premature response to political developments.

Publication of *The Militant Suffrage Movement* occasioned great scrutiny of Billington Greig's role in the movement by the mainstream press. Contemporaries (as well as later historians) tended to reduce the question to one of personal politics, a disagreement among suffragettes. Certainly, Billington Greig's public pronouncements on the movement encouraged this reading. In an article explaining her critique, Billington Greig observed of the militants that "the desire for protest has become stronger than the desire for the suffrage, the means has been preferred upon the end, the chance of early legislation has been sacrificed for a row."[33] Her book, however, was not an isolated critique of militancy motivated by her changing relationship to the movement. Rather, it synthesized growing discontent among suffragettes about the direction militancy was taking. Many suffragettes felt ambivalent about the WSPU's increasing violence.[34] Militants' criticism of WSPU militancy prior to Billington Greig's book had been muted by a refusal on the part of all suffragettes to criticize the WSPU publicly. Indeed, entire organizations were formed on the premise that public criticism of other suffrage organizations' tactics was unacceptable. For example, the New Constitutional Society was founded in 1909 "to promote unity in the Suffrage movement by avoiding criticism of the methods of other Suffrage Societies, and by working with them whenever possible."[35] *The Militant Suffragette Movement* did not reject militancy outright but instead engaged with it as an ongoing practice. Billington Greig's goal in airing her views was to introduce a critical spirit into the discussion and practice of militancy. In this respect, the book was successful. After publication, ambivalence toward WSPU militancy turned into concrete critiques, echoing and amplifying the points Billington Greig had made.

This became evident in 1911. A second Conciliation Bill, introduced by Sir George Kemp in May 1911, proposed that every woman householder would have the parliamentary vote in her division of residence. The bill stipulated that husbands and wives would not be eligible to vote in the same parliamentary division; to exercise the franchise, married women would be required to meet the household qualification in another parliamentary division. Estimates projected that the bill would enfranchise one million women. The bill passed its second reading, and its prospects looked good. Later that year, however, while meeting with a deputation from the People's Suffrage League, Asquith effectively removed the second Conciliation Bill from consideration when he informed members of the deputation that the government would introduce a reform bill in the coming session that would eliminate the numerous qualifications then in use (lodgers, owners, occupiers, and rate payers) and use residence as the primary qualification. He also indicated that the bill would not include a women's suffrage amendment but would leave that question open. At a subsequent deputation with several suffrage organizations, including the NUWSS, the Conservative and Unionist Women's Franchise Association, and the Actresses' Franchise League, the government clarified its position. Asquith emphasized that his government would grant facilities to any bill "which met the qualification of being capable of amendment," asserting also that the government's introduction of a reform bill in no way jeopardized the Conciliation Bill's chances of passage into legislation.[36] These promises further divided suffragists. The WSPU embraced Chancellor of the Exchequer David Lloyd George's accusation that the government had "torpedoed" the Conciliation Bill and escalated its militancy, while other suffragettes and the nonmilitant NUWSS accepted the government's promises and refrained from further action.[37]

In the wake of the second Conciliation Bill's demise, WFL members moved from distancing themselves from the WSPU's accusation that Asquith had torpedoed the Conciliation Bill of 1911 to criticizing the WSPU's attacks on private property.[38] Charlotte Despard noted in her diary the difficulties posed for the WFL's work by WSPU members' use of arson and bombs.[39] Commenting on escalating WSPU violence, WFL member Eunice Murray wrote in her journal in June 1912 that "WSPU tactics are often to me incomprehensible, but I suppose they know their own affairs."[40] Like many suffragettes, Murray opposed WSPU violence yet could not bring herself to condemn it openly.[41] The closest a member of the WFL came to public condemnation of the WSPU came in an article in the *Vote*. Alison Neilans defended the WFL's refusal to attack property, arguing that it did so not out of "respect for plate-glass windows or the usual British idea of 'respectability' and 'womanliness,'" but because it cared "too deeply for [the] Cause to endanger its chance of success, however slender that chance may be."[42]

The reluctance nonviolent militants felt about critizing the WSPU was not shared by other suffragists. In 1912, nonmilitant suffragists joined members of the press, public, and government in critiquing the WSPU's use of violence. In response to the WSPU "window-smashing raids" of late 1911 and early 1912, NUWSS president Millicent Garrett Fawcett decried the situation, observing that a small number of suffragists had "temporarily lost all faith in human honour, in human sense of justice, and are attempting to grasp by violence what should be yielded to the growing conviction that our demand [for women's suffrage] is based on justice and common sense."[43] Suffragist Charlotte Carmichael Stopes's response was more equivocal. In her contribution to Huntly Carter's *Women's Suffrage and Militancy* (1912),a collection of prominent men's and women's responses to militancy, she explained that "the flinging of stones is a primeval sign, . . . as old as the invention of windows. It is a message that some one stands without who has not been able to make himself heard by ordinary means." Throwing stones, she suggested, had worked for men in the past, but it was ultimately a strategy that nonviolent militants wished to avoid. She concluded, saying, "We of the law-abiding societies would rather gain our enfranchisement in a common and ordinary way, and so would the militants."[44] NUWSS propaganda increasingly differentiated between militants' resort to physical force and their own appeals "to the principles of right and reason" (see figure 6.1).[45]

A frequent criticism of the WSPU, from both inside and outside the militant movement, was that it indulged in what Billington Greig identified as "cheap sentiment." WFL member Alison Neilans both borrowed WSPU rhetoric and criticized it in her assertion that the WFL never demanded that members undertake the hunger strike: "No tyranny of tears, of personal affection, of exerted authority, no compulsion of emotional revivalism, is responsible for the deeds our members do. Those who take the danger duty upon their shoulders are volunteers. Their gift of sacrifice is a free-will offering upon the altar of our Cause."[46] Far harsher public critiques were offered by former WSPU member Dora Marsden. In a series of articles in the *Freewoman: A Weekly Feminist Review,* which she edited, Marsden pilloried the WSPU's "simultaneous use of emotional appeal and of virulent scolding" and characterized its militancy as "puerile."[47] Militancy, Marsden contended, fulfilled emotional needs in women who otherwise had no purpose in life.[48]

Suffragettes also criticized what they saw as a narrowing of their agenda to the vote. Here again Billington Greig led the charge, contending that "the movement has allowed itself to be narrowed, lowered, and exploited."[49] A variant of this criticism focused on the WSPU's perceived reluctance to address issues of importance to working-class women and its movement away from issues other than suffrage, especially those relating to women's industrial work.[50] In addition, militants criticized what they saw as a separation of

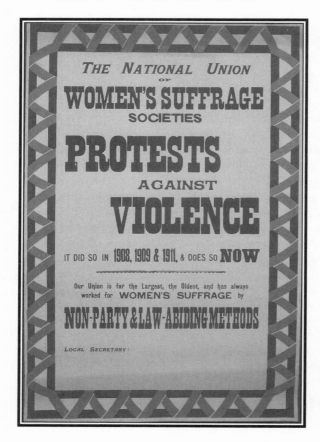

FIGURE 6.1
NUWSS poster
protesting WSPU
violence (1912).
The Women's
Library/Mary Evans
Picture Library.

means from ends: "The fight and the method of fight has been all, the reason and spirit has been nothing to the militants and their supporters."[51] Members of the WFL, especially, urged that protests should "be logical," that is, should make sense to the ordinary person.[52] Too much emphasis, they warned, was placed upon attracting public attention, and not enough thought was given to initiating effective militant protests, that is, protests that would serve their goal of hampering the mechanisms of government.[53]

Despite mounting critiques of violence, suffragettes were not otherwise unanimous in their definition of militancy. Nowhere was this clearer than at the Special Conference convened by the WFL in April 1912. Leading up to the conference, a group emerged from within the WFL, criticizing the organization's unwillingness to challenge the WSPU publicly and attributing that stance to the WFL's president, Charlotte Despard. Seven members of the WFL's National Executive Committee (NEC) circulated a private and confidential letter, accusing Despard of acting without regard for WFL policies on militancy.[54] Edith How Martyn, one of the seven signatories, warned that as long as violent militancy continued, it would be virtually impossible for a women's suffrage bill to pass the House of Commons, partly "because we can never hope to [agitate violently] on a sufficiently large scale, and partly because [such agitation] is a direct appeal to physical force, in which women are admittedly inferior." She maintained that the WFL should continue its passive resistance but should cease to use the designation "militant." She urged the organization to acknowledge that the old methods had all failed.[55] At the conference, the group's attempt to have Despard removed as president failed by a vote of thirty-five to eighteen; subsequently, all seven signatories to the letter resigned from the NEC.[56] The next day the conference agreed to oppose "active" militancy, defined officially as "any kind of protest involving risk of imprisonment, excluding resistance to taxation."[57]

The WSPU, however, made no such resolutions. Between 1909 and 1914, numerous members engaged in acts of physical violence against people and property. These included personal attacks on individuals, including the prime minister and other cabinet ministers, a Holloway Prison medical officer, and a newspaper editor with whose opinions they disagreed. Attacks on property had implications for individuals' personal safety as well. Window breaking involved not only smashing plate glass windows of government office buildings and privately owned shops but also throwing bricks through windows of public halls while ministers spoke to capacity audiences.[58] Nor would it have been apparent to contemporaries that the WSPU's attacks on property would not harm anyone. Increasingly, Christabel Pankhurst used the word "terrorism" to describe the WSPU's actions against the government, implying indiscriminate actions against persons and property with the goal of making the public fearful.[59] By 1913, she had repudiated the notion that women's claims to representation rested on moral force. She insisted "that the politically disinherited ones, whether they are men or whether they are women, are obliged to challenge the physical force used by their tyrant to keep them in bondage."[60] The WSPU's rebellion, she claimed, was a form of terrorism.[61] Beginning in early 1913, WSPU members began to attack personal and public property across the country, cutting telegraph and telephone wires, slashing paintings in public galleries, and setting fire to public buildings and private residences. Historian Andrew Rosen has estimated that the peak of these attacks came in June 1913, when some £54,000 damage was done to a variety of structures in places as various as Oxford, East Lothian, and St. Andrews.[62] The arson campaign continued into July 1914, when it was halted by the coming of war (see figure 6.2).[63]

Eventually even militancy's staunchest supporters had to concede that suffragettes' violence could not be explained solely as a manifestation of moral force. Percy Cohen made this point in May 1913 when he prodded suffragettes to recognize the difference between militant practices like arson and the historical examples of resistance they produced in defense of their actions: "The idealist can prate with success on ideals; but he cannot make ordinary men and women, who have no time for abstractions and the *finesse*

FIGURE 6.2
WSPU arson attack: St. Catherine's church, Hatcham,
London, 6 May 1913. Museum of London.

of a poetic soul, look upon the burning of a railway carriage at Harrow as
the visual embodiment of such a thing as Hampden insurgence."[64] Others
placed suffragette militancy within the broader scope of political problems
facing the state and urged their fellows not to overestimate militancy's effectiveness. A January 1914 editorial in the WFL's paper, the *Vote*, urged suffragettes to continue to seek political methods unique to women but warned that
given tensions in northern Ireland, growing separation between the races in
South Africa, and competition between European powers for military supremacy, "the gentler voice of even the most militant of suffragists will likely
go unheeded."[65]

As critiques of violent militancy increased among suffragettes, it became
clear that new thinking about militancy was changing its practice. An important measure of the vitality of disagreement among militants was the proliferation of militant suffrage organizations between 1911 and 1914. Even
while WSPU violence escalated, numerous nonviolent militant societies attempted to expand the practice of militancy. Unofficial splits emerged within
the WSPU, with new groups breaking away under the leadership of members
Rose Lamartine Yates and Elinor Penn Gaskell.[66] A new organization, the

United Suffragists (US), emerged in February 1914 as a meeting place for militant and nonmilitant suffragists, a return, according to historian Krista Cowman, "to suffrage militancy's earlier passive forms."[67] The United Suffragists counted among its numbers former WSPU members and supporters Frederick and Emmeline Pethick Lawrence, Evelyn Sharp, Barbara Ayrton Gould, and Henry Woodd Nevinson, along with some individuals not previously associated with militancy.[68] The East London Federation of Suffragettes (ELFS), formed in May 1913 as the East London branch of the WSPU, emerged as an independent organization in January 1914 (see figure 6.3).[69] The group attained notoriety in November 1913, when it formed the "People's Army" in the East End in an attempt to protect working-class activists from police violence during suffrage demonstrations. Members of the army drilled in front of East London Federation headquarters and fought with police constables on more than one occasion.[70]

WSPU rhetoric represented dissenters from its policies as splintering off from the one true organization, as a shaking of "rotten fruit" off "the Suf-

FIGURE 6.3
Sylvia Pankhurst addressing the crowd outside WSPU headquarters in Bow, East London, 1912. Museum of London.

frage tree."[71] However, both the proliferation of organizations and the development of new forms of protest between 1911 and 1914 indicate that something more momentous was occurring. Alongside the multiplication of organizations between 1911 and 1914 came a burgeoning discourse on militancy. Nonviolent militants vigorously debated the forms resistance should take. Emmeline Pethick Lawrence reminded readers of *Votes for Women* that violence had played no role in early militancy: "The law—the iniquitous law that extracts from women the duties of citizenship while tyrannously refusing the corresponding rights—was challenged." She pointed to three early methods used by suffragettes: opposition to pro-government candidates at by-elections; organized questioning of cabinet ministers; and resistance of payment of imperial tax, including the insurance poll-tax.[72] Among nonviolent militants, continuity with militancy of the earlier period was maintained, including radical argumentation.[73]

Especially important was the role played by Emmeline and Frederick Pethick Lawrence in editing the newspaper *Votes for Women*. After announcing their estrangement from the WSPU in October 1912, the Pethick Lawrences retained the paper and used it as a forum for discussion of the movement as a whole.[74] Through the paper one can glean fascinating glimpses of the range of militancies between late 1912 and 1914.[75] The Pethick Lawrences consistently cast the militant movement as "robust and wide," vital, and diverse.[76] *Votes for Women,* they urged, would "cast a light to illumine the situation and dispel the ignorance which prevails not only among the outside world, but even among suffragists as to what is being accomplished in the various parts of the Suffrage movement." The paper reported "both law-abiding and revolutionary" action; it deplored "self-righteous criticism" of the movement from within.[77] The paper became a place where new kinds of organizations could be imagined, including what the Pethick Lawrences called "A 'Votes for Women' Fellowship," which would create a forum for militants and nonmilitants alike. *Votes for Women* reported members of the fellowship all over London and its suburbs, England, Scotland, and elsewhere in the world.[78] In January 1913, the paper announced formation of a new Federated Council of women's suffrage societies, which promised unity among the smaller of the militant and nonmilitant suffrage organizations.[79] Discussed was the Suffrage First Committee, which attempted to enlist electors in every constituency to vote for candidates on the basis of their positions on suffrage.[80] The paper also provided a forum for candid discussion between suffrage organizations on the different possible definitions of militancy.[81]

The WFL's paper the *Vote* served a similar purpose, continuing to publish articles of general interest to feminists, as well as providing coverage of a range of militant approaches. Suffrage, social work, and sexual assault received attention in the newspaper's pages, as did children's education and the conditions of working girls in factories. Editorials, essays, and short fiction engaged regularly with the assumptions of militancy, and lively debate was held among correspondents to the paper as to future directions WFL policy should follow. The WFL published information regarding "kindred societies," including the Women Teachers' Franchise Union and the National Federation of Teachers.[82] The *Vote* frequently commented on the movement as a whole, surveying the work of militants and nonmilitants alike and assessing favorably the contributions of all to the larger cause.[83]

Even the *Suffragette,* the WSPU's paper after the split with the Pethick Lawrences in October 1912, exhibited new militancies. It provided weekly news of multiple suffrage organizations, including the Men's Political Union for Women's Enfranchisement, the Suffrage Atelier, the Actresses' Franchise League, Free Church League for Women's Suffrage, Catholic Women's Suffrage Society, Irish Women's Franchise League, Men's Federation for Women's Suffrage, and New Constitutional Society. That these organizations' events received notice in the pages of the paper suggests that members of those organizations continued to read, if not subscribe to, the paper.[84] Creation of the ELFS as a separate organization in January 1914 resulted in yet another suffrage publication in March of that year. The *Woman's Dreadnought,* edited by Sylvia Pankhurst, reported on ELFS activities and provided information on yet further groupings of militants, including the East London Men's Society for Women's Suffrage and the Rebel Social and Political Union.[85] The most innovative aspect of the paper's coverage was its solicitation of multiple perspectives on protests and demonstrations. One such report was published following the 21 May 1914 WSPU deputation to the king at Buckingham Palace. Members of the ELFS present at the protest published statements regarding what they had witnessed, creating a very different experience for the reader of the *Woman's Dreadnought* than that of the *Suffragette.* Rather than presenting events from an omniscient point of view, the paper offered "What Mrs. Drake, of Canning Town, saw," and "What Mrs. Moore, of Bow, saw," portraying ELFS members as authors of their own experiences and reiterating the importance of women's active engagement as citizens.[86]

In the pages of the *Vote* and *Votes for Women,* as well as in personal correspondence and other writings, militants raised a number of critical questions regarding the practice of militancy. General acknowledgment was made of the difficulties experienced by militant organizations that refrained from militancy. Charlotte Despard noted some of the consequences for an organization abstaining from militant action when she observed: "Militancy and defiance, while bringing severe criticism, do also bring public interest, enthusiasm, money, and members. The cold logic of political facts is not inspiring, and a society which applies such logic does not receive much financial assistance from the ordinary public."[87] Yet, non-WSPU militants increasingly questioned the role violence ought to play in militancy. The WFL's National Executive Committee explained that when considering militant action, "the question is not 'Are we content with the situation?' but 'Can militancy improve it?'"[88] Nonviolent militants also revived the question of men's role in the militant movement. From late 1912, the WSPU defined itself as an organization exclusively of women, a notion challenged by other militant organizations.[89]

The WFL, US, and ELFS encouraged men and women to work together for political rights.[90]

Violent militancy was the exception, not the norm, of militancy between 1911 and 1914. While the WSPU introduced ever-escalating forms of militancy, including false fire alarms, setting fire to post boxes, arson, and other forms of property damage, both the WSPU and nonviolent militants continued earlier forms of protest. This included interrupting cabinet ministers at public meetings, and attempts to present petitions to the House of Commons and directly to the monarch.[91] Tax resistance continued and expanded into other financial arenas with the WFL's opposition to the National Insurance Act of 1911. The League's rationale for opposition to the Insurance Act confronted the state's gendered construction of workers' identities, for the bill as proposed failed to include domestic workers and married women.[92] The Middlesbrough Branch of the WFL made a list of additions it saw as necessary to the proposed bill; these included coverage for widows and orphans and England's five million housewives, cash maternity benefit for insured women workers, and an equitable scale of payment for men and women.[93] When the act passed without these additions, the WFL determined it would resist payment of the tax. In June 1912, the WFL's National Executive Committee urged its clerks to file a formal protest against the WFL for failing to do so, hoping thereby to trigger government prosecution.[94] The Insurance Act continued to be a focal point of protest, with a large demonstration in Trafalgar Square in September 1913.[95] The government took action against the WFL in May 1914, instructing Florence Underwood, general secretary, to pay tax on an amount the government estimated was owed by the organization.[96] Resisting payment of national insurance was of a piece with earlier protests impeding functioning of the machinery of the state. The ELFS "No Vote No Rent" protest, under development in 1913 and 1914 but never implemented, also drew upon earlier protests in its assault upon the machinery of government.[97]

Other continuities consisted in militant assaults on the law. In February 1913, the WFL unveiled a new campaign called the "War Against Law," a concerted, multifront assault upon the administration of law in Britain. Members devised this as an explicit criticism of the public's love of sensational militancy.[98] The "War Against Law" made innovative contributions to the treatment of women in the police courts.[99] Members of the League demanded women's right of access to the proceedings of trials involving women, which paved the way for women to be admitted more consistently to suffrage trials.[100] Members also campaigned for improved services for impoverished defendants, including the need for public defenders, and demanded that religious provision be made for prisoners not belonging to the Church of England.[101] The WFL announced it would protest the conviction of prisoners on police evidence alone, as well as the practice of allowing police witnesses to remain in the courtroom to hear evidence they would then be asked to corroborate.[102] These protests were carried out in tandem with the

WFL's exposure of unacceptable conditions in the vans used to transport prisoners.[103] One solution proposed by WFL members for the amelioration of many of these problems was the creation of a women's police force.[104]

Other innovations on earlier themes included obstruction protests in the courts, a type of protest undertaken by both violent and nonviolent militants. Members of the WSPU adopted courtroom disruption as policy in May 1914. At her trial on 22 May, Flora Drummond refused to cooperate with authorities, and women attending the trial interrupted incessantly. The WFL undertook a yet more aggressive campaign against what it saw as the inequitable administration of justice and the abysmal treatment of women by the police in July. In the first of its self-styled obstruction protests, "organised in response to repeated acts of aggression and injustice on the part of police officials, Scotland Yard, and officialdom generally," five members of the WFL chained themselves to the door of the Bow Street Police Court in its temporary quarters in Francis Street, Tottenham Court Road. Their actions effectively locked the doors to the courtroom and impeded the court's proceedings. All five women were arrested outside the police court.[105] The WFL used the arrests as the occasion to comment on the conditions prisoners endured while awaiting trial, between trials, and en route from jail to the courts. They complained about a lack of privacy in jail and the transportation of men and women together in crowded prison vans.[106]

Most notable in the years 1912 to 1914 is the degree to which cooperation between militant organizations increased. This was evident in the manner in which nonviolent militants addressed their reading publics. In October 1912, Emmeline Pethick Lawrence cast the scope of militancy broadly, calling upon all in the women's movement "to adopt the essence of the Militant creed by ceasing to approach politicians as suppliants entreating favour." She urged women to let the government know that they would not accept their continuing disfranchisement and would "maintain their claim by active and persistent opposition." Nor would they "hesitate if necessary for the vindication of the fundamental principle of human liberty to use methods that are in open defiance of the law."[107] Diversity among those women claiming to be militants was acknowledged and even celebrated by the organizations' leadership. In early 1914, when both the US and the ELFS emerged as independent organizations, Charlotte Despard, president of the WFL, urged in an editorial in the *Vote:* "Our societies may be numerous, the methods adopted may vary; that does not trouble us. So far as our sisters in the movement are concerned, we neither praise nor blame. We accept what is done as fellow-soldiers in a great battle."[108]

Despard's acceptance of diversity within militancy was, however, continually debated among militants. One key difference between the WFL and those nonviolent militants allied with *Votes for Women* arose because the latter continued to question cabinet ministers at public meetings even though the questioners frequently faced hostile crowds. Emmeline Pethick Lawrence defended the practice as offering a form of action to "those women and men who, unlike [herself], are conscientiously and temperamentally opposed to any exercise of physical force in the furtherance of a just cause, but are also honestly ashamed of the semblance of acquiescence in wrong which is given when no protest against those who have intrigued and betrayed finds expression in action."[109] Members of the WFL largely agreed with those sentiments, although they continually strove to emphasize that their protests "have been directed against the Government, the law which does not acknowledge the citizenship of women, and the administration of justice when it bears unfairly on women."[110] The emphasis of many nonviolent militants from 1912 and beyond was on the spiritual aspects of militancy rather than their physical manifestations, a shift most notable in the formation of the Spiritual Militancy League, under the leadership of WFL member Mrs. Stanton Coit, at the Ethical Church, Bayswater.[111] Nonviolent militants' refusal to engage in violent militancy led Christabel Pankhurst to critique them publicly and to reject the utility of passive resistance. The moral distinction between active and passive resistance was subtle, she wrote, but "of the two passive resistance approximates more closely to submission. If that be the distinction, then clearly active resistance is grander and more purifying."[112]

Such examples notwithstanding, violent and nonviolent suffragettes came together on issues important to them in the years 1911 to 1914. No better example of cooperation among militants exists than that of the free speech protests of 1913, organized to protest the government's clampdown on the *Suffragette* and outspoken WSPU activists. As WSPU militancy escalated in early April 1913 to include arson, cutting of telegraph lines, and firing of postal boxes, all suffragists began to encounter more aggressive audiences at public meetings. On Sunday, 6 April 1913, suffragists at several London parks, including Hyde Park, Hampstead Heath, and Wimbledon Common, were attacked by hostile crowds.[113] Five men were arrested at Wimbledon Common that afternoon, one for assaulting the suffragettes, the other four for protesting his arrest.[114] At their appearance at Wimbledon Police Court the next day, the chairman of the Wimbledon magistrates used the men's trial as an opportunity to criticize suffragettes for holding meetings that held the potential for violence. The Wimbledon magistrates then appealed to the chief commissioner of police to ban suffrage meetings in parks in the name of public order.[115] Suffragettes were met with similar hostility when they attempted to hold meetings the following Sunday, 13 April, at Hyde Park, Hampstead Heath, and Wimbledon Common.[116] The next day, Police Commissioner Sir Edward Henry informed the WSPU that no meetings could be held in public places because police could not stop ensuing disorder. The prohibition was extended to include the WFL.[117]

Suffragettes responded by holding public meetings in defiance of the ban and to protest suppression of the *Suffragette*. One such meeting, held in Trafalgar Square on 23 April, drew crowds estimated at between two and three thousand. Three members of the WFL were arrested, not for holding an illegal meeting but for obstruction of the police.[118] Protests culminated in a huge demonstration held by the Free Speech Defence Committee in Trafalgar Square on 4 May 1913. Newspaper reports of the demonstration sought to distance women suffragists from the mass of the crowd, estimated at twenty to thirty thousand, which they characterized as "members of trade unions with somewhat revolutionary views."[119] But the participation of numerous suffrage organizations and the personal reminiscences of prominent suffragettes suggest that the demonstration was an important focal point of nonviolent militant protest that spring.[120] Militants were urged to organize around the issue, and suffragette rhetoric was mobilized on behalf of this right.[121] The WFL and nonviolent militants associated with *Votes for Women* held a large public meeting two weeks later, welcoming those women imprisoned on behalf of their free speech agitation. The language speakers used drew upon radical argumentation. An article in the *Vote* described the protest as accomplishing the following: "The strong note of Freedom was struck, a determined fight for liberty, and the recognition of women as part of 'the people.'"[122] Militants thus maintained the model of citizenship as resistance against government operating without consent, rechanneling resistance to instances when the state overstepped its bounds. The protests brought suffragettes together across organizational lines as they used government suppression of their meetings to highlight the state's use of force against women. The free speech protests of 1913 would prove an important model for militancy during the First World War.

During the years from 1910 to 1914, new patterns of resistance to the law emerged, and earlier patterns of militancy were consolidated. While the WSPU has received much attention for its violent methods—mass window breaking, arson, and painting-slashing—and its incendiary, millenarian, and, at times, violently antimale rhetoric, by and large, WSPU militancy was counterproductive after 1912, alienating the public and even women's suffrage supporters in Parliament.[123] But militancy remained a vital force, motivating large numbers of suffragettes to continue to resist the state. Militants fell roughly into two groups in the years between 1910 and 1914. Members of the WPSU, whose development of millenarian and militaristic language came to describe its resistance, created a model of citizenship for women based more on Augustinian notions of "the city of God" than on any of the earlier models invoked by suffragists. This model grew out of suffragettes' analysis of the split between the letter and the spirit of the law and posited a dichotomy between heavenly and earthly kingdoms. Implicitly, the organization began to focus more on the heavenly kingdom than on the earthly one, holding out fulfillment in the act of defiance rather than in the attainment of any specific political goal. Quite in contrast, other militants rejected the use of violence and focused instead upon militancy's effect and their own ultimate goal, the political emancipation of women. Their protests incorporated elements from the earlier militant campaign and negotiated the complexities of claiming a militant identity while pursuing nonviolent policies. All these organizations, from the WFL to the women affiliated with Emmeline and Frederick Pethick Lawrence and their paper, *Votes for Women,* to the ELFS, to the WSPU under the leadership of Christabel and Emmeline Pankhurst, formed a continuum along which suffragettes debated the merits and limits of resistance. These multiple strands of militancy contributed to its overall vitality.

Chapter 7

At War with and for the State, 1914–1918

Britain's declaration of war with Germany in August 1914 spurred reevaluation among suffragettes of the relationship between resistance and citizenship. During four years of war, the British state defined opposition to the war broadly, so that those who voiced opposition to measures deemed necessary for the war effort were imprisoned, fined, and/or subject to community discipline.[1] Suffragettes and suffragists alike returned to a model of citizenship in which service to the nation was the highest value. Ironically, Britain's prosecution of war in South Africa at the turn of the century had galvanized a model of citizenship from which resistance had emerged as an important component, whereas the First World War marked a return to a more traditional notion of citizenship for women, one emphasizing service. This may have had to do with the scale of the Great War, which encompassed civilians in a manner wholly unlike the earlier conflict, which had been an imperial war fought at great distance from the metropole. During the Great War, the government took measures to ensure that all members of the body politic participated on the side of the nation, with tremendous consequences for the practice of citizenship, both during and after the conflict.

The First World War's most important consequence for suffragettes was its realignment of the value placed upon resistance as an active component of citizenship. To a large extent, all militants embraced the service model of citizenship while the nation was at war. At one extreme was the WSPU, which embraced an understanding of service to the nation that could only be characterized as militaristic. Some militants were active in the peace movement, seeking speedy resolution to the conflict. Others, less willing to oppose the war outright, took refuge in a modified service model of citizenship, one that redirected their service away from the nation's war effort and support for combatants to those noncombatants neglected at home, poor women and children. Yet the principle animating prewar militancy, that of resistance, remained an important feature of certain militants' conception of citizenship during the war. Resistance simply took other forms, including opposition to erosion of women's civil liberties.

Campaigning for women's suffrage became a form of resistance once the nation deemed it selfish for women to struggle for political rights during the war. In August 1914, the *Times* reported that several women's organizations, including the Primrose League, the National Liberal Federation, the Conservative and Unionist Women's Franchise Association, the Church League for Women's Suffrage, and the National League for Opposing Women's Suffrage, were to abandon "all outside propaganda work" during the war. The article's title, "Patriotism Before Politics," demonstrated the nation's new priorities.[2] Some suffragists concurred with this assessment, at least initially. The NUWSS under Millicent Garrett Fawcett temporarily "suspended ordinary political work" for the duration of the war.[3] Emmeline Pankhurst declared a suspension not only of WSPU militancy but also of suffrage propaganda during the war.[4] Numerous other suffragists, however, insisted that women had a responsibility to each other, and to the nation, to continue their agitation on behalf of women's political rights. WFL member Nina Boyle urged that the "truest patriotism" would be for "all Suffragists to stand to their guns and man their own forts and not to let themselves be drawn out of their Movement for any purpose whatsoever."[5] The Manchester Men's League for Women's Suffrage spoke for many when it urged "that the worst horrors of war fall upon the women. Help to make this war the last, and to repair its ravages the sooner, by securing for women an effective voice in human affairs through the parliamentary vote."[6] Those women who continued to work for their parliamentary enfranchisement struggled throughout the war against the discourse of patriotism that defined suffrage work as being against the national interest.

But work for suffrage they did, sharing resources and working together to continue to press for women's claim. WSPU members critical of the Pankhursts for abandoning women's suffrage during the war formed new organizations, including the Suffragettes of the WSPU (SWSPU) in October 1915 and the Independent WSPU (IWSPU) in March 1916.[7] The United Suffragists, formed in February 1914, assumed ownership of the paper *Votes for Women* during the war and used it to promote its work for suffrage and other feminist causes.[8] The WFL, SWSPU, IWSPU, and US joined forces on numerous issues during the war. The SWSPU published its newspaper, the *Suffragette News Sheet*, from the WFL offices.[9] WFL branches continued to hold large public, as well as members-only, suffrage meetings.[10] While these meetings rarely received press coverage in the mainstream press, open-air suffrage meetings in London parks, as well as summer and special campaigns, continued throughout the war.[11] Members were encouraged to continue their propaganda on an individual level. The *Vote* urged WFL members in 1916 to "never go out without [a badge]! A badge often gives you an opening for conversation."[12] Also active during the war was the Free Church League for Women's Suffrage, founded in 1910 to promote women's suffrage among male and female adherents of Free Church principles. The organization continued publication of its *Free Church Suffrage Times,* later, the *Coming Day,* during the war.[13] The Catholic Women's Suffrage Society continued its suffrage propaganda work, later becoming St. Joan's Social and Political Alliance.[14] The ELFS similarly continued to hold meetings for women's suffrage and to lobby members of parliament.[15]

Militants faced numerous obstacles in continuing to press their claim. They competed with myriad other demands placed upon suffragists while the nation was at war.[16] They also faced new restrictions on distribution of suffrage materials in public places. In 1917, the WFL challenged a ruling of the London County Council forbidding the sale of literature in parks and open spaces around London. Two members of the WFL sold the *Vote* in Brockwell Park several Sundays in August 1917 in flagrant defiance of the council's regulation. One member was arrested and charged but was released until the validity of the council's ruling could be determined. The case was dismissed by the Central Police Court in October of that year.[17]

Fissures developed during the war in militants' unity on the question of women's suffrage. The US, WFL, IWSPU, and SWSPU maintained support for a parliamentary measure that would grant women suffrage "on the same terms as is or will be granted to men."[18] The WFL discussed adult suffrage in the pages of the *Vote* but remained officially committed to its prewar policy.[19] Members of the WFL also refused to accept the contention that women should be given the vote as a consequence of their war service, urging that they stood "for representation as the right of the people."[20] The ELFS, transformed into the Workers' Suffrage Federation in 1916 (and the Workers' Socialist Federation in 1918), adopted adult suffrage in March 1916 and severed all connections with women's suffrage organizations thereafter.[21]

At the outbreak of war in August 1914, suffragettes articulated strikingly similar analyses of the war's origins. Violent and nonviolent militants alike blamed the war on the masculinization of politics. WFL member Louise Lind-af-Hageby observed in the *Vote* that "men had built up a system of government which was in effect an armed peace, and which was so undermined that it fell to pieces at the first blow."[22] The war was, in the words of Kathleen Tanner, a London member of the WFL, "a war against the ethics women held"; Britain fought "an evil spirit which had taken possession of Germany, the spirit of lust and domination."[23] Militants were quick to note that women were not to blame for the outbreak of war because they lacked the political means to contribute meaningfully to the decision to pursue it. WSPU member Helen Fraser connected women's exclusion from politics to "the forces we women fight in the enemy."[24] ELFS leader Sylvia Pankhurst lamented that "our foreparents suffered generations of persecution to win for the men of our country the forms of democratic Government, but these are discarded and our people are plunged into war with as little choice or foreknowledge as is allowed to those who live under the most absolute of the old despotisms."[25] Christabel Pankhurst went further, casting the war as "God's vengeance upon the people who held women in subjection."[26] Many saw the war as providing fresh opportunities for women to reshape politics after the conflict had ended. Charlotte Despard and Annie A. Smith, editors of the *Vote* during the war, asserted that women would do what was necessary to ensure the survival of their nation, but they were "determined that no man-made laws shall in future prevent their participation in the rights, as well as the responsibilities of citizenship."[27]

Suffragette opposition to the war resurfaced at various times during the conflict. Some militants played an active role in the developing peace movement, seeking speedy resolution to the conflict. Emmeline Pethick Lawrence and others associated with the group around *Votes for Women,* as well as a number of former NUWSS and active WFL members, formed the Women's International League of Great Britain and held a Women's Peace Congress at the Hague in 1915.[28] Charlotte Despard participated increasingly in the antiwar movement, alienating her from the leadership of the WFL.[29] Members of the East London Federation of Suffragettes (later the Workers' Suffrage Federation) held antiwar meetings at London's East India Dock Gates, followed by processions to Victoria Park.[30] With the exception of the ELFS, however, suffragettes focused less on opposing the war than on finding ways to mitigate its effects on women and children.[31] The vast majority of suffragettes spent the war negotiating with the state regarding its demands on women during the conflict.

Historians have long been fascinated with the apparently seamless transition the WSPU made in August 1914 from war with the British government to war against the Germans. They have explained this phenomenon in a number of ways.[32] Jacqueline de Vries has advanced the most compelling explanation of the Pankhursts' seeming about-face from opposition to support for the government in August 1914. She argues that "nationalist patriotism, like militant suffragism, became a kind of religion for Christabel and her followers."[33] The religion of nationalism inflected the rhetoric of other suffragettes as well, most notably that of Nina Boyle, member of the National Executive Committee of the WFL, whose nationalist pronouncements, like her 1915 assertion that "nationality is the strongest feeling human nature knows next to the primeval instinct of sex," alienated her from other WFL members and eventually led to her resignation from the organization in 1918.[34]

Certainly, war gave the WSPU an elegant solution to what was becoming an intractable situation. Government prosecutions in 1913 and 1914 had driven the organization underground and diminished its numbers, but Emmeline and Christabel Pankhurst could not scale back violent militancy without losing face.[35] The outbreak of war presented an opportunity for the organization to turn its energies from assaulting the government to attacking the nation's enemies. In mid-August 1914, Emmeline Pankhurst explained to remaining members of the WSPU that the violence of the war would so supersede that of militancy as to render the latter ineffective; further, if work for the vote had proved futile while the nation was at peace, how much more so during the war. Pankhurst urged those women willing to go to prison for women's rights to redirect that energy toward the war effort.[36] Her rationale provides further explanation for the seeming shift in the organization's emphasis. Suffragettes' resistance to constituted authority had been construed as an obligation of citizenship; once the nation was at war, citizenship's obligation became service. WSPU member M. E. Mansell explained the organization's change of direction as a turn "from the contest against Anti-Suffragism at home to unreservedly take their part by their country's side against the wider Anti-Suffragism threatening the life of nations with the extinction of the great principles of freedom under the iron heel of an imposed Kulturdominion."[37]

Other militants refused to subsume their political demands in the nation's prosecution of war, but they understood the difficulties of pursuing women's political rights during the war. Nonviolent militants fought against what historians Margaret and Patrice Higonnet have called the "organic discourse of wartime patriotism" that discouraged women from pursuing their own rights or needs.[38] Nonviolent militants found themselves in a double bind, for they were limited by their sex in the contributions they could make to the war effort being waged to protect their sex. The range of activities nonviolent militants pursued during the First World War instead offered an indirect challenge to the primacy of war. Their acts contained an implicit criticism of Britain's participation in the war, for these organizations insisted, against the militarist discourse of the state, that women's value to the state should transcend the meanings imposed on that value by the war. These remaining active militants fought against the notion that war was the most important activity in which a society could engage, through continued agitation for women's suffrage, work on behalf of mothers and children, and resistance to government curtailments of women's civil liberties. Charlotte Despard eloquently laid out nonviolent militancy's agenda in the first week of the war as a continuing struggle against the fallacy that the state rested upon physical force. Suffragists' responsibility, she urged, was to attempt to stop the war. If that effort failed, then they must "by every means in our power, while helping so far as we can the innocent sufferers in all such times—the women and children—keep our own flag flying, and emphasise our demand to have a vote in decisions as to momentous events on which hang the destinies of the nation."[39]

Nevertheless, to differing extents all militants embraced the service model of citizenship while the nation was at war. Under the leadership of Christabel and Emmeline Pankhurst, the WSPU embraced a chauvinistic understanding of service to the nation. Both Emmeline and Christabel Pankhurst explicitly rejected service to the nation traditionally deemed "feminine." "'I'm not nursing soldiers,'" Emmeline Pankhurst informed Edith Shackleton of the *Daily Sketch*. "'We have always worked in a national way, and now we feel that our duty is still on national lines, so we are doing everything we can to help recruiting, and make it possible for more and more men to go to fight.'" Pankhurst went on to say that WSPU official Annie Kenney had likened asking WSPU members to knit and nurse to asking cabinet ministers to make army boots and uniforms.[40]

Services the Pankhursts deemed "national" began with active support for military recruitment in the United States and Britain. Christabel Pankhurst undertook a lecture series in the United States in early 1915 in an attempt to enlist American support, but she encountered skepticism from American suffragists about the prospect of U.S. involvement in the war.[41] Emmeline Pankhurst and Flora Drummond spoke at meetings held at theaters and cinemas across England in conjunction with the War Office recruiting campaign.[42] In June and July 1915, with the support of the palace and the government, the WSPU turned its attention to the government's proposal that all men and women must add their names to a national register for military and industrial service.[43] The WSPU sponsored a series of public "At Homes," where they demanded "universal, obligatory war service" for men and women.[44] These meetings culminated in a WSPU presentation of women's demand to work for the nation at the Great Procession of Women. Thirty thousand women in red, white, and blue followed Emmeline Pankhurst in a procession from the Embankment to Whitehall on 17 July 1915, seeking to convince the government and employers to use women's labor in munitions making and other trades associated with the war.[45] The WSPU also actively supported enlisted men, sponsoring a procession in July 1916 to thank soldiers and sailors for their service to the nation.[46]

Emmeline and Christabel Pankhurst strove to ensure that others adhered to their definition of service to the nation. Both women were active in anti-pacifist, anti-German, and anti-Bolshevist propaganda from late 1914 through the end of the war.[47] In private correspondence, on public platforms, and in the pages of the *Suffragette,* later *Britannia,* they repeatedly criticized the Union of Democratic Control, which united Labour and Liberal intellectuals and politicians in seeking an end to the conflict and proposing arbitration between the warring parties.[48] The Pankhursts also worked unofficially for the government at times. In private correspondence with David Lloyd George at the Ministry of Munitions in 1915, Emmeline Pankhurst denounced conscientious objectors in South Wales.[49] Burton Chadwick, at the Ministry of Munitions, assisted Christabel Pankhurst and the WSPU in April 1917 with antipacifist organizing in Liverpool.[50] With government funding, Emmeline Pankhurst and Jessie Kenney organized "a national campaign to combat 'Bolshevism' and explain the urgency of greater production of munitions." The women had access to the prime minister's secretaries at 10 Downing Street, as well as two official organizers.[51] Kenney and Pankhurst traveled to Russia in June 1917 as part of a British contingent hoping to persuade the Russians to remain in the war.[52]

Service also entailed putting women's political demands aside for those of sailors and soldiers. Emmeline and Christabel Pankhurst derided those organizations claiming to "keep the suffrage flag flying." Christabel urged that "there is one flag supremely dear to the true Suffragist and that is the flag of liberty."[53] By 1916, Emmeline was arguing that the government should not jeopardize the enfranchisement of soldiers and sailors by inclusion of women in the proposed reform bill.[54] When it became apparent that women would be enfranchised, Christabel and Emmeline Pankhurst and Flora Drummond formed the National Women's Party in November 1917 so that women "who love their country" could better meet the responsibilities of the parliamentary vote. The group declared that "Victory, National Security, and Social Reform are the watchwords of the Women's Party" and touted their work in "mining, munition-making and other centres of war industry [as having] the object of allaying industrial unrest and counteracting pacifist and pro-German intrigue" (see figure 7.1).[55]

WSPU contributions to the war effort were controversial for two reasons. Many suffragettes deplored the Pankhursts' abandonment of prewar suffrage

FIGURE 7.1
In Manchester, Women's Party members Flora Drummond and Phyllis Ayrton introduce Prime Minister David Lloyd George to a group of munitions workers, September 1918. Mary Evans Picture Library.

principles, and many outside suffrage circles objected to the WSPU's chau-vinism. In the course of questioning the government regarding its suppres-sion of the WSPU's newspaper, *Britannia,* Mr. Handel Booth, M.P., expressed appreciation of the WSPU's support for the nation on the floor of the House of Commons, 15 March 1916.[56] By no means, however, was the WSPU's under-standing of service one embraced fully by the government. A series of gov-ernment raids on *Britannia*'s offices took place between November 1916 and January 1917 after the WSPU criticized what it called the "pro-Germanism" of the Foreign Office. Specifically, Emmeline Pankhurst argued that Foreign Office compromises with the German government were dangerous to British national security. She also hinted that some officials in the Foreign Office were not to be trusted because a number were "half German, or [were] mar-ried to Germans."[57] And Christabel undertook a series of attacks on the gov-ernment's alleged affinities for Germany, darkly warning in an April 1915 ed-itorial in the *Suffragette* that "we will not be Prussianized" (see figure 7.2).

Other militants took refuge in a modified service model of citizenship that redirected their service away from the nation's war effort and support for combatants to those noncombatants neglected at home, poor women and children. Women suffragists collected clothing and food for Belgian refugees in Britain and for the working poor, created jobs for men and women thrown out of work by the war, and sought housing for those dislocated at the war's outset.[58] Historian Jo Vellacott Newberry has characterized the early relief ef-forts of the NUWSS as "war work in only a limited sense," pointing to equal participation of pacifist and nonpacifist members of the NUWSS in efforts to alleviate distress among noncombatants.[59] As historian Sandra Stanley Holton has demonstrated of the NUWSS, "relief work, with all its ambigui-ties, seemed to offer a solution to [the] quandary" posed by the war.[60] A sim-ilar case can be made for the early endeavors of the WFL, ELFS, and United Suffragists. Indeed, for nonviolent militants in late 1914 and early 1915, re-lief work became one way organizations could both widen the scope of their activities to include a measure of work for the nation and simultaneously avoid direct involvement in work underwriting the war. Relief work blurred the distinction between suffrage campaigning and war work so that criticism could not be leveled at the organizations from either without or within.

But relief work represented more than mere acquiescence to a service model of women's citizenship. Implicit in their work for noncombatants was a criticism of the war itself. In word and in deed, nonviolent militants refused to accept that war was the most important activity engaged in by a society, and they resisted the attempt to trivialize feminists' concerns relative to war. While resolving not to be drawn from its main purpose into work that dis-sipated its members' energies, the Middlesbrough Branch of the WFL de-plored the glorification of sons as fighting material.[61] WFL member Mar-garet Hodge criticized British society for allowing war to create "an exciting panorama, which obscures and even actually hides all that is of really vital importance and permanent interest to the human race."[62] Nonviolent mili-

FIGURE 7.2
A suffragette sells a copy of the *Suffragette* newspaper to soldiers, April 1915. Museum of London.

tants articulated their organizational goals in strikingly similar terms. The ELFS, US, WFL, and the Catholic Women's Suffrage Society shared similar approaches to women's service during the war, and all agreed to cease active militancy, keep the suffrage flag flying, and "watch women's interests closely."[63]

Upon the outbreak of war in August 1914, the WFL and ELFS created the first of many relief endeavors aimed at improving the lives of soldiers' dependents. The WFL instituted the Women's Suffrage National Aid Corps (WSNAC); the ELFS transformed a pub, the Gunmakers' Arms, into a clinic and crèche called the Mothers' Arms and created a toy factory in the East End. Between August and December 1914, the WSNAC undertook a variety of projects, among them providing meals for mothers and children; opening workrooms for women thrown out of work by the war; establishing training registries for women workers; distributing shiploads of clothing donated by the colonies, in conjunction with the British Dominions Woman Suffrage Union; and making clothing for children of the very poor.[64] The WSNAC created workrooms on trade union lines, supervised clubs for working people, and operated a convalescent hospital for women and children not admitted to hospitals due to a wartime lack of beds.[65] The WSNAC, however, had ceased operation by 1916, to be replaced by the WFL's Nine Elms Settlement House.[66]

Located in Battersea, an area of Southwest London that was home to gas-workers, hawkers, and transport and rail workers, the settlement eventually included a guest house, which provided accommodation for children whose mothers were recuperating from illness or childbirth. Also associated with the settlement were a milk depot, distributing milk at low cost to mothers and children; a vegetarian restaurant, serving penny and halfpenny meals to children once a day; and a clinic, offering services to children and babies of the community.[67] By the end of 1917, the settlement could feed up to two hundred children per day, and the milk depot had expanded its clientele to seventy-seven women (see figure 7.3).[68] The East London Federation of Suffragettes undertook similar work in London's East End. Members served on local distress committees and created milk centers, cost price restaurants, and crèches at the Mothers' Arms.[69] The organization agitated to keep food and rent prices at prewar levels and attempted to find employment for men and women thrown out of work by the transition to war.[70] The WSNAC and ELFS occasionally worked together.[71]

FIGURE 7.3
Mrs. Despard's clinic and children's center,
at 2, Currie Street, Battersea, during the war.
Museum of London.

Yet the principle that animated prewar militancy, that of resistance, remained an important feature of many militants' understanding of citizenship during the war. Suffragettes were careful to separate their relief work from their work as militants. Some were critical of those who attempted to combine the two. Lena Ashwell, founder of the Women's Emergency Corps (WEC), an organization of suffragists dedicated to assisting the nation at war, acknowledged this tension in a letter to former WSPU organizer Ada Flatman in October 1914 when she noted that one of the WEC's workers had "not been very wise having been selling *Votes for Women* with a W.E.C. badge on her arm!"[72] Suffragettes refused to set aside their demands for the right to engage fully as citizens, especially while they were providing vital services to the nation at war. Resistance took familiar forms, such as tax resistance and opposition to erosion of women's civil rights; it also manifested itself in the continued struggle for women's suffrage.

Suffragettes professed ambivalence about tax resistance after August 1914. The WTRL suspended activities during the war, while other suffrage organizations left it to individuals to decide if they would persist in that strategy.[73] Many members of the WFL and US chose to continue their tax resistance during the war as a form of opposition to the government that continued to deny women the right of citizenship.[74] The WFL actively supported its members who resisted payment of taxes, such as Dr. Winifred Patch, as well as nonmembers, like Evelyn Sharp of the United Suffragists.[75] One WFL member explained her continued tax resistance in terms of the necessity of vigilance: "Though we may cheerfully waive our individual rights as citizens, and bow to exigencies of martial law when called upon to do so, yet it is of extreme importance that we should not lose sight of the great constitutional principles on which our liberties are based."[76]

Much more prominent than tax resistance, however, were campaigns suffragettes mounted against the state's encroachment on citizen rights. These campaigns took a number of forms, some emphasizing themes familiar within the women's movement, others occasioned by issues arising during the war. Suffragettes organized campaigns against legislation (proposed and passed) that would limit women's movements or activities. The government devoted much attention to issues around sexuality and alcohol; some of the first battles militants fought were on those grounds. Later struggles focused on freedom of speech and anticonscription.

Government attempts to regulate women's sexuality took a number of forms during the war, and the government and military did not always agree on strategies toward that end.[77] Suffragettes mounted three campaigns in the area of sexuality during the war. They strenuously resisted military attempts to reintroduce the Contagious Diseases Acts in 1914 and 1917, and they vigorously protested legislative efforts to pass the Criminal Law Amendment Bill in 1917 and to implement Regulation 40D of the Defence of the Realm Act (DORA) in 1918. Each of these attempts to suspend civil liberties in the name of protecting the troops from exposure to prostitution was met with opposition from suffragettes. The WFL played a prominent role in organizing these campaigns, although members of many other militant organizations actively opposed the measures as well.

Attempts to reintroduce elements of the Contagious Diseases Acts brought militants together in early October 1914 when Miss Hare of Brighton, active in the Women's Police Volunteers, a WFL initiative to create a female constabulary, called suffragettes' attention to the recommendations of the Plymouth Watch Committee to its town council that the acts be reestablished in that town. Members of the WFL, ELFS, Catholic Women's Suffrage Society, British Dominions Woman Suffrage Union (after 1916 the British Dominions Woman Citizens' Union) together opposed reinstitution of the acts, sending telegrams to the Plymouth Town Council opposing the action.[78] Members of several suffrage organizations requested permission to lay the matter in writing before the prime minister.[79] Speaking on behalf of the government, Maurice Bonham Carter informed the women that the Plymouth Town Council had deferred the Watch Committee's recommendations for further consideration, as no local body could reinstate the Contagious Diseases Acts without an act of Parliament. The WFL pointed out that, since local authorities had the power to impose other kinds of restrictions on women, such as closing public houses and placing towns under military law, a reinstatement of the Contagious Diseases Acts could certainly be passed under these guises. Despite Asquith's protestations that the special acts of Parliament passed for the duration of the war could not reintroduce the Contagious Diseases Acts, by December 1914, the acts were reestablished in a new form.[80] A commanding officer in Cardiff, on the strength of existing provisions of DORA, had passed a decree that "'women of a certain class'" should not be allowed outdoors between 7:00 P.M. and 8:00 A.M.; the police would determine who was a member of "the class in question." Suffragettes protested the action, but the decree remained in place.[81] Subsequent deputations of the ELFS, Northern Men's Federation for Women's Suffrage, US, and WFL to the War Office had little effect.[82]

In November 1916, the WFL convened an emergency conference of women's organizations to discuss the pending Criminal Law Amendment Bill (CLAB) and its recommendations for the compulsory notification of venereal diseases. Suffragettes opposed compulsory examinations of anyone for venereal diseases, the proposed punishment of keepers of "disorderly houses," and measures enabling magistrates to incarcerate girls up to the age of nineteen.[83] The conference sent a manifesto to the press laying out its objections.[84] The WFL, League of Justice, Free Church League for Women's Suffrage, SWSPU, Women's International League, British Dominions Woman Suffrage Union, Actresses' Franchise League, Hastings and St. Leonard's Women's Suffrage Propaganda League, Irishwomen's Suffrage Federation, Hendon Women's Franchise Society, and the IWSPU all organized deputations to the home secretary and Local Government Board in November and December 1916.[85] The Home Office introduced the CLAB in February

1917, and suffragettes campaigned against it throughout the spring. Herbert Samuel, home secretary, received a deputation against the bill in March 1917, and a mass public meeting of those opposed to the bill was held in London that month. A wide range of organizations participated, from the Actresses' Franchise League to the Association of Women Pharmacists, the Scottish Women's Liberal Federation, and the Women's International League.[86] Soon after, provisions of the bill seen to be implementing the Contagious Diseases Acts by other means were withdrawn.[87]

In March 1918, suffragettes protested provisions of Regulation 40D of DORA. The first regulations under DORA had been initiated by the government in 1914 as a means of protecting the nation during the war, and much of this legislation entailed the temporary suspension of individual civil liberties. Regulation 40D provided explicitly for the incarceration and examination of any woman suffering from venereal disease who had sexual intercourse with a member of His Majesty's forces. A number of organizations, including the WFL, Women's International League, IWSPU, and Association for Moral and Social Hygiene, worked together to oppose this policy.[88] Beginning in March 1918, the WFL led opposition to the French *maisons tolérées*, licensed brothels providing "disease-free" prostitutes for use by French and British troops in France. The WFL met with members of Parliament and representatives of a range of women's organizations at the House of Commons to protest the government's actions. Represented were the WFL, NUWSS, Association for Moral and Social Hygiene, Women's Cooperative Guild (WCG), Women's Local Government Society, and the National British Women's Temperance Association.[89] Further large public meetings were held in London against the legislation in July and September 1918.[90]

Suffragettes also fought government attempts to regulate the sale of alcohol to women. No longer subject to the authority of the single male in the home, women became increasingly vulnerable to government efforts to become a substitute authority figure.[91] Public discussion of women's drinking had begun immediately upon the declaration of war and would continue throughout its duration. A 1914 editorial in the *Times* argued that efforts should be made to control the drinking of women on separation allowances, who, it was claimed, suddenly had much more money to spend because they no longer had men or responsibilities at home. This editorial was published amid early attempts to restrict women's access to public houses in October 1914.[92]

In October 1914, the WFL formed a deputation to the mayor of Plymouth with representatives of the WCG and the Free Church League for Women's Suffrage when it learned that the Plymouth Watch Committee would bar women from public houses between 6:00 P.M. and 9:00 A.M. WFL member Nina Boyle informed General Penton, commanding officer for Plymouth, that the decree banning women from public houses "seemed to be perilously near the mark of special legislation penalising women."[93] Rhetorically the WFL maintained this position during the war, but it had more success in the formation of the "alternative" public house. WFL member Emily Juson Kerr opened the first Tipperary Room, an "alternative public house" for women at the Baths, Black's-road, Hammersmith, London, on October 28, 1914.[94] Nonalcoholic refreshments were provided at cost, and a nursery for mothers was maintained on the premises.[95] The Tipperary Rooms were advertised as offering "the women, whose husbands, fathers and brothers are defending their country, a place where they will find a brightness, companionship, recreation, war news and refreshments, free from the temptations of the public house."[96] The Tipperary Rooms never fell under the WFL's direct control, but the two continued to work together during the war.[97] The WFL also undertook its own form of the alternative public house. In March 1915, at Charlotte Despard's urging that the public house be reorganized "on sane, clean and wholesome lines," the North London Branches of the WFL opened the "Despard Arms" in a room rented from the Esperance Club.[98]

But the efforts of the Tipperary League and other organizations like them proved insufficient to quell fears of women's drinking. In November 1914, the commissioner of police, Alderman Edward Johnson, the London chair of the Board of Licensed Victuallers' Central Protection Society, and Frank P. Whitbread of the London Brewers' Council agreed that all establishments licensed in the Metropolitan Police District would not serve alcohol to women on or off the premises before 11:30 A.M.[99] Speaking on behalf of the WSPU, Flora Drummond praised the move and urged that men's sacrifice as combatants required women to make the minimal effort of giving up alcohol during the war.[100] Other suffragettes, however, protested the "insult" done to women by the proposed legislation.[101]

Other campaigns mounted by suffragettes between 1914 and 1918 excoriated the government for not appreciating fully the contributions women made to the war effort and challenged the government's right to force citizens to undertake particular forms of service to the nation, especially when not adequately compensated. As soon as the first male volunteers enlisted, suffragettes began to critique government handling of financial compensation of soldiers' and sailors' dependents. Florence Underwood, general secretary of the WFL, lamented the government's unwillingness to provide for combatants' dependents and criticized the bureaucratic hoops through which soldiers' and sailors' wives were forced to jump to secure the miserly allowances the government provided.[102] Suffragettes also criticized local governments' attempts to regulate the behavior of soldiers' wives. At a demonstration in Trafalgar Square on 24 January 1915, the WFL, ELFS, Northern Men's Federation for Women's Suffrage, and US, passed a resolution protesting "illegal restrictions and penalties for women," as well as a resolution against all legislation by which "soldiers' wives are insulted, restrictions are enforced against women only, and vice is regulated in a way that protects men only." A similar meeting was held in Edinburgh.[103] The protest in London was followed the next day by a deputation of women's organizations to the War Office. Charlotte Despard introduced the group, which was composed of representatives of the WFL, ELFS, US, and the Soldiers' Wives, Preston. The deputation demanded that the War Office withdraw the Army Council Circular regarding cessation of payments to the unworthy and that commanding officers not impose arbitrary restrictions on women's alcohol consumption. B. B. Cubitt, assistant secretary, received the deputation, promising to make inquiries regarding implementation of the order.[104]

Suffragettes not only were critical of government treatment of combatants' dependents but also refused to assist the government in recruiting for military and industrial service. At the outset of the war, WFL member Margaret Wynne Nevinson declined invitations to address recruiting meetings in Trafalgar Square on the grounds that she could not encourage others to do what she was protected by her age and sex from doing herself.[105] The WFL explicitly asked noncombatants to refrain from encouraging men to enlist. Noting that suffragettes had resented men's attempts to instruct them as to their duties to the nation, an editorial in the *Vote* urged that suffragettes should refrain from urging upon men "a course of action for which they feel no sense of vocation."[106] The Sheffield Branch of the WFL refused to assist its local Labour Exchange in securing girls for filling shells in Lancashire.[107] Members of the ELFS held regular meetings against conscription in 1915 and 1916, and one member was arrested, convicted, and sentenced to six months' imprisonment in March 1916 for "'making statements likely to prejudice recruiting.'"[108]

Early in 1915, the Board of Trade appealed for women to register at Labour Exchanges for war service in industry, agriculture, and munitions manufacture. The government followed this appeal with the threat of compulsory registration for women. Nonviolent militants contended that women should not have to take work under any conditions the government might see fit to create while serving the nation at war. Instead, they insisted that women's war work should be treated as if it were to continue after the war: that women receive equal pay for equal work; that they be considered after the war for jobs they held during the war; and that they be given proper pay during training.[109] The WFL, ELFS, US, and Irish Women's Franchise League issued manifestos demanding the vote and equal pay for equal work as conditions for women's compulsory war service. The WFL's manifesto attempted to separate "nation" and "government," asserting support for Britain as a country, but not for the current government, which had violated women's citizenship.[110] In March 1915 a number of militants joined the Workers' War Emergency Committee in a national conference of women's organizations to discuss the mobilization of women during the war. Before that conference could meet, however, Lloyd George reached agreement with the men's unions at the Treasury, and Walter Runciman had called a meeting of women's organizations at the Board of Trade. At the meeting, held at the Treasury from March 17 to 19, Arthur Henderson and other trade union leaders agreed to the government's terms for labor during the war: unions involved in work essential to the war effort would surrender the right to strike;

disputes would be arbitrated; and "present trade practices" would be relaxed. All these provisions were understood by both sides to be for the duration of the war only.[111] At Runciman's meeting with women's organizations at the Board of Trade on 13 April 1915, the government announced that those women on its Special Register would be pressed into service only if the lists provided by local Labour Exchanges proved insufficient to meet its needs. It was also proposed that local women arrange for housing women workers where necessary; that men's jobs be held open for men after the war; and that women be paid the same rate as men for government jobs involving piecework. No special conditions were laid down by the government regarding timework. Represented at the conference were a number of organizations, including numerous suffrage groups, Mothers' Unions, and the Women's Trades Union League.[112]

The WFL attempted to preempt government's military and civilian conscription by creating its own national service organization in June 1915, the WFLNSO. Members hoped to avoid compulsory service and to use women where they were best suited rather than simply wherever the government needed bodies. The WFLNSO was organized to act as a union of sorts for women workers, and as such it aimed at ending disparities in training between the sexes; promoting employment on the basis of skill rather than sex; and emancipating women politically.[113] By January 1916, the organization had fallen apart and all connections between the NSO and the WFL severed amid charges that members of the WFLNSO had attempted to dissociate the organization from the cause of suffrage.[114]

Opposition to its plan notwithstanding, the government went ahead with compulsory registration. National Registration Day, 15 August 1915, required all male and female citizens between the ages of fifteen and sixty-five to register for national service.[115] Suffragettes responded in a variety of ways. While the WSPU actively promoted registration for men and women in military and industrial service, the ELFS protested the Registration Act, staging a demonstration in conjunction with Suffragette Crusaders, US, the Amalgamated Society of Toolmakers, Engineers and Machinists, the British Socialist Party, and the National Union of Gasworkers.[116] At the meeting participants passed resolutions urging that no register be passed without safeguards, that Parliament implement legislation forbidding sweated labor, that women receive equal pay for equal work, and that women be enfranchised immediately.[117] The WFL exhibited more ambivalence over the question. When a referendum taken of WFL branches revealed that no majority existed in support of resistance to national registration, the National Executive Committee determined that individuals could take action on their own behalf, but the WFL would not support their cases officially.[118] Other suffragettes resisted registration. Using language reminiscent of prewar protests, members of the SWSPU urged, "No Vote. No Register."[119]

One wartime organization created with assistance from suffragettes highlighted the many ambiguities of women attempting to claim citizenship during war. The Women's Police Volunteers (WPV), a special constabulary to protect women, was proposed as a means of ending violence against women and the sexual subjection of women by men. Although a number of suffragettes were involved in the formation of the WPV at the beginning of the war, early conflict on the question of women's civil liberties alienated many militants from the organization. In August 1914, the mayor of Finsbury called a meeting to establish a special constabulary.[120] WFL member Nina Boyle took that opportunity to propose that women be allowed to serve on the new force, to offer their particularly feminine skills in aiding women and children. Women police could be useful in providing "for the information of distressed or destitute women (according as they may be wives of soldiers, sailors, Territorials, unemployed, or themselves discharged from work)," as well as information pertaining to hospitals, ambulance-vans, fire stations, and public telephones.[121] This initiative overlapped with another already under way. Margaret Damer Dawson, active on the Criminal Law Amendment Committee and in the National Vigilance Association before the war, had begun organizing women patrols in response to allegations that white slave traders were kidnapping Belgian women refugees from English train stations.[122] To avoid a duplication of efforts, the two organizations amalgamated, with Damer Dawson as chief and Boyle as deputy.[123] Despite opposition to Boyle's participation on the force from the police commissioner, Sir Edward Henry, the WPV trained in London, beginning in October 1914.[124]

On 27 November 1914, three members of the WPV, including Damer Dawson, Mary Allen, a former member of the WSPU, and Ellen Harburn, a member of the WFL, were assigned to work in Grantham, a town about 110 miles north of London in Lincolnshire, where approximately twenty-five thousand troops were temporarily stationed under the command of Damer Dawson's brother-in-law, Staff Captain Kensington. The general officer, Brigadier General Hammersley, had recently imposed a curfew on Grantham's female residents, ordering them to stay indoors between 7:00 P.M. and 6:00 A.M. As commanding officer, Hammersley authorized the police to enter houses in the area if deemed necessary to enforce the order. The WPV were chosen to accompany the police on their raids. In her autobiography, Mary Allen recorded this use of the WPV as a triumph, recounting that "we received the first mark of confidence—the military authorities conferring upon us the right to enter any house, building or land within a six-mile radius of the Army Post Office."[125] Nina Boyle, however, was horrified by the use of the WPV to enforce such a blatant restriction of women's civil liberties, and by February 1915 she was urging Damer Dawson to resign as chief of the corps. Boyle vowed the WPV would "continue its work on the lines originally laid down, i.e., for the service of women, and not to assist the present authorities in carrying out laws and regulations known to be unjust and improper."[126] Pushed to a vote, the corps opted overwhelmingly in favor of remaining under the control of Damer Dawson, who immediately reformed the group under the name of the Women Police Service, effectively ending its association with the WFL. Boyle repeatedly reminded readers of the *Vote* that the WFL broke with the WPV because the organization aided the government in violating women's civil rights.[127] The WPV remained active in Brighton and in parts of London until 1916, continuing its rota of the criminal courts, patrolling public gardens and parks, and establishing a mounted section devoted to the welfare of animals.[128]

The troubled history of the WPV thus provides insight into the arenas of struggle in which suffragettes struggled to keep prewar principles alive during the war. Resisting the state's curtailment of women's civil liberties proved to be as important a site for women's practice of citizenship, if not more so, than suffragettes' work for their political rights during the war, for in the final analysis, women's demands were not instrumental in shaping the legislation on enfranchisement emerging during the war. Far more important to the government was the status of the nation's fighting men, many of whom had remained voteless because their military service precluded fulfillment of the residency requirements of the Reform Act of 1884. By August 1916, the issue of electoral reform had been handed to a special conference chaired by the Speaker of the House of Commons, James W. Lowther. The committee reported in January 1917, recommending a form of female enfranchisement similar to that proposed by W. H. Dickinson's 1913 bill proposing a household franchise, that is, one providing for the enfranchisement of women who held the household qualification in their own right or were married to men who did.[129] Parliamentary enfranchisement thus would be granted to women above the age of thirty who already possessed the local government vote or to those who were married to men who already had the local government vote.[130] Other significant aspects of the bill proposed by the committee were its recommendations to retain only three of the many qualifications of the previous act, those of residence, business occupation, and university representation. It abolished all or parts of some sixty statutes treating franchise and registration, creating in their place a simpler and more uniform system. The proposed bill would add some two million men and about six million women, more than doubling the electorate.[131] Prime Minister Lloyd George accepted a deputation of women's organizations on the proposed bill in March 1917, but by that time women's electoral concerns had become marginal within the overall scheme of franchise reform.[132] The bill that became the Representation of the People Act (1918) thus granted a form of female suffrage that would have been unacceptable to suffragists prior to the war and which was, on the whole, greeted with little enthusiasm by suffragettes. The war had taken its toll.

Conclusion

Fetishizing Militancy, 1918–1930

The 1920s proved to be a key decade in the reformulation of the meaning of citizenship in Britain. In the increasingly retrospective glance of that decade, the act of militancy became separated from its underlying motivation of resistance. Subsequent discussions of the prewar suffrage movement fetishized militancy at the expense of the political rationale underlying individual acts of resistance. The consequence of this was twofold: suffragettes were made out to be irrational political actors, and their emphasis on citizenship as engagement with the state dwindled. This shift in the meaning of citizenship occurred at a time when the meaning of the vote was itself diminished. Women were granted the vote in 1918, at a point when many historians believe that party organization and the manipulation of public opinion had come to matter far more than did individual voters.

The act of militancy, unhinged from its foundation in a constitutional or moral principle of dissent, became central to postwar representations of the movement. Fixation on the act of militancy acted as a fetish in the Freudian sense, "drawing attention away from that which was most troubling to something seemingly more benign."[1] Suffragettes' insistence on the radical notion of resistance to government operating without citizens' consent figures nowhere in postwar accounting of militancy. Some suffragettes themselves understood this aspect of postwar discourse; as one disillusioned WSPU member noted to another in 1961, "All that is left of what was once a vital movement is now nothing more than a coterie worshipping a sort of 'Sacred Cow'—the militant tactics which were far less important than the movement's objectives."[2]

Central to the fetishization of militancy was the process of memorialization. By the 1930s, former suffragettes' postwar representations of the prewar women's movement conformed to a single narrative, one elevating cer-

135

tain forms of resistance and neglecting others. The act of militancy, narrowly defined as violence against property, followed by arrest, imprisonment, hunger strike, and forcible feeding, came to be seen as the only legitimate expression of resistance. Other forms of militant protest, such as tax resistance or the presentation of petitions to the prime minister, rarely arose in postwar representations of militancy.[3] This was the case for a number of reasons. Nonviolent militancy tended to be overshadowed in light of more spectacular forms of violent protest such as arson or window breaking. Additionally, memorialization of the suffrage movement took place within the context of national memorialization of the First World War, which permeated every aspect of British culture.[4] Some of the forms suffragettes chose to use for remembering their comrades were similar to those used by former combatants. The "Roll of Honour of Suffragette Prisoners," akin to "Rolls of Honour" for those killed in combat, published in British newspapers during the war, documented those women imprisoned prior to 1914 for their militant activism.

Former militants took active roles in producing postwar commemorations of their movement, some historians would argue, to the exclusion of all other political activism in the 1920s and 1930s.[5] Members of the Suffragette Fellowship, founded to guard the memory of the militant suffrage movement, undertook a variety of commemorative measures in the 1920s and beyond. They collected materials for an archive, now located at the Museum of London. In the late 1920s, members successfully lobbied Parliament to install a statue of Emmeline Pankhurst in Victoria Tower Gardens in 1930.[6] Many of these same women actively tended the statue and its surrounding landscaping for the following three decades. The statue became a focal point for former suffragettes' activities from its unveiling in 1930 well into the 1970s (see figure 8.1).[7] Members of the Suffragette Fellowship protested in the 1950s when officials of the Ministry of Works redesigned Victoria Tower Gardens to accommodate a grouping of Rodin's *Burghers of Calais,* ensuring that Pankhurst's statue received a more prominent placement in the gardens. Members also took active roles in shaping television, radio, and film productions treating the suffrage movement. On more than one occasion, the BBC canceled production plans because of opposition to its representations by former suffragettes. Writers at the BBC found they had to negotiate the shoals of prewar factionalism among suffragettes, as well as field charges that the organization did not take women's struggles for political rights seriously enough.[8]

One consequence of the ceaseless activity of the Suffragette Fellowship was that militancy's variety became reduced in the recounting. In its version of the story, Emmeline Pankhurst became single-handedly responsible for British women acquiring the vote. This had become a theme of postwar discourse on the suffrage movement as early as the late 1920s and was recognized by former militants themselves, as in Emmeline Pethick Lawrence's 1929 observation that Emmeline Pankhurst had become "the embodiment

FIGURE 8.1
Former suffragettes at Mrs. Pankhurst's statue,
ca. 1945. Museum of London.

and representative" of the militant movement.[9] Mrs. Pankhurst's unique significance was reiterated by former suffragettes in numerous radio productions and press publications throughout the next thirty years.[10] Some former
suffragettes chafed at the difficulties surrounding any attempt to commemorate the efforts of other women active in the militant campaign, but to little
effect.[11] The proposals of a committee, formed in 1958 to make additions to
the site of Emmeline Pankhurst's statue, exposed the bitterness many former
suffragettes felt at how their movement had been represented by some of
their colleagues. The proposal, to add bronze medallions honoring Christabel Pankhurst and depicting the Holloway prisoners' brooch, elicited strong
comments from those who believed that too much attention had been given
to violent militancy, and not enough credit had been given to nonviolent militants and those who had opposed militancy altogether.[12] Former WSPU
member Theresa Garnett asserted that the committee's suggestions were "an
affront to all the women who fought, but did not agree with the later methods of the WSPU." She reminded readers that those opposed to the use of
violence "were and still are in the majority."[13] This discussion among former

137

suffragettes took place within the pages of the *Women's Freedom League Bulletin,* the successor to the WFL's paper, the *Vote,* and consequently had little impact on wider public portrayals of militancy.

Representation of the prewar movement within the popular press in the 1920s and 1930s bore a striking resemblance to former WSPU members' accounts of the prewar movement. At times the two overlap significantly, in telling and interpretation. One barometer of this was the newspaper coverage of the tenth anniversary of the first extension of the suffrage to women at the age of thirty, which coincided with the tense waiting period leading up to passage of the Equal Franchise Act of 1928. Every major newspaper carried stories of commemorative dinners staged by former suffragettes, reporting in admiring or condescending tones upon the speeches, toasts, and political utterances made by these women. Former suffragettes emerge from these accounts seemingly titillated by militancy. At one meeting in Craig's Court Restaurant in February 1928, attended by approximately 150 former suffragettes, discussion revolved around the chair's instructions to speakers to "'tell the most humorous or thrilling experience [of militancy] you ever had.'"[14] Suffragettes went on record as marveling at their prewar selves. At the Craig's Court Restaurant dinner, Irene Middleton, described as having "served one bleak Christmas in Holloway," commented that "'looking back on those W.S.P.U. days it all seems mad, but well worth while.'"[15] "'It all seems mad'" had the effect of diminishing the rational causes of women's political dissent, while overemphasizing the heady physicality of women's violent resistance. Speakers at commemorative dinners only grudgingly included nonviolent militants in the pantheon of suffrage heroines. "'Altogether,' Mrs. How-Martyn told the *Evening Standard,* 'there will be 150 of us. We do not feel there is any disgrace attaching to the odd fifty or so who will be sitting down with us who did not go to gaol.'"[16]

The tendency of former suffragettes to fetishize militancy plays neatly into the postwar assertion, made repeatedly by politicians, journalists, and former suffragettes themselves, that the war, and women's work for the nation during the war, was responsible for the partial enfranchisement of women at the age of thirty.[17] Women's agitation in the prewar period and their attempts to use dissent as a means of reconfiguring the state to accommodate gender difference were no longer seen as playing a role in the campaign. A movement with roots in the 1860s paled in comparison to a four-year period in which women made the "ultimate sacrifice" for the nation—whether rolling bandages, driving ambulances, or sending sons, husbands, lovers, or brothers to the front. By the late 1920s, suffragettes' success was defined in the popular imagination by their willingness to abandon suffrage work and take up the cause of the nation. Virtually every account published in a major newspaper of the passage of the 1918 Representation of the People Act emphasized the role played by the war in the shift of opinion on the question of women's enfranchisement. A "woman correspondent" for the *Manchester Guardian* in February 1928 asserted confidently that "it was the magnificent work done by women of all classes during the war—thanks very largely to the organisation and initiative of suffrage societies—that changed the attitude of the nation and secured" passage of the Reform Act by a large majority.[18] Even those suffragettes who insisted that militancy, or, rather, the government's fear of revived militancy, resulted in women's enfranchisement attributed the shift in public opinion to women's war work.[19]

Postwar emphasis on women's work during the war had the paradoxical effect of negating the dynamism of and conflict within the prewar women's movement, which had laid the groundwork for the successes of 1918 and 1928 through its emphasis on an active citizenship defined as countering the primacy of state authority rooted in physical force. Suffragettes' postwar accounts of their movement corroborated that shift. Numerous suffragette autobiographies published in the 1920s and after emphasized the role of the war in changing public opinion on the question of women's enfranchisement.[20] Additionally, and not incidentally, postwar emphasis on women's war work overlooked the significant fact that those women enfranchised in 1918—women over the age of thirty—were not necessarily the same women providing essential services to the nation at its time of need.[21] A great many of the women working in munitions and industry during the war were not enfranchised by the provisions of the 1918 act. And politicians' political goal of keeping the numbers of enfranchised women below those of men, whose numbers had shrunk so dramatically during the war, received little mention in the press or from suffragists, who prior to the war would have resisted attempts to limit their numbers in such a way.

The fetishistic quality of militancy and an overemphasis on the war's effects culminated in a prevalent theme of postwar representations of the prewar movement—discussion of the relative lack of significance of the enfranchisement of women. Passage of the second Representation of the People Act in 1928 (enfranchising women and men from the age of twenty-one) became an occasion for analyzing the effects of the earlier franchise extension. Commentators and former suffragettes themselves repeatedly observed how little the political process had changed between 1918 and 1928 as a consequence of the earlier Representation of the People Act. Journalist Shaw Desmond, writing for the *Evening Standard* in January 1928, recounted lessons of the six years he spent covering the WSPU's activities in the period before the war, only to conclude that the idealistic hopes suffragists had for the franchise had not been fulfilled. "Man-made law" had not been destroyed, and society had yet "to be regenerated." Christabel Pankhurst, he observed, had made her disillusionment apparent. Desmond went on to assert, "I do know that giving women the vote did not make a ha'porth of difference to anybody, least of all to the women themselves." Enumerating the ways in which women's suffrage had not made a difference, he noted their enlistment into "the orthodox camps of men's politics" and their concern for the home, "dress and entertainment" above politics.[22] Ironically, his points were corroborated by former suffragettes and anxious supporters of the Equal

Franchise Bill, who were determined to emphasize the smallness of women's "direct political influence," lest the bill not pass.[23] Young women in the late 1920s reassured men that women voters would not outnumber men if enfranchised at the same age.[24] Even those who defended the vote as "the outward and visible sign of the inward and spiritual grace of citizenship" tended to emphasize the ways in which the vote would not make a significant difference in legislation.[25] The women elected to Parliament in the first half decade after 1918 tended not to represent their candidacies as leading the way to the feminine transformation of politics.[26] This analysis continued well into the 1960s. BBC materials provided to secondary school students assured them that women voters never formed a block defined by gender, nor had they voted only for women or in opposition to men (see figure 8.2).[27]

Looking back from the vantage point of the 1930s, many former suffragettes themselves assessed the meaning of the vote and found it lacking. Sylvia

FIGURE 8.2
Suffragists during the Equal Political Rights campaign
of 1927, which culminated in passage of the
Representation of the People Act (1928)
enfranchising women and men at the age of
twenty-one. Mary Evans Picture Library.

Pankhurst penned her musings on "Women's Citizenship" on the twenty-first anniversary of Emily Wilding Davison's death at the Derby. She posed the question: "Are we satisfied with the result? Have we achieved what we desired from women's citizenship for the nation and for the world?" She, for one, was not. "Amongst crowds of young women, the emancipation of today," she wrote, "displays itself mainly in cigarettes and shorts . . . and other absurdities of dress and deportment, which betoken the slave woman's sex appeal rather than the free woman's intelligent companionship."[28]

In fetishizing militancy, postwar representations of the prewar movement lost sight of the most significant aspects of the militant movement: its dynamism, and the range of practices constituting militancy. Representations of the movement crystallized into the simple dichotomy of constitutional versus militant; all differences among suffragettes on fundamental questions such as the use of violence disappeared. This was partly due to militants' extreme efforts to claim responsibility for the vote, but it was largely due to separation of the act of militancy from its rationale. The act of militancy, in short, did not make good politics in the context of the 1920s and 1930s. Militancy was appropriated by radicals in the communist and labor movements in those decades, and most suffragettes did not wish to see connections between their agitation and movements inspired by the revolution in Russia.

During these decades, there was also general acknowledgment of the diminishing value of the vote, for men and women. The vote held significantly less meaning for individuals in 1920 than it had held in the nineteenth century, largely due to the professionalization of electoral politics and the emergence of new media, such as film and radio that packaged politics as "a set of images for mass consumption."[29] Contemporary press accounts emphasized the relative insignificance of the twentieth-century voter. The *Evening Standard* asserted with confidence in 1928: "No one can doubt that the individual elector is to-day of less importance than he was sixty years ago."[30] The *Manchester Guardian* agreed with this assessment, locating the shift in the years between 1918 and 1928. "The most superficial observer cannot but see that [between 1918 and 1928] the power of the executive has mightily increased, while that of the House of Commons and the people which it is supposed to represent has proportionately diminished."[31] The advent of mass communications and the manipulation of public opinion, the evolution and entrenchment of the party system, and the privatization of the practice of citizenship all contributed to this development.[32]

The emergence of fascism in the 1920s and 1930s cast suffrage militancy in a far different light. By the mid-1930s, former militants began to look to contemporaries less like benign autocrats and more like protofascists. In 1935, suffragist Cicely Hamilton criticized the militant movement's emphasis on the sacrifice of individuality in the service of the collective, characterizing it as "the first indication of the dictator movements." A "magnificent demagogue," Emmeline Pankhurst became the "forerunner of Lenin, Hitler, Mussolini."[33] Extreme political and religious allegiances of suffragettes like

Christabel Pankhurst, Mary Allen, and Mary Richardson contributed to a public sense that militancy's excesses were potentially lethal to democratic institutions.[34]

Related to fascism's development, a kind of general disillusionment with democracy in the 1920s and 1930s made militancy's idealism seem dangerous. Public discourse on citizenship in the late 1920s cast women as too irrational to vote responsibly. Editorials and cartoons in the months leading up to passage of the 1928 Representation of the People Act lampooned the "flapper vote," suggesting that increasing the number of women voters would result in more handsome men in Parliament.[35] But gender was only part of the critique leveled by public opinion makers. All discussion of women's suffrage took place within a broader public discussion of the limitations of universal suffrage. A significant strand within British liberalism itself questioned universal suffrage as a means to obtaining democracy. This strand, dating back to J. S. Mill's *Considerations on Representative Government* (1861), resurfaced in the mid-1920s around discussion of the second Representation of the People Act and continued into the 1930s.

In a series of articles in the *Evening Standard* in 1927 and 1928, the Very Reverend W. R. Inge, dean of St. Paul's, cataloged democracy's ills. Reiterating Mill's concern that women and people of color were not fit for citizenship, he warned in April 1927 that universal suffrage would mean the end of parliamentary government because it would include as voters those unfit for the practice of citizenship.[36] The next year, he characterized the "flapper vote" as "the last kick of that discredited theory—doctrinaire democracy." "Human beings," he asserted, "are born unequal, and the only persons who have a right to govern their neighbours are those who are competent to do so. Universal suffrage has always brought with it the end of popular government."[37]

Mainstream historical accounts of the 1930s posited a kind of "disillusionment with democracy," which authors projected back on to the Edwardian age. Books as various as G. M. Young's *Portrait of an Age* (1936), George Dangerfield's now-classic *Strange Death of Liberal England* (1935), and F. J. C. Hearnshaw's collection of essays, *Edwardian England* (1933), argued that early twentieth-century British political culture displayed little faith in democracy. Hearnshaw characterized the militants as "belligerent suffragettes . . . favoured by the immunities of their sex, [who] displayed a progressive recklessness and irrationality; a destructive and abusive Bedlam seemed let loose."[38] And while he admired their energy, Dangerfield wrote of suffragettes' activism as events "which, working with the pointless industry of termites, slowly undermined England's parliamentary structure until, but for the providential intervention of a world war, it would certainly have collapsed."[39]

From this historical distance, however, the ferment at the beginning of the century around expansion of the electorate reads less as an expression of "disillusionment" or "pessimism" about democracy on the part of the disenfranchised than a vital and vibrant moment for discussions of democracy, and not, it must be noted, among women alone. Suffragettes' very public confrontation with the state over its refusal to give them parliamentary representation forced members of the public more generally to reconsider citizenship's embodiment and contributed in no small way to vital debates about the relationship between voting and citizenship, and that between individuals and the state.

For some forty years now, historians have debated the effectiveness of militancy in securing the parliamentary vote for women.[40] This book, however, has been concerned less with militancy's effectiveness than with the relationship suffragettes asserted between resistance and citizenship. It has been concerned with those men and women in late-Victorian and Edwardian Britain who believed that active, engaged participation in the public sphere—with force if necessary—would improve political life for all. The success of liberal democratic citizenship in constituting the voter as the passive bearer of rights has obscured the vitality of this and other radical attempts to rethink suffrage at the beginning of the twentieth century. That liberal democratic citizenship has for so long been the standard by which citizenship is measured in no way diminishes suffragettes' struggles. Drawing attention to their attempts to define citizenship through the act of resistance thus highlights a significant chapter in British political history and suggests alternative trajectories for democracy's development.

Notes

INTRODUCTION

1. *The Times*, 26 June 1909, p. 12.

2. See Sandra Stanley Holton, *Suffrage Days: Stories from the Women's Suffrage Movement* (London: Routledge, 1996).

3. Millicent Garrett Fawcett and Frances Power Cobbe suggested the possibility of women's use of violence in *The Woman Question in Europe: A Series of Original Essays*, ed. Theodore Stanton (London, 1884; reprint, New York: Source Book Press, 1974).

4. Sandra Stanley Holton, *Feminism and Democracy: Women's Suffrage and Reform Politics in Britain, 1900–1918* (Cambridge: Cambridge University Press, 1986); Jane Rendall, "Citizenship, Culture and Civilisation: The Languages of British Suffragists, 1866–1874," in *Suffrage and Beyond: International Feminist Perspectives*, ed. Caroline Daley and Melanie Nolan (New York: New York University Press, 1994), pp. 127–50; and Cheryl Jorgensen-Earp, *The Transfiguring Sword: The Just War of the Women's Social and Political Union* (Tuscaloosa: University of Alabama Press, 1997).

5. Angela V. John and Claire Eustance, eds., *The Men's Share? Masculinities, Male Support and Women's Suffrage in Britain, 1890–1920* (London: Routledge, 1997).

6. Anna Clark, "Gender, Class and the Constitution: Franchise Reform in England, 1832–1928," in *Re-reading the Constitution: New Narratives in the Political History of England's Long Nineteenth Century*, ed. James Vernon (Cambridge: Cambridge University Press, 1996), pp. 230–53.

7. Martin Pugh, *The Making of Modern British Politics, 1867–1939* (Oxford: Blackwell, 1982; 2d edition 1993), pp. 5–10, 249–52.

8. For a critique of this view, see James Vernon, *Politics and the People: A Study in English Political Culture, c. 1815–1867* (Cambridge: Cambridge University Press, 1993), pp. 1–9.

9. Antoinette Burton, *Burdens of History: British Feminists, Indian Women, and Imperial Culture, 1865–1915* (Chapel Hill: University of North Carolina Press, 1994); Vernon, *Politics and the People;* Catherine Hall, Keith McClelland, and Jane Rendall, *Defining the Victorian Nation: Class, Race, Gender and the Reform Act of 1867* (Cambridge: Cambridge University Press, 2000); Duncan Tanner, *Political Change and the Labour Party, 1900–1918* (Cambridge: Cambridge University Press, 1990).

10. Barbara Caine, *English Feminism, 1780–1980* (New York: Oxford University Press, 1997), pp. 144–45.

11. June Purvis, "A 'Pair of . . . Infernal Queens'? A Reassessment of the Dominant Representations of Emmeline and Christabel Pankhurst, First Wave Feminists in Edwardian Britain," *Women's History Review* 5, no. 2 (1996): 259–80.

12. For an important exception, see Hall, McClelland, and Rendall, *Defining the Victorian Nation.*

13. See Ursula Vogel, "Is Citizenship Gender-specific?" in *The Frontiers of Citizenship,* ed. Ursula Vogel and Michael Moran (New York: St. Martin's Press, 1991), p. 61.

14. Martin Durham, "Suffrage and After: Feminism in the Early Twentieth Century," in *Crises in the British State, 1880–1930,* ed. Mary Langan and Bill Schwarz (London: Hutchinson, 1985), pp. 179–91; June Hannam, "Women and Politics," in *Women's History: Britain, 1850–1914,* ed. June Purvis (New York: St. Martin's Press, 1995), pp. 217–46.

15. Holton, *Feminism and Democracy;* Rendall, "Citizenship, Culture and Civilisation," pp. 127–50; Joan Williams, "Domesticity as the Dangerous Supplement of Liberalism," *Journal of Women's History* 2, no. 3 (1991): 69–88.

16. James Meadowcroft, *Conceptualizing the State: Innovation and Dispute in British Political Thought 1880–1914* (Oxford: Clarendon Press, 1995); S. J. D. Green and R. C. Whiting, eds., *The Boundaries of the State in Modern Britain* (Cambridge: Cambridge University Press, 1996); W. H. Greenleaf, *The British Political Tradition* (London: Methuen, 1983); Jose Harris, "Society and the State in Twentieth-Century Britain," in *The Cambridge Social History of Britain, 1750–1950,* ed. F. M. L. Thompson (Cambridge: Cambridge University Press, 1990), 3:63–177.

17. Marian Sawer, "Gender, Metaphor and the State," *Feminist Review,* no. 52 (1996): 119–20.

18. Jane Lewis, *Women and Social Action in Victorian and Edwardian England* (Stanford, Calif.: Stanford University Press, 1991); Philippa Levine, *Victorian Feminism, 1850–1900* (London: Hutchinson, 1987). Not that feminists wholeheartedly embraced the movement of the state into what was seen as women's sphere; see M. J. D. Roberts, "Feminism and the State in Later Victorian England," *Historical Journal* 38, no. 1 (1995): 85–110.

19. For militancy as aberration, see Martin Pugh, *The March of the Women: A Revisionist Analysis of the Campaign for Women's Suffrage, 1866–1914* (Oxford: Oxford University Press, 2000), pp. 172–223, and Brian Harrison, *Prudent Revolutionaries: Portraits of British Feminists Between the Wars* (Oxford: Clarendon Press, 1987), pp. 41–43, 53–56; for militancy as culmination, see Martha Vicinus, *Independent Women: Work and Community for Single Women, 1850–1920* (Chicago: University of Chicago Press, 1985), p. 250.

20. Sowon Park, "When Mother Joined the Suffragettes: The Spectacle of Women Through the Gaze of History" (paper presented at Lucy Cavendish College, Cambridge University, 13 February 2001). [Available on-line at www.lucy- cav.cam.ac.uk/cwl/op/SowonPark.htm].

21. On the former, see Lisa Tickner, *The Spectacle of Women: Imagery of the Suffrage Campaign, 1907–1914* (London: Chatto and Windus, 1987); on the latter, see Vicinus, *Independent Women,* pp. 247–80; see also Maud Ellman, *The Hunger Artists: Starving, Writing and Imprisonment* (Cambridge, Mass.: Harvard University Press, 1993); Mary Jean Corbett, *Representing Femininity: Middle-Class Subjectivity in Victorian and Edwardian Women's Autobiographies* (New York: Oxford University Press, 1992).

22. Tickner, *Spectacle of Women,* p. ix.

23. See Barbara Green, *Spectacular Confessions: Autobiography, Performative Activism, and the Sites of Suffrage, 1905–1938* (New York: St. Martin's Press, 1997), pp. 16, 30, 56–57.

24. See David Mitchell, *Queen Christabel: A Biography of Christabel Pankhurst* (London: Macdonald and Jane's, 1977); and more recently, Pugh, *The March of the Women.*

25. Gareth Stedman Jones, *Languages of Class: Studies in English Working-Class History, 1832–1982* (Cambridge: Cambridge University Press, 1983); Vernon, *Politics and the People;* Patrick Joyce, *Visions of the People: Industrial England and the Question of Class, 1848–1914* (Cambridge: Cambridge University Press, 1991); James Epstein, *Radical Expression: Political Language, Ritual, and Symbol in England, 1790–1850* (New York: Oxford University Press, 1994); Anna Clark, *The Struggle for the Breeches: Gender and the Making of the British Working Class* (Berkeley: University of California Press, 1995); Eugenio F. Biagini and Alistair J. Reid, *Currents of Radicalism: Popular Radicalism, Organised Labour and Party Politics in Britain, 1850–1914* (Cambridge: Cambridge University Press, 1991); Stefan Collini, *Public Moralists: Political Thought and Intellectual Life in Britain, 1850–1930* (Oxford: Clarendon Press, 1991).

26. Ruth Lister, *Citizenship: Feminist Perspectives* (New York: New York University Press, 1997), p. 1.

27. Carole Pateman, *The Disorder of Women: Democracy, Feminism and Political Theory* (Stanford, Calif.: Stanford University Press, 1989); Pateman, *The Sexual Contract* (Stanford, Calif.: Stanford University Press, 1988); Chantal Mouffe, ed., *Dimensions of Democracy: Pluralism, Citizenship, Community* (London: Verso, 1992); Nancy Fraser, *Unruly Practices: Power, Discourse and Gender in Contemporary Social Theory* (Minneapolis: University of Minnesota Press, 1989).

28. Lister, *Citizenship,* pp. 13–14; Adrian Oldfield, *Citizenship and Community: Civic Republicanism and the Modern World* (London: Routledge, 1990); Chantal Mouffe, "Feminism and Radical Politics," in *Feminists Theorize the Political,* ed. Judith Butler and Joan W. Scott (New York: Routledge, 1992), pp. 369–84.

29. Mary Dietz, "Context Is All: Feminism and Theories of Citizenship," *Daedalus* 116, no. 4 (1987): 5.

30. Mary Shanley, "Afterword: Feminism and Families in a Liberal Polity," in *Families, Politics, and Public Policy: A Feminist Dialogue on Women and the State,* ed. Irene Diamond (New York: Longman, 1983), p. 360.

31. Susan James, "The Good-Enough Citizen: Female Citizenship and Independence," in *Beyond Equality and Difference: Citizenship, Feminist Politics and Female Subjectivity,* ed. Gisela Bock and Susan James (London: Routledge, 1992), p. 48.

CHAPTER 1

1. For the parliamentary context, see Brian Harrison, "Women's Suffrage at Westminster, 1866–1928," in *High and Low Politics in Modern Britain: Ten Studies,* ed. Michael Bentley and John Stevenson (Oxford: Clarendon Press, 1983), pp. 80–122; Martin Pugh, *Women's Suffrage in Britain* (London: Historical Association, 1980). For suffrage as social movement, see Sophia A. van Wingerden, *The Women's Suffrage Movement in Britain, 1866–1928* (Hampshire: Macmillan, 1999); Leslie Parker Hume, *The National Union of Women's Suffrage Societies, 1897–1914* (New York: Garland, 1982); Andrew Rosen, *"Rise Up, Women!": The Militant Campaign of the Women's Social and Political Union, 1903–1914* (London: Routledge and Kegan Paul, 1974).

2. Constance Rover, *Women's Suffrage and Party Politics in Britain, 1866–1914* (London: Routledge and Kegan Paul, 1967); David Morgan, *Suffragists and Liberals: The Politics of Woman Suffrage in England* (Totowa, N.J.: Rowman and Littlefield, 1975); Sandra Stanley Holton, *Feminism and Democracy: Women's Suffrage and Reform Politics in Britain, 1900–1918* (Cambridge: Cambridge University Press, 1986).

3. George Dangerfield, *The Strange Death of Liberal England* (London, 1935; reprint, London: Granada, 1983); Martin Pugh, *The March of the Women: A Revisionist Analysis of the Campaign for Women's Suffrage, 1866–1914* (Oxford: Oxford University Press, 2000); Mary Langan and Bill Schwarz, eds., *Crises in the British State, 1880–1930* (London: Hutchinson, 1985).

4. See Hugh Cunningham, *The Challenge of Democracy: Britain, 1832–1918* (London: Longman, 2001), pp. 125–28.

5. Jonathan Parry, *The Rise and Fall of Liberal Government in Victorian Britain* (New Haven, Conn.: Yale University Press, 1993), p. 7.

6. Jon Lawrence, *Speaking for the People: Party, Language and Popular Politics in England, 1867–1914* (Cambridge: Cambridge University Press, 1998), p. 170. See also T. A. Jenkins, *The Liberal Ascendancy, 1830–1886* (New York: St. Martin's Press, 1994), p. 72.

7. Jose Harris, "Society and the State in Twentieth-Century Britain," in *The Cambridge Social History of Britain, 1750–1950*, ed. F. M. L. Thompson (Cambridge: Cambridge University Press, 1990), 3: 65–70; Parry, *Rise and Fall of Liberal Government*, pp. 3–6.

8. Mary Dietz, "Context Is All: Feminism and Theories of Citizenship," *Daedalus* 116, no. 4 (1987): 3–5; see also Peter Clarke, "The Edwardians and the Constitution," in *Edwardian England*, ed. Donald Read (New Brunswick, N.J.: Rutgers University Press, 1982), pp. 50–51.

9. Pat Thane, "The British Imperial State and the Construction of National Identities," in *Borderlines: Genders and Identities in War and Peace, 1870–1930*, ed. Billie Melman (New York: Routledge, 1998), p. 29.

10. James A. Epstein, *Radical Expression: Political Language, Ritual, and Symbol in England, 1790–1850* (New York: Oxford University Press, 1994), pp. 7–8.

11. Catherine Hall, "The Rule of Difference: Gender, Class and Empire in the Making of the 1832 Reform Act," in *Gendered Nations: Nationalisms and Gender Order in the Long Nineteenth Century*, ed. Ida Blom, Karen Hagemann, and Catherine Hall (Oxford: Berg, 2000), p. 111.

12. Ibid., pp. 112–21.

13. Parry, *Rise and Fall of Liberal Government*, pp. 78–89; Michael Willis, *Democracy and the State, 1830–1945* (Cambridge: Cambridge University Press, 2001), pp. 7–9; Cunningham, *Challenge of Democracy*, p. 33; Ian Machin, *The Rise of Democracy in Britain, 1830–1918* (Hampshire: Macmillan, 2001), pp. 20–21.

14. Hall, "Rule of Difference," pp. 107, 111.

15. Rover, *Women's Suffrage and Party Politics*, p. 3.

16. Kathryn Gleadle, *The Early Feminists: Radical Unitarians and the Emergence of the Women's Rights Movement, 1831–1851* (New York: St. Martin's Press, 1995); Anna Clark, *The Struggle for the Breeches: Gender and the Making of the British Working Class* (Berkeley: University of California Press, 1995); Barbara Taylor, *Eve and the New Jerusalem: Socialism and Feminism in the Nineteenth Century* (London: Virago, 1983). See also Helen Rogers, *Women and the People: Authority, Authorship and the Radical Tradition in Nineteenth-Century England* (Aldershot, Hampshire, England: Ashgate, 2000).

17. Harris, "Society and the State," p. 66.

18. Eugenio F. Biagini, "Liberalism and Direct Democracy: John Stuart Mill and the Model of Ancient Athens," in *Citizenship and Community: Liberals, Radicals, and Collective Identities in the British Isles, 1865–1931,* ed. Eugenio F. Biagini (Cambridge: Cambridge University Press, 1996), pp. 36–37.

19. Keith McClelland, "Rational and Respectable Men: Gender, the Working Class, and Citizenship in Britain, 1850–1867," in *Gender and Class in Modern Europe,* ed. Laura L. Frader and Sonya O. Rose (Ithaca, N.Y.: Cornell University Press, 1996), pp. 280–93; see also Catherine Hall, Keith McClelland, and Jane Rendall, *Defining the Victorian Nation: Class, Race, Gender and the Reform Act of 1867* (Cambridge: Cambridge University Press, 2000), pp. 71–118.

20. Cunningham, *Challenge of Democracy,* pp. 103–5.

21. Stuart Hall and Bill Schwarz, "State and Society, 1880–1930," in Langan and Schwarz, *Crises in the British State,* p. 12.

22. Hall, McClelland, and Rendall, *Defining the Victorian Nation,* pp. 130–36.

23. Jane Rendall, "John Stuart Mill, Liberal Politics, and the Movements for Women's Suffrage, 1865–1873," in *Women, Privilege, and Power: British Politics, 1750 to the Present,* ed. Amanda Vickery (Stanford, Calif.: Stanford University Press, 2001), pp. 177–78; Machin, *Rise of Democracy in Britain,* p. 64.

24. Hall, McClelland, and Rendall, *Defining the Victorian Nation,* p. 139; Philippa Levine, *Victorian Feminism, 1850–1900* (London: Hutchinson, 1987), p. 63.

25. Hall, McClelland, and Rendall, *Defining the Victorian Nation,* p. 156.

26. Helen Taylor, "The Claim of Englishwomen to the Suffrage Constitutionally Considered" (1867), in *Before the Vote Was Won: Arguments for and Against Women's Suffrage,* ed. Jane Lewis (London: Routledge and Kegan Paul, 1987), pp. 26–27.

27. Millicent Garrett Fawcett, "England: The Women's Suffrage Movement," in *The Woman Question in Europe: A Series of Original Essays,* ed. Theodore Stanton (London, 1884; reprint, New York: Source Book Press, 1974), p. 5.

28. Barbara Bodichon, "Reasons for the Enfranchisement of Women" (paper presented at the National Association for the Promotion of Social Science), October 1866, reprinted in *Barbara Leigh Smith Bodichon and the Langham Place Group,* ed. Candida Ann Lacey (London: Routledge and Kegan Paul, 1986), pp. 104, 108.

29. Richard Marsden Pankhurst, "The Right of Women to Vote Under the Reform Act, 1867," *Fortnightly Review,* 1 September 1868, pp. 250–54.

30. Levine, *Victorian Feminism,* pp. 63–66; Pugh, *The March of the Women,* pp. 10–29.

31. Hall, McClelland, and Rendall, *Defining the Victorian Nation,* pp. 157–59; Patricia Hollis, *Ladies Elect: Women in English Local Government, 1865–1914* (Oxford: Clarendon Press, 1987), pp. 7–10.

32. Martha Vicinus, *Independent Women: Work and Community for Single Women, 1850–1920* (Chicago: University of Chicago Press, 1985), pp. 211–46.

33. Linda Walker, "Party Political Women: A Comparative Study of Liberal Women and the Primrose League, 1890–1914," in *Equal or Different: Women's Politics, 1800–1914,* ed. Jane Rendall (Oxford: Basil Blackwell, 1987), pp. 165–66.

34. W. S. B. McLaren, "The Political Emancipation of Women" (London: Women's Printing Society, ca. 1888), p. 6.

35. David Rubinstein, *Before the Suffragettes: Women's Emancipation in the 1890s* (New York: St. Martin's Press, 1986), p. 157.

36. Jonathan Schneer, "The Politics of Feminism in 'Outcast London': George Lansbury and Jane Cobden's Campaign for the First London County Council," *Journal of British Studies* 30 (1991): 63–82.

37. Moisei Ostrogorski, *The Rights of Women: A Comparative Study in History and Legislation*, 2d ed. (London: George Allen and Unwin, 1908), p. 196.

38. Willis, *Democracy and the State*, pp. 23–24; Machin, *Rise of Democracy in Britain*, pp. 94–102; Cunningham, *Challenge of Democracy*, pp. 120–28.

39. Martin Pugh, "The Limits of Liberalism: Liberals and Women's Suffrage, 1867–1914," in Biagini, ed., *Citizenship and Community*, p. 56.

40. Duncan Tanner, *Political Change and the Labour Party, 1900–1918* (Cambridge: Cambridge University Press, 1990), pp. 111–23; see also Jon Lawrence, "The Dynamics of Urban Politics, 1867–1914," in *Party, State and Society: Electoral Behavior in Britain Since 1820*, ed. Jon Lawrence and Miles Taylor (Aldershot, Hants, England: Scolar Press, 1997), p. 87.

41. Millicent Garrett Fawcett, "Home and Politics: An Address Delivered at Toynbee Hall and Elsewhere" (London: Women's Printing Society, 1889), pp. 3–4.

42. Barbara Caine, *Victorian Feminists* (Oxford: Oxford University Press, 1992), p. 41.

43. Mrs. William Grey, "Is the Exercise of the Franchise Unfeminine?" (London: London National Society for Women's Suffrage, 1870); Gwenllian F. Morgan, "The Duties of Citizenship: The Proper Understanding and Use of the Municipal and Other Franchises for Women" (1896), in Lewis, *Before the Vote Was Won*, pp. 465–71.

44. Marian Sawer, "Gender, Metaphor and the State," *Feminist Review*, no. 52 (1996): 121.

45. Stefan Collini, *Public Moralists: Political Thought and Intellectual Life in Britain, 1850–1930* (Oxford: Clarendon Press, 1991), pp. 91–118.

46. Josephine Butler, "Introduction," in *Women's Work and Women's Culture: A Series of Essays*, ed. Josephine Butler (London: Macmillan, 1869), p. xxv.

47. A. V. Dicey, "Woman Suffrage," *Quarterly Review*, 210, no. 418 (January 1909), pp. 277, 288.

48. Michael Freeden, "The New Liberalism and Its Aftermath," in *Victorian Liberalism: Nineteenth-Century Political Thought and Practice*, ed. Richard Bellamy (London: Routledge, 1990), pp. 175–76.

49. See "Law," in Elizabeth K. Helsinger, Robin Lauterbach Sheets, and William Veeder, *The Woman Question: Society and Literature in Britain and America, 1837–1883* (New York: Garland, 1983), 2:3–55.

50. Barbara Caine, *English Feminism, 1780–1980* (New York: Oxford University Press, 1997), pp. 66–68; Mary Lyndon Shanley, *Feminism, Marriage, and the Law in Victorian England* (Princeton, N.J.: Princeton University Press, 1989), pp. 23–29.

51. Shanley, *Feminism, Marriage, and the Law*; see also Lee Holcombe, *Wives and Property: Reform of the Married Women's Property Law in Nineteenth-Century England* (Toronto: University of Toronto Press, 1983).

52. Olive Banks, *Becoming a Feminist: The Social Origins of "First Wave" Feminism* (Athens: University of Georgia Press, 1986), pp. 82–85.

53. Sandra Stanley Holton, *Suffrage Days: Stories from the Women's Suffrage Movement* (London: Routledge, 1996), pp. 36–47; Lucy Bland, "The Married Woman, the 'New Woman' and the Feminist: Sexual Politics of the 1890s," in Rendall, *Equal or Different*, pp. 141–64.

54. Freeden, "The New Liberalism and Its Aftermath," pp. 175–92; see also Pugh, "The Limits of Liberalism," pp. 45–65.

55. Jenkins, *Liberal Ascendancy*, p. 138; Parry, *Rise and Fall of Liberal Government*, p. 306; Lawrence, *Speaking for the People*, p. 195.

56. Lawrence, *Speaking for the People,* p. 195.

57. Rodney Barker, "Socialism and Progressivism in the Political Thought of Ramsay MacDonald," in *Edwardian Radicalism, 1900–1914: Some Aspects of British Radicalism,* ed. A. J. A. Morris (London: Routledge and Kegan Paul, 1974), pp. 114–15; Duncan Tanner, "Ideological Debate in Edwardian Labour Politics: Radicalism, Revisionism and Socialism," in *Currents of Radicalism: Popular Radicalism, Organised Labour, and Party Politics in Britain, 1850–1914,* ed. Eugenio F. Biagini and Alistair J. Reid (Cambridge: Cambridge University Press, 1991), pp. 271–93.

58. For the range of concerns engaging progressives, see Joy Dixon, *Divine Feminine: Theosophy and Feminism in England* (Baltimore: Johns Hopkins University Press, 2001), pp. 121–22.

59. Collini, *Public Moralists,* p. 181–82.

60. Ignota [Elizabeth C. Wolstenholme Elmy], "Privilege v. Justice to Women," *Westminster Review,* August 1899, p. 140.

61. Collini, *Public Moralists,* pp. 128–29.

62. Sandra Stanley Holton, "Now You See It, Now You Don't: The Women's Franchise League and Its Place in Contending Narratives of the Women's Suffrage Movement," in *The Women's Suffrage Movement: New Feminist Perspectives,* ed. Maroula Joannou and June Purvis (Manchester: Manchester University Press, 1998), p. 22.

63. "How to Injure a Good Cause," *Woman's Herald,* 12 November 1892, p. 3.

64. Hester Leeds, "Origin and Growth of the Union" (London: Union of Practical Suffragists, 1898); Miss Priestman, "Women and Votes" (London: Union of Practical Suffragists, 1897); see also Dora Montefiore, *From a Victorian to a Modern* (London: E. Archer, 1927), p. 40.

65. "Its Origin and Its Work; Report of the Women's Emancipation Union Presented at the Meeting" (Congleton, England: WEU, 1892), 1:2.

66. Charlotte Carmichael Stopes, "The Women's Protest" (paper read at the WEU's London conference, 15 October 1896), p. 2.

67. Eunice Guthrie Murray diaries, vol. I, 9 February 1897, p. 31.

68. Sandra Stanley Holton, "'To Educate Women into Rebellion': Elizabeth Cady Stanton and the Creation of a Transatlantic Network of Radical Suffragists," *American Historical Review* 99, no. 4 (1994): 1134.

69. Hume, *National Union of Women's Suffrage Societies,* pp. 226–27.

70. Holton, *Suffrage Days,* p. 90.

CHAPTER 2

1. Millicent Garrett Fawcett, *What I Remember* (London: T. Fisher Unwin, 1925), p. 149. Fawcett first made this argument in *Women's Suffrage: A Short History of a Great Movement* (London: T. C. And E. C. Jack, 1912; reprint, New York: Source Book Press, 1970), pp. 58–60. See also David Rubinstein, *A Different World for Women: The Life of Millicent Garrett Fawcett* (Columbus: Ohio State University Press, 1991), p. 120.

2. NUWSS conference report, 1900, in NUWSS, Central and East of England Society for Women's Suffrage, Occasional Paper, 12 March 1900. See also Minutes of the National Executive Committee, 7 December 1899, GB/106/2/NWS/A/1, Box 83, The Women's Library; the North of England Society for Women's Suffrage *Annual Reports,* 1899–1900, 1900–1901, and 1902, in the Women's Suffrage Collection, Manchester Central Library, microform, part 1, M/50/1/4/27, 28, 29, and 30. For historians' accounting of suffrage campaigning during these years, see Jill Liddington and

Jill Norris, *One Hand Tied Behind Us: The Rise of the Women's Suffrage Movement* (London: Virago, 1978), pp. 76–83, 143–66; June Hannam, *Isabella Ford* (Oxford: Basil Blackwell, 1989), pp. 83–91.

3. See Sandra Stanley Holton, *Suffrage Days: Stories from the Women's Suffrage Movement* (London: Routledge, 1996), p. 105; and Holton, "Now You See It, Now You Don't: The Women's Franchise League and Its Place in Contending Narratives of the Women's Suffrage Movement," in *The Women's Suffrage Movement: New Feminist Perspectives,* ed. Maroula Joannou and June Purvis (Manchester: Manchester University Press, 1998), pp. 15–36.

4. Bernard Porter, "The Pro-Boers in Britain," in *The South African War: The Anglo-Boer War, 1899–1902,* ed. Peter Warwick (London: Longman, 1980), pp. 240–41. See also John W. Auld, "The Liberal Pro-Boers," *Journal of British Studies* 14, no. 2 (1975): pp. 78–101; and Richard Price, *An Imperial War and the British Working Class: Working-Class Attitudes and Reactions to the Boer War, 1899–1902* (London: Routledge and Kegan Paul, 1974).

5. Stephen Koss, *The Pro-Boers: The Anatomy of an Antiwar Movement* (Chicago: University of Chicago Press, 1973).

6. Paul Ward, *Red Flag and Union Jack: Englishness, Patriotism, and the British Left, 1881–1924* (Bury St. Edmunds, Suffolk: Boydell Press, 1998), p. 58.

7. Catherine Hall, "Rethinking Imperial Histories: The Reform Act of 1867," *New Left Review* 208 (1994): 3–29. David Brooks argues that the South African War's "shadow remained over the country at least until 1914," in *The Age of Upheaval: Edwardian Politics, 1899–1914* (Manchester: Manchester University Press, 1995), p. 5.

8. Antoinette Burton, *Burdens of History: British Feminists, Indian Women, and Imperial Culture, 1865–1915* (Chapel Hill: University of North Carolina Press, 1994), pp. 41–52.

9. Shula Marks and Stanley Trapido, "The Politics of Race, Class, and Nationalism," in *The Politics of Race, Class, and Nationalism in Twentieth-Century South Africa,* ed. Shula Marks and Stanley Trapido (London: Longman, 1987), pp. 3–4; Leonard Thompson, *A History of South Africa,* rev. ed. (New Haven, Conn.: Yale University Press, 1995), pp. 110–21.

10. This phrase from the Pretoria Convention of 3 August 1881 is quoted in Byron Farwell, *The Great Anglo-Boer War* (New York: Norton, 1990), p. 19.

11. Iain R. Smith, *The Origins of the South African War, 1899–1902* (London: Longman, 1996), pp. 228–29, 253; Thompson, *History of South Africa,* pp. 136–40.

12. The dispatch reached Chamberlain on 5 May 1899 but was not made public until after the conclusion of the Bloemfontein conference. Milner's dispatch is quoted in Farwell, *Great Anglo-Boer War,* p. 33.

13. See Smith, *Origins of the South African War,* p. 1; Thompson, *History of South Africa,* p. 141.

14. Smith, *Origins of the South African War,* p. 420; see *Times,* 24 May 1899, which provided a detailed accounting of the white man's vote in all its permutations from the 1850s.

15. H. Paul, "The Conservatism of President Kruger," *Contemporary Review,* July 1899, 1–13; F. E. Garrett, "The Inevitable in South Africa," *Contemporary Review,* October 1899, 457–81.

16. Holton, *Suffrage Days,* p. 40.

17. Barbara Caine, *English Feminism, 1780–1980* (New York: Oxford University Press, 1997), pp. 122–23.

18. Ray Strachey, *Millicent Garrett Fawcett* (London: John Murray, 1931), pp. 185–86.

19. Josephine Butler to Stanley Butler, 18 December and 25 December 1899, Josephine Butler Autograph Letter Collection (hereafter JBALC), the Women's Library.

20. Josephine Butler, *Native Races and the War* (London: Gay and Bird, 1900), p. 110. My reading of this text owes much to Antoinette Burton, "'States of Injury': Josephine Butler on Slavery, Citizenship, and the Boer War," in *Women's Suffrage in the British Empire: Citizenship, Nation, and Race,* ed. Ian Christopher Fletcher, Laura E. Nym Mayhall, and Philippa Levine (London: Routledge, 2000), pp. 18–32. See also Barbara Caine, *Victorian Feminists* (Oxford: Oxford University Press, 1992), pp. 173–74.

21. Josephine Butler to Millicent Garrett Fawcett, 20 June 1900 (JBALC). See also H. J. Wilson to Miss Forsaith, 7 January 1901 (JBALC), regarding opposition of workers within the international movement to Butler's position on the war.

22. Burton, "'States of Injury,'" pp. 18–19.

23. Strachey, *Millicent Garrett Fawcett,* p. 185.

24. Hobhouse's research was funded by the South African Women and Children Distress Fund, and excerpts from her report were reproduced in a number of British publications in 1901; see Stephen Koss, ed., *The Pro-Boers: The Anatomy of an Antiwar Movement* (Chicago: University of Chicago Press, 1973), pp. 194–207.

25. Campbell-Bannerman used the phrase "methods of barbarism" in a speech before the National Reform Union, 14 June 1901; see Koss, *Pro-Boers,* p. xxxvii.

26. On the relationship between cleanliness and civilization, see Anne McClintock, *Imperial Leather: Race, Gender and Sexuality in the Colonial Context* (New York: Routledge, 1995), pp. 207–31.

27. Millicent Garrett Fawcett, "Report on the Concentration Camps in South Africa by the Committee of Ladies Appointed by the Secretary of State for War Containing Reports on the Camps in Natal, the Orange River Colony, and the Transvaal," (London: HMSO, 1902). Fawcett's personal copy of the report, into which photographs have been interleaved, is held at the Women's Library (GB/106/7/MGF/90B/1). For Fawcett's comments on education, see p. 5; on hygiene, pp. 14–17.

28. See, for example, Sophia Jex-Blake's letter to the *Times,* 30 August 1902.

29. Fawcett, *What I Remember,* pp. 149–50.

30. Frances Power Cobbe, "Criminals, Idiots, Women, and Minors. Is the Classification Sound? A Discussion on the Laws Concerning the Property of Married Women" (Manchester: A. Ireland, 1869).

31. "Women and the War," *Englishwoman's Review,* 17 April 1900, pp. 77–82.

32. J. E. Hand, ed., *Good Citizenship* (London: G. Allen, 1899); "Women as Citizens," *Englishwoman's Review,* 16 October 1899, pp. 283–84. On the importance of duty to nineteenth-century liberal feminist definitions of citizenship, see Jane Rendall, "Citizenship, Culture and Civilisation: The Languages of British Suffragists, 1866–1874," in *Suffrage and Beyond: International Feminist Perspectives,* ed. Caroline Daley and Melanie Nolan (New York: New York University Press, 1994), pp. 127–50.

33. Quoted in Strachey, *Millicent Garrett Fawcett,* p. 186.

34. Butler, *Native Races and the War,* pp. 133–34.

35. "Women's Work and the War," *Englishwoman's Review,* 15 October 1900, p. 230.

36. See Emmeline Pethick Lawrence, *My Part in a Changing World* (London: Victor Gollancz, 1938), pp. 122–24; Frederick Pethick Lawrence, *Fate Has Been Kind* (London: Hutchinson, 1943), pp. 53–61; Henry Woodd Nevinson, *Fire of Life* (London: Camelot Press, 1935), p. 94; Elizabeth Wolstenholme Elmy, manuscript draft of poem published under pseudonym, "Ignota," in *Westminster Review,* Additional Manuscripts

47452, and Elizabeth Wolstenholme Elmy to Harriet McIlquham, 10 February 1900, Additional Manuscripts 47452, in Elizabeth Wolstenholme Elmy Papers, British Library (hereafter Elmy Papers).

37. On the range of possibilities among the Edwardian left, see Samuel Hynes, *The Edwardian Turn of Mind* (Princeton, N.J.: Princeton University Press, 1968), pp. 87–88; on radicals' attempts to unite politics and religion, see Bernard Porter, *Critics of Empire: British Radical Attitudes to Colonialism in Africa, 1895–1914* (London: Macmillan, 1968), pp. 156–68.

38. On Frederick Pethick Lawrence's relationship to the *Echo*, see Pethick Lawrence, *Fate Has Been Kind*, pp. 52–67, and Pethick Lawrence, *My Part in a Changing World*, pp. 122–24. On the *New Age*, see Alvin Sullivan, ed., *British Literary Magazines: The Victorian and Edwardian Age* (Westport, Conn.: Greenwood Press, 1983), 3:250–66.

39. *Echo*, 11 and 29 September 1899.

40. *New Age*, 15 and 29 June 1899.

41. *New Age*, 24 August 1899.

42. *New Age*, 14 September 1899.

43. *New Age*, 6 and 20 July 1899.

44. *New Age*, 14 September 1899.

45. For her influence, see Dora Montefiore, *From a Victorian to a Modern* (London: E. Archer, 1927); E. Sylvia Pankhurst, *The Suffragette Movement: An Intimate Account of Persons and Ideals* (London: Longman, 1931; reprint, London: Virago, 1977); Christabel Pankhurst, *Unshackled: The Story of How We Won the Vote*, ed. F. W. Pethick Lawrence (London: Hutchinson, 1959), and June Hannam and Karen Hunt, *Socialist Women: Britain, 1880s to 1920s* (London: Routledge, 2002).

46. Porter, *Critics of Empire*, pp. 162–63. Hobson's opinions were published first in his reports from South Africa while a correspondent for the *Manchester Guardian* and in the *Ethical World;* his book, *The War in South Africa: Its Causes and Effects*, was published in London in 1900 and exercised great influence on subsequent studies of the war.

47. Dora Montefiore, "Women Uitlanders," *Ethical World*, 14 October 1899, pp. 642–43, reprinted as a pamphlet by the Union of Practical Suffragists (London, 1899).

48. Miss Priestman, "Women and Votes" (London: Union of Practical Suffragists, 1897), in Elmy papers, Additional Manuscripts 47451. See also Holton, *Suffrage Days*, p. 106.

49. Montefiore, *From a Victorian to a Modern*, pp. 72–76.

50. Dora Montefiore, "Shall Women Refuse Their Taxes?" *Woman's Signal*, 17 June 1897, p. 383.

51. Montefiore, *From a Victorian to a Modern*, pp. 72–82.

52. Ibid., pp. 74–76; Pankhurst, *Suffragette Movement*, p. 214. See *Times*, 25 May 1906 and 14 July 1906.

53. The significance of suffragettes' arguments basing citizenship upon women's consent has received scant attention from historians; what analysis has been provided has focused on the question of sexual consent and its relationship to women's representation. See Carole Pateman, "Women and Consent," in her *The Disorder of Women: Democracy, Feminism, and Political Theory* (Stanford, Calif.: Stanford University Press, 1980), pp. 71–89.

54. See, for example, Elizabeth C. Wolstenholme Elmy, "Woman's Franchise: The Need of the Hour" (London: ILP, 1906), p. 12; Emmeline Pethick Lawrence, "The Faith That Is in Us" (London: Woman's Press, 1908); Christabel Pankhurst, "Window Breaking: To One Who Has Suffered" (London: WSPU, 1912–13), reprinted in *Suf-*

frage and the Pankhursts, ed. Jane Marcus (London: Routledge and Kegan Paul, 1987), pp. 183–84; "The Deserters," *Votes for Women,* 5 March 1912, p. 376; W. Lyon Blease, "Concerning the Status of Political Prisoners" (London: National Political Reform League, 1910), pp. 8–9, 15–17; Marion Holmes, "The A.B.C. of Votes for Women" (London: WFL, 1910), p. 1.

55. A point much of the WSPU's early activism strove to make; see Ian Christopher Fletcher, "'A Star Chamber of the Twentieth Century': Suffragettes, Liberals, and the 1908 'Rush the Commons' Case," *Journal of British Studies* 35, no. 4 (1996): 504–30.

56. *New Age,* 6 and 20 July, 3 and 24 August, 2 November 1899.

57. *New Age,* 21 June 1900.

58. Saul Dubow, "Colonial Nationalism, the Milner Kindergarten and the Rise of 'South Africanism,' 1902–10," *History Workshop Journal* 43 (1997): 55–57.

59. Pat Thane, "The British Imperial State and the Construction of National Identities," in *Borderlines: Genders and Identities in War and Peace, 1870–1930,* ed. Billie Melman (New York: Routledge, 1998), pp. 30–32.

60. Fawcett, *Women's Suffrage,* p. 58.

61. Henry Woodd Nevinson, *Essays in Rebellion* (London: James Nisbet, 1913), p. 22; see also James Bryce, *The Hindrances to Good Citizenship* (Oxford: Oxford University Press, 1909).

62. George William Byrt, *John Clifford: A Fighting Free Churchman* (London: Kingsgate Press, 1947).

63. James D. Hunt, *Gandhi and the Nonconformists: Encounters in South Africa* (New Delhi: Promilla, 1986), p. 85; Hunt, *Gandhi in London,* rev. ed. (Springfield, Va.: Nataraj Books, 1993), pp. 55–98.

64. Andrew Chadwick, *Augmenting Democracy: Political Movements and Constitutional Reform During the Rise of Labour, 1900–1924* (Aldershot, Hampshire, England: Ashgate, 1999), p. 6.

65. Duncan Tanner, *Political Change and the Labour Party, 1900–1918* (Cambridge: Cambridge University Press, 1990), pp. 19–43.

66. Thomas James Cobden Sanderson, *The Journals of Thomas James Cobden Sanderson* (London: Richard Cobden Sanderson, 1926), 23 January 1902 and 8 November 1902; 2:17, 39–40.

67. Pankhurst, *Suffragette Movement,* p. 127.

68. Stanton Coit in the *Ethical World,* January 1900, quoted in I. D. MacKillop, *The British Ethical Societies* (Cambridge: Cambridge University Press, 1986), pp. 111–12.

69. See F. W. Pethick Lawrence and Joseph Edwards, eds., *The Reformers' Year Book* (formerly *Labour Annual*) (London: Taylor, Garnett, and Evans, 1903–1909); see also Tierl Thompson, ed., *Dear Girl: The Diaries and Letters of Two Working Women, 1897–1917* (London: Women's Press, 1987).

70. "Women and the Franchise," *Reformers' Year Book,* 1905, p. 148.

71. Karen Hunt, *Equivocal Feminists: The Social Democratic Federation and the Woman Question, 1884–1911* (Cambridge: Cambridge University Press, 1996), p. 161.

72. For two excellent treatments of socialist men and women's struggles with these questions, see Hannam and Hunt, *Socialist Women,* pp. 105–33; and Hunt, *Equivocal Feminists,* pp. 152–84.

73. Florence Balgarnie, "The Women's Suffrage Movement in the Nineteenth Century," in *The Case for Women's Suffrage,* ed. Brougham Villiers [Frederick John Shaw] (London: T. Fisher Unwin, 1907), p. 41; Charlotte Despard, "The Next Step to Adult Suffrage," *Reformers' Year Book,* 1907, p. 153.

74. Brougham Villiers [Frederick John Shaw], "Introduction," in *The Case for Women's Suffrage,* p. 21.

75. Krista Cowman, "'Incipient Toryism'? The Women's Social and Political Union and the Independent Labour Party, 1903–14," *History Workshop Journal* 53 (2002): 129–48; see also June Hannam, "'In the Comradeship of the Sexes Lies the Hope of Progress and Social Regeneration': Women in the West Riding ILP, c. 1800–1914," in *Equal or Different: Women's Politics, 1880–1914,* ed. Jane Rendall (Oxford: Basil Blackwell, 1987), pp. 214–38.

76. Pankhurst, *Unshackled,* p. 49.

77. Although she was formally charged with "spitting at a policeman," Pankhurst noted in retrospect that "it was not a real spit but only, shall we call it, a 'pout,' a perfectly dry purse of the mouth. I could not really have done it, even to get the vote, I think. Anyhow, there was no need, my technical assault was enough" (Pankhurst, *Unshackled,* p. 52). See also Pankhurst, *Suffragette Movement,* pp. 189–92.

CHAPTER 3

1. Andrew Rosen, *"Rise Up, Women!": The Militant Campaign of the Women's Social and Political Union, 1903–1914* (London: Routledge and Kegan Paul, 1974), p. 65.

2. The definitive account of the WSPU remains Rosen, *"Rise Up, Women!"* For the Women's Freedom League, Women's Tax Resistance League, and United Suffragists, see articles by Claire Eustance, Hilary Frances, and Krista Cowman, in *The Women's Suffrage Movement: New Feminist Perspectives,* ed. Maroula Joannou and June Purvis (Manchester: Manchester University Press, 1998), pp. 51–64, 65–76, 77–88. On the Men's Political Union, see Sandra Stanley Holton, "Manliness and Militancy: The Political Protest of Male Suffragists and the Gendering of the 'Suffragette' Identity," in *The Men's Share? Masculinities, Male Support and Women's Suffrage in Britain, 1890–1920,* ed. Angela V. John and Claire Eustance (London: Routledge, 1997), pp. 110–57. On the East London Federation of Suffragettes, see Ian Bullock and Richard Pankhurst, eds., *Sylvia Pankhurst: From Artist to Anti-Fascist* (New York: St. Martin's Press, 1992). On the Independent WSPU and the Suffragettes of the WSPU, see Jacqueline de Vries, "Gendering Patriotism: Emmeline and Christabel Pankhurst and World War One," in *This Working-Day World: Women's Lives and Culture(s) in Britain, 1914–1945,* ed. Sybil Oldfield (London: Taylor and Francis, 1994), p. 79.

3. Leslie Parker Hume, *The National Union of Women's Suffrage Societies, 1897–1914* (New York: Garland, 1982); and Sandra Stanley Holton, *Feminism and Democracy: Women's Suffrage and Reform Politics in Britain, 1900–1918* (Cambridge: Cambridge University Press, 1986).

4. Ian Christopher Fletcher, "'A Star Chamber of the Twentieth Century': Suffragettes, Liberals, and the 1908 'Rush the Commons' Case," *Journal of British Studies* 35, no. 4 (1996): 504–30.

5. David Rubinstein, *Before the Suffragettes: Women's Emancipation in the 1890s* (New York: St. Martin's Press, 1986), pp. 139–47. This was certainly an argument made by contemporaries; see Ethel Hill and Olga Fenton Shafer, *Great Suffragists — and Why: Modern Makers of History* (London: H. J. Drane, 1909), pp. 20–21.

6. Martin Pugh, *The March of the Women: A Revisionist Analysis of the Campaign for Women's Suffrage, 1866–1914* (Oxford: Oxford University Press, 2000), pp. 120–44.

7. Numerous arguments have been advanced for the origins of militancy. See es-

pecially Brian Harrison, "The Act of Militancy: Violence and the Suffragettes, 1904–1914," in his *Peaceable Kingdom: Stability and Change in Modern Britain* (Oxford: Clarendon Press, 1982), pp. 26–81; and Sandra Stanley Holton, "'In Sorrowful Wrath': Suffrage Militancy and the Romantic Feminism of Emmeline Pankhurst," in *British Feminism in the Twentieth Century,* ed. Harold L. Smith (Amherst: University of Massachusetts Press, 1991), pp. 7–24.

8. Hugh Cunningham, *The Challenge of Democracy: Britain, 1832–1918* (London: Longman, 2001), p. 205.

9. Constance Rover, *Women's Suffrage and Party Politics in Britain, 1866–1914* (London: Routledge and Kegan Paul, 1967), pp. 146–67.

10. Pugh, *The March of the Women,* pp. 136–44; Rover, *Women's Suffrage and Party Politics,* pp. 117–42.

11. Mabel Atkinson, "Women and the Revival of Interest in Domestic Politics," in *The Case for Women's Suffrage,* ed. Brougham Villiers [Frederick John Shaw] (London: T. Fisher Unwin, 1907), pp. 122–23, 134.

12. Ibid., p. 128.

13. Homer Lawrence Morris, *Parliamentary Franchise Reform in England from 1885 to 1918* (New York: Columbia University Press, 1921; reprint, New York: AMS Press, 1969), pp. 32–34.

14. Pugh, *The March of the Women,* p. 136.

15. Emmeline Pankhurst, "The Present Position of the Movement," in Villiers, *The Case for Women's Suffrage,* p. 45; see also Morris, *Parliamentary Franchise Reform,* pp. 45–46, 56–59, 69–70.

16. Krista Cowman, "'Incipient Toryism'? The Women's Social and Political Union and the Independent Labour Party, 1903–14," *History Workshop Journal* 53 (2002): 137–39.

17. Holton, *Feminism and Democracy,* p. 76.

18. These were bills introduced by Radical Liberals W. H. Dickinson (1907), Henry York Stanger (1908), and Geoffrey Howard (1909); see Morris, *Parliamentary Franchise Reform,* pp. 42–55.

19. Lisa Tickner, *The Spectacle of Women: Imagery of the Suffrage Campaign 1907–1914* (London: Chatto and Windus, 1987).

20. Patrick Joyce, *Visions of the People: Industrial England and the Question of Class, 1848–1914* (Cambridge: Cambridge University Press, 1991), pp. 27–55; Joyce, *Democratic Subjects: The Self and the Social in Nineteenth-Century England* (Cambridge: Cambridge University Press, 1994), pp. 176–204; James Vernon, *Politics and the People: A Study in English Political Culture, c. 1815–1867* (Cambridge: Cambridge University Press, 1993), pp. 295–330.

21. F. W. Pethick Lawrence, "Preface," *Reformers' Year Book,* 1907, ed. F. W. Pethick Lawrence and Joseph Edwards (London: Taylor, Garnett, and Evans, 1907), pp. 6–7; see also Ronald H. Kidd, "For Freedom's Cause: An Appeal to Working Men" (London: Woman's Press, 1912).

22. Florence Fenwick Miller, "Real Representative Government" (London: WSPU, 1907); Christabel Pankhurst, "The Policy of Revolt," *Votes for Women,* 19 November 1909, p. 120.

23. Maude FitzHerbert, "When Women Are Citizens," *Women's Franchise,* 28 November 1907, p. 251.

24. E. Sylvia Pankhurst, "The Treatment of Political Prisoners," *Votes for Women,* 7

January 1909, p. 252; Christabel Pankhurst, "Suffragettes and Cabinet Ministers," *Votes for Women,* 4 June 1909, p. 756; Anne Cobden Sanderson, letter to the *Times,* 1 October 1909.

25. Annie Kenney's speech from Dock at the Newington Sessions, 26 March 1912, in "Women's Social and Political Emancipation: The Suffragette Fellowship Collection in the Museum of London," Harvester Microfilm (hereafter Suffragette Fellowship Archive), 57.70/10.

26. Elizabeth C. Wolstenholme Elmy, "Women's Franchise: The Need of the Hour" (London: ILP, 1907), p. 3.

27. Emmeline Pethick Lawrence, "The Meaning of the Woman's Movement" (London: Woman's Press, 1907), pp. 6–7; see Charlotte Carmichael Stopes, "The Constitutional Basis of Women's Suffrage" (Edinburgh: Darien Press, 1908), p. 3.

28. Emmeline Pethick Lawrence, "Women or Kaffirs?" *Votes for Women,* 9 July 1909, p. 912.

29. F. W. Pethick Lawrence, "Do Militant Tactics Pay?" *Votes for Women,* 19 November 1908, p. 129.

30. See Catherine Hall, Keith McClelland, and Jane Rendall, *Defining the Victorian Nation: Class, Race, Gender and the Reform Act of 1867* (Cambridge: Cambridge University Press, 2000), p. 221; Joyce, *Democratic Subjects,* p. 134.

31. WFL General Election Leaflet, No. 5, "Who Are the People?" in Suffragette Fellowship Archive, 50.82/557i; also in Suffragette Fellowship Archive: NWSPU, "What Liberal Statesmen say about Militant Action," 50.82/622; WSPU, "Manifesto," 50.82/549. See also Chrystal MacMillan, "The Struggle for Political Liberty" (London: Woman's Press, 1909), pp. 1, 2, 12; Alison Neilans, "Ballot Box Protest: Defence at Old Bailey" (London: WFL, 1910), pp. 8–9.

32. WFL General Election Leaflet No. 6, "What About Representative Government?" Suffragette Fellowship Archive, 50.82/557j.

33. Emmeline Pethick Lawrence, "The Will of the People," *Votes for Women,* 16 July 1908, p. 312.

34. F. E. M. Macaulay, "Women Demonstrators of the Past," *Votes for Women,* 8 October 1908, p. 21.

35. Helena Normanton, "Magna Carta and Women," *Englishwoman,* 26, no. 77 (May 1915), p. 10.

36. MacMillan, "Struggle for Political Liberty," pp. 5, 9; Neilans, "Ballot Box Protest," p. 6.

37. Emmeline Pethick Lawrence, "The New Crusade" (London: NWSPU, 1907), p. 8; J. Keir Hardie, "Radicals and Reform" (Manchester: National Labour Press, 1912), p. 1.

38. WFL General Election Leaflet No. 3, "Why the Lords Threw Out the Budget," in Suffragette Fellowship Archive, 50.82/557g; see also H. N. Brailsford, "Militant Suffragists in Newcastle," *Newcastle Daily Chronicle,* 11 October 1909.

39. "Fossils," *Women's Franchise,* 5 March 1908, p. 419.

40. Christabel Pankhurst, "Shall This Country Lead the Way? Mr. Asquith's Opportunity," *Votes for Women,* 3 September 1908, p. 427.

41. Teresa Billington Greig, misc. manuscript notes, n.d., Teresa Billington Grieg papers, box 399, "ws misc," the Women's Library.

42. Helen Taylor, "The Claim of Englishwomen to the Suffrage Constitutionally Considered," *Westminster Review* (1867); reprinted in *Before the Vote Was Won: Arguments*

for and Against Women's Suffrage, ed. Jane Lewis (London: Routledge and Kegan Paul, 1987), pp. 24, 36–37.

43. Marion Holmes, "The A.B.C. of Votes for Women" (London: WFL, 1910), p. 11; Charlotte Despard, "Woman in the Nation" (London: WFL, 1910); Harriet McIlquham, "The Enfranchisement of Women: an Ancient Right, a Modern Need" (Congleton, England: WEU, 1891), pp. 5–8; Charlotte Carmichael Stopes, *British Freewomen: Their Historical Privilege* (London: Swann Sonnenschein, 1894), pp. 136–37; Millicent Garrett Fawcett, "Home and Politics: An Address Delivered at Toynbee Hall and Elsewhere" (London: Women's Printing Society, 1889), pp. 2–3.

44. Ian Christopher Fletcher, "'Prosecutions . . . Are Always Risky Business': Labor, Liberals, and the 1912 'Don't Shoot' Prosecutions," *Albion* 28, no. 2 (1996): 251–78.

45. MacMillan, "Struggle for Political Liberty," p. 4.

46. WFL, "Women and the Law Courts" (London: WFL, 1907).

47. WFL, "Boycott the Census" (1911), Suffragette Fellowship Archive, 50.82/461.

48. Vida Goldstein to editor of *Daily Telegraph* (Sydney), 26 November 1911 (in Vida Goldstein, box 67, 7/VDG, the Women's Library). See also M.L., "Tactics," *Women's Franchise,* 27 February 1908, p. 407; Christabel Pankhurst, "Political Notes," *Votes for Women,* 9 July 1908, p. 297; Teresa Billington Greig, "Suffragist Tactics: Past and Present" (London: WFL, 1909), p. 12; Hardie, "Radicals and Reform," p. 4.

49. Christabel Pankhurst, "The Value of Militant Methods," *Votes for Women,* 24 September 1908, p. 473.

50. Christabel Pankhurst, "The Title Deeds of Political Liberty," *Votes for Women,* 10 September 1908, p. 441.

51. Robert F. Cholmeley, "Women's Suffrage: The Demand and Its Meaning" (London: Woman Citizen Society, 1909), p. 5.

52. Laurence Housman, "The Physical Force Fallacy" (London: The Women's Press, 1912), p. 4.

53. Clipping from *Eastbourne Chronicle,* dated 29 May 1909, in Maude Arncliffe Sennett, vol. 7 (59), British Library. See also Holmes, "The A.B.C. of Votes for Women," p. 11; Billington Greig, "Suffragist Tactics," p. 9.

54. H. N. Brailsford, "Milestones in the Movement," *Votes for Women,* 25 February 1910, p. 341.

55. Here, I draw upon Vernon, *Politics and the People,* in which he argues that competing groups in nineteenth-century Britain articulated their own understanding of the public political sphere through the discourse of popular constitutionalism (p. 7). See also Anna Clark, "Gender, Class and the Constitution: Franchise Reform in England, 1832–1928," in *Re-reading the Constitution: New Narratives in the Political History of England's Long Nineteenth Century,* ed. James Vernon (Cambridge: Cambridge University Press, 1996), pp. 239–53. That such a reading had racialized implications is clear; see Antoinette Burton, *Burdens of History: British Feminists, Indian Women, and Imperial Culture, 1865–1915* (Chapel Hill: University of North Carolina Press, 1994), pp. 52–59. Militancy incorporated, rather than challenged, the narratives of constitutionalism. For a different view, see Sandra Stanley Holton, "British Freewomen: National Identity, Constitutionalism and Languages of Race in Early Suffragist Histories," in *Radical Femininity: Women's Self-Representation in the Public Sphere,* ed. Eileen Janes Yeo (Manchester: Manchester University Press, 1998), pp. 163–67.

56. The following treat this protest: E. Sylvia Pankhurst, *The Suffragette: The History of the Women's Militant Suffrage Movement, 1905–1910* (London: Gray and Hancock,

1911), pp. 260-321; Constance Lytton, *Prisons and Prisoners: Some Personal Experiences* (London: William Heinemann, 1914, reprint, London: Virago, 1988), pp. 18-30; Emmeline Pankhurst, *My Own Story* (London: Eveleigh Nash, 1914), pp. 116-30; E. Sylvia Pankhurst, *The Suffragette Movement: An Intimate Account of Persons and Ideals* (London: Longman, 1931; reprint, London, Virago, 1977), pp. 288-93; Emmeline Pethick Lawrence, *My Part in a Changing World* (London: Victor Gollancz, 1938), pp. 194-207; Frederick Pethick Lawrence, *Fate Has Been Kind* (London: Hutchinson, 1943), pp. 79-80; Christabel Pankhurst, *Unshackled: The Story of How We Won the Vote* (London: Hutchinson, 1959), pp. 102-12.

57. *Times,* 14 October 1908.

58. Ibid.

59. Pethick Lawrence, *My Part in a Changing World,* p. 205.

60. See Rosen, *"Rise Up, Women!"* pp. 109-17; Holton, *Feminism and Democracy,* p. 46; Fletcher, "'Star Chamber,'" 506-7.

61. F. W. Pethick Lawrence, "The Trial of the Suffragist Leaders" (1908), in *Suffrage and the Pankhursts,* ed. Jane Marcus (London: Routledge and Kegan Paul, 1987), p. 58.

62. Rosen, *"Rise Up, Women!"* p. 111; on the WFL's invocation of 13 Charles II (1661), see "The Right to Petition. Our Statutory Rights" (London: WFL, 1909), in Suffragette Fellowship Archive, 50.82/589.

63. *Times,* 22 October 1908.

64. Christabel Pankhurst, "The Militant Methods of the N.W.S.P.U. (Being the Verbatim Report of a Speech of Christabel Pankhurst, at the St. James' Hall, on October 15th, 1908)," reprinted in Marcus, *Suffrage and the Pankhursts,* p. 48.

65. Pankhurst, "Militant Methods," p. 49. For a provocative and innovative discussion of the rhetorical strategies of the WSPU in the later years of militancy, see Cheryl Jorgensen-Earp, *The Transfiguring Sword: The Just War of the Women's Social and Political Union* (Tuscaloosa: University of Alabama Press, 1997).

66. Rohan McWilliam, "Radicalism and Popular Culture: The Tichborne Case and the Politics of 'Fair Play,' 1867-1886," and Duncan Tanner, "Ideological Debate in Edwardian Labour Politics: Radicalism, Revisionism and Socialism," both in *Currents of Radicalism: Popular Radicalism, Organised Labour and Party Politics in Britain, 1850-1914,* ed. Eugenio F. Biagini and Alistair J. Reid (Cambridge: Cambridge University Press, 1991), pp. 44-64, 271-293.

67. Rosen, *"Rise Up, Women!"* pp. 110-117.

68. WFL, *Report for the Year 1908, and the Fourth Annual Conference* (London: WFL, 1909), pp. 10-11 (hereafter *AR1908*). See also *Times,* 29 and 30 October 1908.

69. Jane Marcus, "Rereading Suffrage and the Pankhursts," in Marcus, *Suffrage and the Pankhursts,* p. 9. See also Claire Eustance, "Protests from Behind the Grille: Gender and the Transformation of Parliament, 1867-1918," *Parliamentary History* 16, no. 1 (1997): 107-26.

70. Teresa Billington-Greig, "The 'Grille' Protest," *Women's Franchise,* 5 November 1908, p. 211.

71. *Times,* 29 October 1908.

72. *AR1908,* pp. 10-11; *Report from the Select Committee, 1908, on House of Commons (Admission of Strangers),* PP1908 (HC371) ix.1, p. 23; Norman Wilding and Philip Laundy, *An Encyclopedia of Parliament* (London: Cassell, 1968), pp. 415-16.

73. Burton, *Burdens of History,* pp. 63-96. The phrase comes from Billington-Greig, "The 'Grille' Protest," p. 211.

74. Barbara Green, *Spectacular Confessions: Autobiography, Performative Activism, and the Sites of Suffrage, 1905–1938* (New York: St. Martin's Press, 1997), p. 7.

75. The Grille Protest occasioned a formal breach between the WFL and the NUWSS, the latter using the October 1908 protest as justification for ending its affiliation with *Women's Franchise,* the newspaper carrying news of suffragist activism between 1907 and 1909. The NUWSS continued to distance itself from the methods of the WFL in public statements and letters to members of parliament; see *Women's Franchise,* 21 January 1909, and *Times,* 12 and 20 November 1908.

76. "Women's Suffrage," *Englishwoman's Review,* 15 October 1909, p. 247.

77. "Women's Suffrage," *Englishwoman's Review,* 15 January 1909, pp. 34–37, and Millicent Garrett Fawcett, *Women's Suffrage: A Short History of a Great Movement* (London: T. C. And E. C. Jack, 1912; reprint, New York: Source Book Press, 1970), p. 61; F. W. Pethick Lawrence, "Elements of the Woman Suffrage Demand," *Votes for Women,* 7 May 1909, p. 623.

78. *Times,* 13 October 1908.

79. *Times,* 13 October 1908; WFL, *AR1908,* p. 11.

80. *Times,* 26 June 1909.

81. Rosen, *"Rise Up, Women!"* p. 118.

82. "The Writing on the Wall," *Votes for Women,* 9 July 1909, p. 905.

83. "The Eve of the Deputation," *Votes for Women,* 2 July 1909, pp. 873.

84. *Times,* 25 June 1909.

85. *Times,* 30 June 1909.

86. *Daily Chronicle,* 30 June 1909.

87. *Times,* 30 June 1909.

88. *Times,* 1 July 1909.

89. *Daily Chronicle,* 1 July 1909.

90. *Daily Telegraph,* 1 July 1909.

91. *Times,* 1 July 1909.

92. *Daily Telegraph,* 1 July 1909.

93. "The Besieged House," *Women's Franchise,* 8 July 1909, p. 673. The WFL's petition is found in Suffragette Fellowship Archive, 50.82/588, pp. 12–13, and *Women's Franchise,* 15 July 1909, p. 686.

94. *Times,* 6 July 1909; WFL, "Why We Petition the King," in Suffragette Fellowship Archive, 50.82/587.

95. "'The Humble Petition and Advice,'" *Women's Franchise,* 15 July 1909, pp. 685–86. At that meeting, Gladstone informed the women that it was "a new point of law" to argue for the king's acceptance of a deputation under the Act of 1661; see the transcript of this meeting in the Home Office files, Public Record Office (hereafter PRO): HO 45/10338/139199/63a. See also correspondence between the Home Office and the WFL, dated 23 July, 3 and 9 August 1909, PRO: HO 45/10338/139199/64 and /67.

96. *Times,* 10, 13, 17, and 24 July 1909.

97. The longest a single deputation waited was on 14 July, when the women remained on the pavement from 2:50 P.M. until the House rose the next day at 9:15 A.M.; *Report of the Women's Freedom League for the Year 1909 and of the Fifth Annual Conference* (London, 1910), 45.

98. *Times,* 10 July 1909.

99. Ibid.

100. The petition was a mainstay of early-nineteenth-century radical protest; see James A. Epstein, *Radical Expression: Political Language, Ritual, and Symbol in England, 1790–1850* (New York: Oxford University Press, 1994), p. 15.

101. K.M., "History-Making and Magisterial-Heckling," *Women's Franchise*, 22 July 1909, p. 698; "The Deputation of June 29," *Votes for Women*, 2 July 1909, pp. 869–70.

102. Tickner, *Spectacle of Women*, pp. 213–26.

103. M. Nelson, "The Siege," *Women's Franchise*, 29 July 1909, p. 709; M. Nelson, "The Siege," *Women's Franchise*, 12 August 1909, p. 727.

104. A key component of WFL rhetoric was the significance of women's roles within the family; see Despard, "Woman in the Nation"; Eunice Murray, "Why I Want the Vote," *Vote*, 2 April 1910, p. 272.

105. See Tickner, *Spectacle of Women*, p. 226.

106. Wells described the women of the picket as "women of all sorts, though of course the independent worker-class predominated," in *The New Machiavelli* (London: John Lane, 1911), pp. 430–31.

107. On the gendering of suffrage militancy, see Holton, "Manliness and Militancy," pp. 110–34. On the gendering of citizenship, see Anna Clark, "Manhood, Woman-hood, and the Politics of Class in Britain, 1790–1845," and Keith McClelland, "Rational and Respectable Men: Gender, the Working Class, and Citizenship in Britain, 1850–1867," both in *Gender and Class in Modern Europe*, ed. Laura L. Frader and Sonya O. Rose (Ithaca, N. Y.: Cornell University Press, 1997), pp. 263–79, 280–93.

108. See WFL handbills from the "Siege" in Suffragette Fellowship Archive, including "Is Political Agitation a Crime?" (50.82/557d); "An Appeal to the Voters," (50.82/557k); and "Who Are the People?" (50.82/557i).

109. "The Besieged House," *Women's Franchise*, 8 July 1909, p. 673.

110. "Humble Petition and Advice," *Women's Franchise*, 15 July 1909, p. 685.

111. "Correspondence with the Prime Minister," *Women's Franchise*, 19 August 1909, p. 735.

112. *Times*, 19, 20, and 28 August 1909.

113. T. M. Healy, "Defence at Bow Street" (London: WFL, 1909), p. 1.

114. Ibid., pp. 2–4, 10–11.

115. *Times*, 4 September 1909.

116. The two women remained at large until their appeal was heard; "The Women and the Case," *Women's Franchise*, 9 September 1909, p. 765.

117. *Times*, 2 December 1909; 15 January 1910.

118. See Helen Blackburn, *Women's Suffrage: A Record of the Women's Movement in the British Isles with Biographical Sketches of Miss Becker* (London: Williams and Norgate, 1902), pp. 82–88.

119. Laurence Housman, "A Question for 'Constitutionals,'" *Votes for Women*, 24 February 1911, p. 335; Christabel Pankhurst, "Title Deeds of Political Liberty," *Votes for Women*, 10 September 1908, p. 441.

120. Mrs. Darent Harrison, "John Hampden" (London: WTRL, 1913), p. 2.

121. "WSPU," *Women's Franchise*, 14 November 1907, p. 227.

122. "No Vote—No Tax," *Women's Franchise*, 19 December 1907, p. 287.

123. "The Sinews of War—An Appeal," *Women's Franchise*, 20 February 1908, p. 392.

124. Charlotte Despard, "Women Pay the Piper, Men Call the Tune," *Women's Franchise*, 16 January 1908, p. 335.

125. Hilary Frances, "'Pay the Piper, Call the Tune!': The Women's Tax Resistance League," in Joannou and Purvis, *The Women's Suffrage Movement*, p. 69.

126. Laurence Housman, "No Truce to Tax-Resistance," *Votes for Women,* 11 August 1911, p. 735.

127. Margaret Kineton Parkes, "Why We Resist Our Taxes" (London: WTRL, 1911).

128. Edith How Martyn to Miss Strachey, London Society for Women's Suffrage, 20 February 1911, in LSWS, box 154 (4), the Women's Library.

129. "No Votes for Women—No Census" (London: WFL, 1911).

130. Housman, *Unexpected Years,* pp. 242–44. See also Charlotte Despard to Mrs. Saul Solomon, 9 February 1911, in Fawcett Autograph Collection, Militants (20D). For WSPU instructions on using the census form to register protest, see Emily Wilding Davison papers, IND/EWD/C7/1/C/7/1, Box 554, the Women's Library.

131. *Times,* 7 and 14 April 1911.

132. See Laurence Housman, "News from No-Man's Land," *Vote,* 4 March 1911, p. 223; Laurence Housman, "Official Blackmail," *Vote,* 1 April 1911, p. 271.

133. Burton, *Burdens of History,* p. 33.

CHAPTER 4

1. Christabel Pankhurst, "The Legal Disabilities of Women," in *The Case for Women's Suffrage,* ed. Brougham Villiers [Frederick John Shaw] (London: T. Fisher Unwin, 1907), pp. 84–86.

2. Suffragists and suffragettes alike made this argument; for the suffragist case, see Bertha Mason, *The Story of the Women's Suffrage Movement* (London: Sharratt and Hughes, 1912), p. 40.

3. See Lee Holcombe, *Wives and Property: Reform of the Married Women's Property Law in Nineteenth-Century England* (Toronto: University of Toronto Press, 1983).

4. Ian Christopher Fletcher, "'Prosecutions . . . Are Always Risky Business': Labor, Liberals, and the 1912 'Don't Shoot' Prosecutions," *Albion* 28, no. 2 (1996): 251–78.

5. Jane Rendall, "Who Was Lily Maxwell? Women's Suffrage and Manchester Politics, 1866–1867," in *Votes for Women,* ed. June Purvis and Sandra Stanley Holton (London: Routledge, 2000), p. 57.

6. Ibid., p. 75; E. Sylvia Pankhurst, *The Suffragette Movement: An Intimate Account of Persons and Ideals* (London: Longman, 1931; reprint, London: Virago, 1977), pp. 37–42; Helen Blackburn, *Women's Suffrage: A Record of the Women's Movement in the British Isles with Biographical Sketches of Miss Becker* (London: Williams and Norgate, 1902), pp. 72–74.

7. Pankhurst, *Suffragette Movement,* p. 42; see Blackburn, *Women's Suffrage,* Appendix E, for locations, numbers of women's claims, and revising barristers' responses, pp. 258–61.

8. Blackburn, *Women's Suffrage,* pp. 82–83.

9. Justice Willes, Master of the Rolls, quoted in Pankhurst, *Suffragette Movement,* p. 45.

10. See, for example, E. Sylvia Pankhurst, "The History of the Suffrage Movement. Chapter II.—Decisions of the Courts," *Votes for Women,* November 1907, pp. 24–25; J. Keir Hardie, "The Citizenship of Women" (London: ILP, 1906), pp. 9–10.

11. Charlotte Carmichael Stopes, *The Sphere of "Man" in Relation to That of "Woman" in the Constitution* (London: T. Fisher Unwin, 1907), p. 11.

12. Ibid., 5.

13. Charlotte Carmichael Stopes, "The Constitutional Basis of Women's Suffrage" (Edinburgh: Darien Press, 1908), p. 9.

14. Emmeline Pethick Lawrence, "Women's Fight for the Vote" (London: Woman's Press, 1910), p. 9; J. Keir Hardie, "The Labour Party and Women's Suffrage" (London: Central Society for Women's Suffrage, 1912), p. 4; E. Sylvia Pankhurst, "The History of the Suffrage Movement. III.—From 1868 to 1871," *Votes for Women,* December 1907, p. 40.

15. Pankhurst, *Suffragette Movement,* pp. 42–47.

16. Quoted in Ray Strachey, *"The Cause": A Short History of the Women's Movement in Great Britain* (London: G. Bell and Sons, 1928; reprint, London: Virago, 1978), p. 116.

17. Pamphlet literature of the period is strewn with references to these cases; see Hardie, "Citizenship of Women," p. 114; Charlotte Carmichael Stopes, *British Freewomen: Their Historical Privilege* (London: Swann Sonnenschein, 1894), pp. 170–76; Annie Chapman and Mary Wallis Chapman, *The Status of Women Under the English Law* (London: G. Routledge, 1909), p. 67.

18. Harriet McIlquham, "The Enfranchisement of Women: An Ancient Right, a Modern Need" (Congleton, England: WEU, 1891), p. 15.

19. The origins of this campaign are not clear; the court case may have originated with the 1902 presentation of a women's suffrage petition to the House of Commons on behalf of a deputation representing women graduates of several universities. Women graduates of the Universities of London, Victoria, Durham, Edinburgh, Glasgow, Aberdeen, St. Andrews, Wales, and Royal University of Ireland argued that they were qualified to vote on account of their university educations, and they urged the necessity of women's suffrage because children's education rested largely in women's hands. Sir Robert Fitzgerald presided over the 20 March 1902 deputation (North of England Society for Women's Suffrage *Annual Report* 1902, Manchester Central Library, reel 3).

20. Scottish Women Graduates Committee, "Report of the Scottish Women Graduates Appeal in the House of Lords" (London: Woman Citizen Publishing Society, 1908), p. 1 (hereafter SWGA).

21. *Manchester Guardian,* 11 November 1908.

22. Printed appeal, Committee of Women Graduates of Scottish Universities, January 1906. In Fawcett Autograph Collection, Women's Suffrage (1B2).

23. Amelia Hutchison Stirling, "Precedent *v.* Principle," *Englishwoman's Review,* 16 April 1906, pp. 74–77.

24. SWGA, p. 4.

25. J. Chrystal MacMillan, "The Scottish Women Graduates' Lawsuit," *Votes for Women,* December 1907, p. 34; *Times,* 11 November 1908.

26. *Englishwoman's Review,* 15 January 1908, pp. 23–24.

27. "Progress of Women. The Scottish Graduates," *Votes for Women,* 1 October 1908, p. 7. Appellants were Margaret Nairn, M.A., Edinburgh; Frances Simson, M.A., Edinburgh; Chrystal MacMillan, M.A., B.Sc., Edinburgh; Francis Helen Melville, M.A., St. Andrew's; Elsie Inglis, B.M., M.S., Edinburgh; see "The Case of the Scottish Graduates," *Votes for Women,* 19 November 1908.

28. J. Chrystal MacMillan to Eunice Murray, 19 November 1908, Fawcett Autograph Collection, Women's Suffrage (1B2).

29. SGWA, preface.

30. *Manchester Guardian,* 11 November 1908.

31. SWGA, p. 13; *Times,* 11 November 1908.

32. SWGA, pp. 20–21.

33. Ibid., p. 22.

34. Ibid., pp. 27–28.

35. Ibid., p. 33.

36. *Englishwoman's Review,* 15 January 1908, p. 3.

37. Miss J. Chrystal MacMillan (Honorary Secretary and Treasurer, Committee of Women Graduates of Scottish Universities) to Elizabeth Wolstenholme Elmy, 9 March 1906, Elmy papers, Additional Manuscripts 47454.

38. *Manchester Guardian,* 13 November 1908.

39. *Times,* 11 and 13 November 1908.

40. *Manchester Guardian,* 11 November 1908.

41. Ibid.

42. *Times,* 11 December 1908; see also "The Scottish Graduates' Case," *Votes for Women,* 17 December 1908, p. 196.

43. SWGA, pp. 52–57; *Manchester Guardian,* 11 December 1908.

44. *Times,* 11 December 1908; "The Scottish Graduates' Case," p. 196.

45. Elizabeth C. Wolstenholme Elmy used the phrase in correspondence to *Votes for Women,* 24 December 1908, p. 210, as did Christabel Pankhurst, "The Legal Disabilities of Women," in Villiers, *Case for Women's Suffrage,* p. 86.

46. Robin West, *Narrative, Authority, and Law* (Ann Arbor: University of Michigan Press, 1993), pp. 93–94.

47. Stefan Collini, *Public Moralists: Political Thought and Intellectual Life in Britain 1850–1930* (Oxford: Clarendon Press, 1991), p. 257.

48. Florence Fenwick Miller, "Real Representative Government" (London: WSPU, 1907).

49. West, *Narrative, Authority, and Law,* p. 3.

50. Collini, *Public Moralists,* p. 257.

51. Chrystal MacMillan, "The Struggle for Political Liberty" (London: Women's Press, 1909), pp. 14–15.

52. *Votes for Women,* 24 December 1908, p. 210.

53. E. Sylvia Pankhurst, *The Suffragette: The History of the Women's Militant Suffrage Movement, 1905–1910* (London: Gray and Hancock, 1911), pp. 358–59.

54. "The Appeal of the Scottish Women Graduates," *Englishwoman's Review,* 15 January 1908, pp. 3–4.

55. Millicent Garrett Fawcett, *Women's Suffrage: A Short History of a Great Movement* (London: T. C. and E. C. Jack, 1912; reprint, New York: Source Book Press, 1970), p. 11.

56. Teresa Billington Greig, misc. ms notes, box 399, the Women's Library.

57. West, *Narrative, Authority, and Law,* pp. 93–94; Anne Bottomley and Joanne Conaghan, "Feminist Theory and Legal Strategy," in their *Feminist Theory and Legal Strategy* (Oxford: Blackwell, 1993), pp. 1–7.

58. Holcombe, *Wives and Property,* p. 218; Mary Lyndon Shanley, *Feminism, Marriage, and the Law in Victorian England* (Princeton, N.J.: Princeton University Press, 1989), p. 8.

59. Barbara Leigh Smith Bodichon, "A Brief Summary, in Plain Language, of the Most Important Laws Concerning Women: Together with a Few Observations Thereon" (1854), reprinted in *Barbara Leigh Smith Bodichon and the Langham Place Group,* ed. Candida Ann Lacey (London: Routledge and Kegan Paul, 1986), pp. 23–35; Frances Power Cobbe, "Criminals, Idiots, Women, and Minors. Is the Classification Sound? A Discussion on the Laws Concerning the Property of Married Women" (Manchester: A. Ireland, 1869).

60. See W. G. Earengey, "Woman Under the Law" (London: WFL, 1909); J. W. F. Jacques, "Women: And the Unfair Position They Occupy at the Present Time from a Legal Point of View" (London: NUWSS, 1912); Sydney Herbert Mellone, "The Position and Claims of Women: A Historical Survey with Reference to Present Conditions" (London: Woman's Press, 1909); Frederick Pethick Lawrence, "Is the English Law Unjust to Women?" (London: Woman's Press, 1909); Henry H. Schloesser, "The Legal Status of Women in England" (London: Woman's Press, 1907).

61. John notes that 10 percent of the first three hundred members of the Men's League for Women's Suffrage were lawyers; Angela V. John, "Between the Cause and the Courts: The Curious Case of Cecil Chapman," in *A Suffrage Reader: Charting Directions in British Suffrage History,* ed. Claire Eustance, Joan Ryan, and Laura Ugolini (London: Leicester University Press, 2000), pp. 146–47. Of the pamphlet writers mentioned above, Frederick Pethick Lawrence and Henry Schloesser were barristers; J. W. F. Jacques first published his pamphlet in the proceedings and resolutions of the 36th Provincial Meeting of the Law Society, 1911. Other types of professional expertise were acknowledged as well; Sydney Herbert Mellone, for example, held the M.A. and the D.Sc. and had been an examiner in philosophy in the Universities of St. Andrews, Edinburgh, and London.

62. Emmeline Pethick Lawrence, "The Written Law," *Votes for Women,* 21 July 1911, p. 691.

63. Arthur Rackham Cleveland, *Woman Under the English Law: From the Landing of the Saxons to the Present Time* (London: Hurst and Blackett, 1896), p. v.

64. See, for example, Earengey, "Woman Under the Law," and Jacques, "Women."

65. Rev. F. Lewis Donaldson, "The Religion of Women's Suffrage" (London: Central Society for Women's Suffrage, 1905), p. 4.

66. Schloesser, "Legal Status of Women in England," p. 1.

67. Anon., "Woman's Position Under Laws Made by Man" (London: Women's National Anti-Suffrage League, 1908).

68. Margaret Wynne Nevinson, "Woman—the Spoilt Child of the Law," *Vote,* 2 April 1910, p. 273.

69. Cicely Hamilton, "Legal Privileges of Married Women," *Women's Franchise,* 10 October 1907, p. 168.

70. Pethick Lawrence, "Is the English Law Unjust to Women?"

71. See *Manchester Guardian,* 22 June 1906; see also MEPO 2/1016/15, 23 June 1906; 2/2016/12 and /18, 26 June 1906; and HO 45/10345/141956, PRO.

72. D Division Metropolitan Police, 21 June 1906, MEPO 2/1016/11–14; Wontner & Sons, Solicitors, to Chief Clerk, Metropolitan Police, 5 July 1906, MEPO 2/1016/25–28; Billington's statement appears also in HO 45/10345/141956/3, 23 June 1906, PRO.

73. Those arrested were Mary Gawthorpe, Emmeline Pethick Lawrence, Annie Kenney, Dora Montefiore, Adela Pankhurst, Teresa Billington, Edith How Martyn, Irene Fenwick Miller, Minnie Baldock, and Anne Cobden Sanderson; *Manchester Guardian,* 25 October 1906.

74. *Manchester Guardian,* 25 October 1906; see also "Women and Women's Work," in *The Reformers' Year Book,* ed. F. W. Pethick Lawrence and Joseph Edwards (London: Taylor, Garnett, and Evans, 1907), pp. 149–50.

75. Inspector Jarvis reported that "each of them denied the right of his Worship to try their case because they had no vote and consequently no voice in making the laws

and elected to go to prison." Cannon Row, A Division, 24 October 1906, MEPO 2/1016/32–34, PRO.

76. Wontner and Sons to Chief Clerk, Metropolitan Police Office, New Scotland Yard, 25 October 1906, MEPO 2/1016/35–36, PRO.

77. WFL, "Women and the Law Courts" (London: WFL, 1907).

78. *Manchester Guardian,* 15 November 1907.

79. "Police Court Protests," *Women's Franchise,* 21 November 1907, p. 239; *Manchester Guardian* 15 November 1907.

80. Circular letter, marked "private and confidential," from Edith How Martyn and Teresa Billington Greig, 17 November 1907, in "Women's Social and Political Emancipation: The Suffragette Fellowship Collection in the Museum of London," Harvester Microfilm, reel 2, group D, vol. III, p. 13.

81. Unattributed newspaper article, 25 November 1907, Maude Arncliffe Sennett, vol. 2 (31), British Library; see also *Manchester Guardian,* 25 November 1907.

82. Mary Phillips, "Woman's Point of View," *Forward,* 30 November 1907, p. 8.

83. "At Greenwich Police Court," *Women's Franchise,* 28 November 1907, p. 253; see also *Manchester Guardian,* 25 November 1907.

84. *Manchester Guardian,* 15 November 1907.

85. "Women's Parliament and the House of Commons," *Votes for Women,* March 1908, pp. 82–83.

86. James A. Epstein, *Radical Expression: Political Language, Ritual, and Symbol in England, 1790–1850* (New York: Oxford University Press, 1994), pp. 32–33. On trials as protest and performance, see Susan F. Hirsch and Mindie Lazarus-Black, "Performance and Paradox: Exploring Law's Role in Hegemony and Resistance," in their *Contested States: Law, Hegemony, and Resistance* (New York: Routledge, 1994), p. 14.

87. Charlotte Despard, "President's Address" (March 1913), from *Report of the Women's Freedom League for the Year 1912 and of the Eighth Annual Conference* (London: WFL, 1913), p. 7.

88. Ian Christopher Fletcher, "'A Star Chamber of the Twentieth Century': Suffragettes, Liberals, and the 1908 'Rush the Commons' Case," *Journal of British Studies* 35, no. 4 (1996): 504–30.

89. Emmeline Pethick Lawrence, *My Part in a Changing World* (London: Victor Gollancz, 1938), p. 209.

90. See the *Times, Manchester Guardian, Daily Mirror, Daily Telegraph,* 22–26 October 1908.

91. *Daily Telegraph,* 22 October 1908.

92. *Daily Telegraph,* 26 October 1908.

93. *Daily Telegraph,* 22 October 1908.

94. *Daily Telegraph,* 26 October 1908.

95. *Daily Telegraph,* 30 October 1908.

96. "At Bow Street," *Votes for Women,* 5 March 1909, p. 406.

97. *Manchester Guardian,* 26 February 1909.

98. *Daily Telegraph,* 1 November 1909.

99. William Grantham to HG, 25 November 1909, HO 144/1047/185574/13, PRO.

100. Cheryl Jorgensen-Earp characterizes the trial as "truly the centerpiece of the militant movement," in *Speeches of the Militant Suffragettes* (Cranbury, N.J.: Associated University Presses, 1999), p. 150.

101. *Times*, 15 May 1912.

102. *Daily Chronicle*, 16 May 1912.

103. *Daily Chronicle*, 17 May 1912.

104. *Daily Chronicle*, 18 May 1912.

105. Ibid.

106. *Manchester Guardian*, 22 May 1912.

107. *Manchester Guardian*, 16 May 1912.

108. *Standard*, 17 May 1912.

109. *Standard*, 18 May 1912.

110. *Standard*, 21 May 1912.

111. *Times*, 15 May 1912.

112. *Standard*, 22 May 1912.

113. *Standard*, 17 May 1912.

114. *Standard*, 22 May 1912.

115. *Standard*, 21 May 1912.

116. *Standard*, 22 May 1912.

117. *Standard*, 18 May 1912.

118. Andrew Rosen, *"Rise Up, Women!": The Militant Campaign of the Women's Social and Political Union, 1903–1914* (Routledge and Kegan Paul, 1974), p. 166.

119. *Standard*, 23 May 1912.

120. "Introduction," *Suffrage Speeches from the Dock (Conspiracy Trial, Old Bailey, May 15th–22nd, 1912)* (London: WSPU, 1912), p. 2.

CHAPTER 5

1. Joan Wallach Scott, "'A Woman Who Has Only Paradoxes to Offer': Olympe de Gouges Claims Rights for Women," in *Rebel Daughters: Women and the French Revolution*, ed. Sara E. Melzer and Leslie W. Rabine (New York: Oxford University Press, 1992), p. 102.

2. Emmeline Pankhurst, "Victory Is Assured," *Suffragette*, 13 February 1914, p. 397.

3. See Wendy Parkins, "Protesting Like a Girl: Embodiment, Dissent and Feminist Agency," *Feminist Theory* 1, no. 1 (2000): 59–78; Caroline Howlett, "Writing on the Body? Representation and Resistance in British Suffragette Accounts of Forcible Feeding," *Genders* 23 (1996): 3–41.

4. *Votes for Women*, 16 July 1909.

5. Andrew Rosen, *"Rise Up, Women!": The Militant Campaign of the Women's Social and Political Union, 1903–1914* (London: Routledge and Kegan Paul, 1974), pp. 123–24, 191–93.

6. Most notably, Constance Lytton, *Prisons and Prisoners: Some Personal Experiences* (London: William Heinemann, 1914; reprint, London: Virago, 1988).

7. Mary Jean Corbett, *Representing Femininity: Middle-Class Subjectivity in Victorian and Edwardian Women's Autobiographies* (New York: Oxford University Press, 1992); Jane Marcus, "The Asylums of Antaeus: Women, War, and Madness—Is There a Feminist Fetishism?" in *The New Historicism*, ed. H. Aram Veeser (New York: Routledge, 1989); Marcus, "Rereading Suffrage and the Pankhursts," in *Suffrage and the Pankhursts*, ed. Jane Marcus (London: Routledge and Kegan Paul, 1987), pp. 1–17; Barbara Green, *Spectacular Confessions: Autobiography, Performative Activism, and the Sites of Suffrage, 1905–1938* (New York: St. Martin's Press, 1997).

8. Lisa Tickner, *The Spectacle of Women: Imagery of the Suffrage Campaign, 1907–1914* (London: Chatto and Windus, 1987), p. 107.

9. Suffragists celebrated historical, mythical, and biblical women in numerous media, including plays, processions, pamphlets, and *tableaux vivants*. See Tickner, *Spectacle of Women;* and Antoinette Burton, *Burdens of History: British Feminists, Indian Women, and Imperial Culture, 1865–1914* (Chapel Hill: University of North Carolina Press, 1994).

10. Christabel Pankhurst, "Militant Methods," ca. 1909, reprinted in Marcus, *Suffrage and the Pankhursts*, pp. 117–19; Millicent Garrett Fawcett, *Women's Suffrage: A Short History of a Great Movement* (London: T. C. and E. C. Jack, 1912; reprint, New York: Souce Book Press, 1970), pp. 59–60.

11. E. Sylvia Pankhurst, *The Suffragette Movement: An Intimate Account of Persons and Ideals* (London: Longman, 1931; reprint, London: Virago, 1977), p. 468. An exhaustive list of those who have examined aspects of the symbolism of Joan of Arc within the British suffrage movement would be impossible. The most thorough analysis is Sheila Stowell, "Dame Joan, Saint Christabel," *Modern Drama* 37, no. 3 (1994): 421–36.

12. Sheila Stowell, *A Stage of Their Own: Feminist Playwrights of the Suffrage Era* (Ann Arbor: University of Michigan Press, 1992), p. 45.

13. Tickner, *Spectacle of Women*, p. 208.

14. In January 1914, Despard read and commented upon biographies of Joan of Arc by Anatole France, Mark Twain, and Andrew Lang; Charlotte Despard, diary, D2479/1/2, 1914 Despard, Public Record Office of Northern Ireland, Belfast.

15. This literature is vast and varies widely in depth of analysis. Nadia Margolis's *Joan of Arc in History, Literature, and Film* (New York: Garland, 1990) provides an excellent guide. The most useful surveys on the reception of Joan in England include Frances Gies, *Joan of Arc: The Legend and the Reality* (New York: Harper and Row, 1981); Marina Warner, *Joan of Arc: The Image of Female Heroism* (New York: Knopf, 1981); W. S. Scott, *Jeanne d'Arc* (London: Harrup, 1974); Charles Wayland Lightbody, *The Judgements of Joan* (Cambridge, Mass.: Harvard University Press, 1961); and Herbert Thurston, "Blessed Joan of Arc in English Opinion," *Month* 113 (May 1909): 449–64.

16. Lightbody, *Judgements of Joan*, p. 162.

17. Warner, *Joan of Arc*, pp. 242–44.

18. Lightbody, *Judgements of Joan*, p. 164; Gies, *Joan of Arc*, p. 252.

19. Lord Ronald Gower, *Joan of Arc* (London: John C. Nimmo, 1893), p. 2.

20. *Times*, 3 August 1909.

21. Nadia Margolis, "The 'Joan Phenomenon' and the French Right," in *Fresh Verdicts on Joan of Arc*, ed. Bonnie Wheeler and Charles T. Wood (New York: Garland, 1996), p. 265. See also Martha Hanna, "Iconology and Ideology: Images of Joan of Arc in the Idiom of the Action française, 1908–1931," *French Historical Studies* 14, no. 2 (1985): 215–39.

22. Margolis, "The 'Joan Phenomenon,'" p. 269.

23. Kenneth L. Woodward, *Making Saints* (New York: Simon and Schuster, 1990), pp. 16–18, 78–85; Warner, *Joan of Arc*, pp. 263–64.

24. Woodward, *Making Saints*, p. 18.

25. Ibid., p. 64.

26. Stowell, "Dame Joan," p. 429; Sandra Stanley Holton, "'In Sorrowful Wrath': Suffrage Militancy and the Romantic Feminism of Emmeline Pankhurst," in *British Feminism in the Twentieth Century*, ed. Harold L. Smith (Amherst: University of Massachusetts Press, 1991), p. 15.

27. Christabel Pankhurst, *Unshackled: The Story of How We Won the Vote* (London: Hutchinson, 1959), p. 282.

28. Burton, *Burdens of History,* pp. 55–56.

29. Kelly DeVries, "A Woman as Leader of Men: Joan of Arc's Military Career," in Wheeler and Wood, *Fresh Verdicts,* pp. 3–18.

30. Christabel Pankhurst, "Joan of Arc," *Suffragette,* 9 May 1913, p. 501.

31. Tickner, *Spectacle of Women,* pp. 122–31; Antoinette Burton, "The Feminist Quest for Identity: British Imperial Suffragism and 'Global Sisterhood,' 1900–1915," *Journal of Women's History* 3, no. 2 (1991): 67.

32. Mary Richardson to Kitty Marion, quoted in Martha Vicinus, *Independent Women: Work and Community for Single Women, 1850–1920* (Chicago: University of Chicago Press, 1985), p. 355.

33. Lytton, *Prisons and Prisoners,* p. 276.

34. Woodward, *Making Saints,* pp. 52–54.

35. Millicent Garrett Fawcett, "Joan of Arc," in her *Five Famous French Women* (London: Cassells, 1905); reprinted as "Joan of Arc," NUWSS, 1912, p. 31. Fawcett engaged with Joan of Arc as early as 1902, when Mrs. Arthur Lyttelton invited her to speak on Joan in Portsmouth during weekly lectures for educated young married women and girls (Mrs. Arthur Lyttleton to Millicent Garrett Fawcett, 28 February 1902, Fawcett Autograph Collection). See also discussion of Joan's worthiness for elevation to status of venerable in the liberal feminist *Englishwoman's Review,* 14 April 1904, pp. 132–33.

36. Fawcett, "Joan of Arc," pp. 5, 15.

37. Editorial, "The Bugler Girl," *Common Cause,* 14 November 1913, p. 572; Emmeline Pankhurst used this phrase to describe a change in WSPU policy at a February 1912 meeting; quoted in Pankhurst, *Suffragette Movement,* p. 372.

38. Emmeline Pankhurst, "Defence" (Tuesday, 21 May 1912), reprinted in Marcus, *Suffrage and the Pankhursts,* p. 128.

39. Mrs. Saul Solomon, "Breaking to Mend," *Vote,* 1 August 1913, pp. 230–31.

40. Mohandas Gandhi, "When Women Are Manly, Will Men Be Effeminate?" *Indian Opinion,* 2 February 1907, translated from Gujarati, and reprinted in *Gandhi on Women,* compiled by Pushpa Joshi (Ahmedabad: Navajivan Publishing House, 1988), p. 5.

41. Literature on the visual presentation of suffragettes is growing; see Joel H. Kaplan and Sheila Stowell, *Theatre and Fashion: Oscar Wilde to the Suffragettes* (Cambridge: Cambridge University Press, 1994); Katrina Rolley, "Fashion, Femininity, and the Fight for the Vote," *Art History* 13, no. 1 (1990): 48–70; Marcus, "The Asylums of Antaeus," pp. 132–51; see also Sandra Stanley Holton, "Manliness and Militancy: The Political Protest of Male Suffragists and the Gendering of the 'Suffragette' Identity," in *The Men's Share? Masculinities, Male Support and Women's Suffrage in Britain, 1890–1920,* ed. Angela V. John and Claire Eustance (London: Routledge, 1997), pp. 110–34.

42. See Tickner, *Spectacle of Women,* pp. 213–26.

43. Mary Poovey, *Uneven Developments: The Ideological Work of Gender in Mid-Victorian England* (Chicago: University of Chicago Press, 1988), pp. 164–98; Vicinus, *Independent Women,* pp. 19–21.

44. Poovey, *Uneven Developments,* p. 169.

45. "Caxton Hall 'Wednesdays,'" *Vote,* 7 March 1913, p. 315.

46. Solomon, "Breaking to Mend," pp. 230–31.

47. See Marion Holmes's series of popular pamphlets, the "cameo-life sketches": *Elizabeth Fry, Florence Nightingale, Frances Mary Buss, Josephine Butler,* and *Lydia Becker* (London, WFL, 1911–13).

48. See the advertising for both NUWSS and WFL on all the "Cameo Life-Sketch" pamphlets.

49. My thanks to Antoinette Burton on this point, personal correspondence, 13 November 1996.

50. Margaret Wynne Nevinson, "The Suffragists' Bazaar," *Women's Franchise,* 26 March 1908, p. 456.

51. The photographs were printed in *Vote* weekly between 12 March and 30 April 1910; see Edith How Martyn, "Suffragette Jam and Marmalade," *Vote,* 26 March, 1910, p. 261.

52. H. W. Nevinson, *Essays in Freedom* (London: Duckworth, 1909), p. xv.

53. H. W. Nevinson, *Essays in Rebellion* (London: James Nisbet, 1913), p. x.

54. On this tendency more generally, see Thomas Holt, *The Problem of Freedom: Race, Labor, and Politics in Jamaica and Britain, 1832–1938* (Baltimore: Johns Hopkins University Press, 1992); Orlando Patterson, "Slavery: The Underside of Freedom," in *Out of Slavery: Abolition and After,* ed. Jack Hayward (London: Frank Cass, 1985), pp. 7–29; David Brion Davis, *The Problem of Slavery in the Age of Revolution, 1770–1823* (Ithaca, N.Y.: Cornell University Press, 1966). For the range of meanings attached to the idea of slavery, see Carl Plasa and Betty J. Ring, *The Discourse of Slavery: Aphra Behn to Toni Morrison* (London: Routledge, 1994).

55. See especially Kathryn Gleadle, *The Early Feminists: Radical Unitarians and the Emergence of the Women's Rights Movement, 1831–1851* (New York: St. Martin's Press, 1995); Burton, *Burdens of History;* Moira Ferguson, *Subject to Others: British Women Writers and Colonial Slavery, 1670–1834* (New York: Routledge, 1992); Clare Midgley, *Women Against Slavery: The British Campaigns, 1780–1870* (London: Routledge, 1992); Vron Ware, *Beyond the Pale: White Women, Racism and History* (London: Verso, 1992); Jane Rendall, *The Origins of Modern Feminism: Women in Britain, France and the United States, 1760–1860* (London: Macmillan, 1985).

56. See Midgley, *Women Against Slavery;* Sandra Stanley Holton, "'To Educate Women into Rebellion': Elizabeth Cady Stanton and the Creation of a Transatlantic Network of Radical Suffragists," *American Historical Review* 99, no. 4 (1994): 1112–36.

57. The analogy of slavery would become increasingly sexualized between 1861 and 1914; see Judith R. Walkowitz, *City of Dreadful Delight: Narratives of Sexual Danger in Late-Victorian London* (Chicago: University of Chicago Press, 1992). For the range of meanings feminists invoked, see Barbara Leigh Smith Bodichon, "Of Those Who Are the Property of Others, and of the Great Power That Holds Others as Property" (1863), in *Barbara Leigh Smith Bodichon and the Langham Place Group,* ed. Candida Ann Lacey (London: Routledge and Kegan Paul, 1986), pp. 84–96; Josephine Butler, "Social Purity" (n.d.), Annie Besant, "Marriage: As It Was, As It Is, and As It Should Be" (1882), and Elizabeth C. Wolstenholme Elmy, *Phases of Love* (1897), all in *The Sexuality Debates,* ed. Sheila Jeffreys (London: Routledge and Kegan Paul, 1987), pp. 170–89, 391–445, and 341–52.

58. James Walvin, "The Public Campaign in England Against Slavery, 1787–1834," in *The Abolition of the Atlantic Slave Trade: Origins and Effects in Europe, Africa, and the Americas,* ed. David Eltis and James Walvin (Madison: University of Wisconsin Press, 1981), p. 69.

59. Patterson, "Slavery," pp. 8–9.

60. Lee Holcombe makes this point in *Wives and Property: Reform of the Married Women's Property Law in Nineteenth-Century England* (Toronto: University of Toronto Press, 1983), p. 149.

61. F. W. Pethick Lawrence, "Women and Physical Force" (London: Woman's Press, n.d.).

62. Charlotte Carmichael Stopes, "The Constitutional Basis of Women's Suffrage" (Edinburgh: Darien Press, 1908), p. 10.

63. Chrystal MacMillan, "The Struggle for Political Liberty" (London: Woman's Press, 1909), p. 4. See also Rev. F. Lewis Donaldson, "The Religion of Women's Suffrage" (London: Central Society for Women's Suffrage, 1905), p. 7.

64. Annie Besant, "Legalisation of Female Slavery," in Jeffreys, *Sexuality Debates*, pp. 95–96.

65. Butler, "Social Purity," p. 184.

66. Christabel Pankhurst, *The Great Scourge and How to End It* (London: E. Pankhurst, 1913), pp. ix–x.

67. Ibid., p. 20.

68. Ibid., p. 37.

69. A point made by Cicely Hamilton, *Marriage as a Trade* (London: Chapman and Hall, 1909), p. 19.

70. Pankhurst, *Great Scourge,* p. 115.

71. Ibid., pp. 146–47.

72. For examples of Emmeline Pankhurst's invocations of white slavery, see "Great Meeting at the Albert Hall," *Suffragette,* 25 October 1912, p. 16; Emmeline Pankhurst, "Why We Are Militant," *Suffragette,* 21 November 1913, p. 127.

73. Dora Marsden, "Views and Comments," *The Egoist* 12, no. 1 (1914).

74. Rebecca West, "On Mentioning the Unmentionable: An Exhortation to Miss Pankhurst," *Clarion,* 26 September 1913, reprinted in *The Young Rebecca: Writings of Rebecca West, 1911–1917,* ed. Jane Marcus (New York: Viking, 1982), p. 204.

75. The term "organic freedom" is Orlando Patterson's; see "Slavery" pp. 8–9.

76. John Stuart Mill, *The Subjection of Women,* ed. by Susan M. Okin (London, 1869; reprint, Indianapolis: Hackett, 1988), pp. 6–14.

77. See Gwenllian E. F. Morgan, "The Duties of Citizenship" (1896), in *Before the Vote Was Won: Arguments for and Against Women's Suffrage,* ed. Jane Lewis (London: Routledge and Kegan Paul, 1987), p. 466.

78. Andrew Vincent and Raymond Plant, *Philosophy, Politics and Citizenship: The Life and Thought of the British Idealists* (Oxford: Basil Blackwell, 1984).

79. See Laura E. Nym Mayhall, "The Rhetorics of Slavery and Citizenship: Suffragist Discourse and Canonical Texts in Britain, 1880–1914," *Gender and History* 13, no. 3 (2001): 489–93.

80. Dora Montefiore, *From a Victorian to a Modern* (London: E. Archer, 1927), pp. 100–105; Montefiore, *Serf Life in Russia* (London: W. Heinemann, 1906).

81. See Henry Woodd Nevinson, *Fire of Life* (London: Camelot Press, 1935), p. 210. See also his book *A Modern Slavery* (London: Harper, 1906).

82. Marion Holmes, "The A.B.C. of Votes for Women" (London: WFL, 1910), p. 1.

83. Charlotte Despard, "The Ethics of Resistance," *Vote,* 20 January 1912, p. 150.

84. Robert F. Cholmeley, "A State of Mind," *Englishwoman* 5, no. 15 (April 1910), p. 305.

CHAPTER **6**

1. Christabel Pankhurst, "The Martyr Spirit," *Suffragette,* 28 March 1913, p. 384.

2. Christabel Pankhurst, "Why the Union Is Strong," *Suffragette,* 20 December 1912, p. 160.

3. WFL, *Report for the Year 1908 and of the Fourth Annual Conference* (London: WFL, 1909), p. 4.

4. Emmeline Pethick Lawrence, "Christians, Awake!" *Votes for Women,* 27 December 1912, p. 194.

5. Charlotte Despard, "Our Responsibility," *Vote,* 11 November 1909, p. 34.

6. Emmeline Pethick Lawrence, "Militant Men," *Votes for Women,* 1 September 1911, p. 770.

7. W. F. Cobb, "Women and Brute Force" (London: Woman's Press, 1912).

8. Charlotte Carmichael Stopes, "The Constitutional Basis of Women's Suffrage" (Edinburgh: Darien Press, 1908), p. 10.

9. Margaret Kineton Parkes, "Why We Resist Our Taxes" (London: WTRL, 1911), p. 7; see also Mrs. Darent Harrison, "The Right to Resist" (London: WTRL, 1913).

10. Laurence Housman, "A Question for 'Constitutionals,'" *Votes for Women,* 24 February 1911, p. 335.

11. Charlotte Despard, "Militant Policy of the WFL," *Vote,* 13 February 1914, p. 259.

12. Cheryl Jorgensen-Earp, *The Transfiguring Sword: The Just War of the Women's Social and Political Union* (Tuscaloosa: University of Alabama Press, 1997), pp. 100–101.

13. Clipping from *Eastbourne Gazette,* 2 June 1909, quoting Charlotte Despard, in Maude Arncliffe Sennett, vol. 7, p. 59, British Library.

14. Martin Pugh, *The March of the Women: A Revisionist Analysis of the Campaign for Women's Suffrage, 1866–1914* (Oxford: Oxford University Press, 2000), pp. 55–57.

15. A. MacCallum Scott, "The Physical Force Argument Against Woman Suffrage" (London: National League for Opposing Woman Suffrage, 1912), p. 4.

16. Heber Hart, "Woman Suffrage: A National Danger" (London: P. S. King and Son, 1912), p. 23.

17. Laurence Housman, "The Relations of Physical Force to Political Power," *Votes for Women,* 29 April 1910, p. 491.

18. Sidney Low, "The Physical Force Argument," *Votes for Women,* 4 June 1909, p. 751.

19. A point not missed by nonmilitants; see A. Maude Royden, "The True End of Government" (London: NUWSS, 1912).

20. Caroline Morrell, *"Black Friday": Violence Against Women in the Suffragette Movement* (London: Women's Research and Resources Centre, 1981); Andrew Rosen, *"Rise Up, Women!": The Militant Campaign of the Women's Social and Political Union, 1903–1914* (London: Routledge and Kegan Paul, 1974), pp. 138–42.

21. See, for example, statements regarding Teresa Billington Greig's June 1906 arrest in Cavendish Square (26 June 1906, HO45/10345/141956/12); complaints regarding police brutality during 13 February 1907 arrests of suffragists (19 February 1907, MEPO 2/1016/41, /42, /43); and complaints against police officers for treatment of suffragists during 20 March 1907 meeting (28 March 1907, MEPO 2/1016/2, /3).

22. Suffragists' Vigilance League, "To Split the Marble Walls of Wrong," leaflet accompanying correspondence to Home Office, 20 July 1909, MEPO 144/1038/180782/36, PRO.

23. M. M. Farquharson, quoted in *Manchester Guardian*, 17 May 1912.

24. Ian Christopher Fletcher, "Liberalism and the Rule of Law: Protest Movements, Public Order, and the Liberal Government, 1905–14" (Ph.D. diss., John Hopkins University, 1990), p. 102.

25. For a description of the conditions of prison life for suffragettes, see Elizabeth Crawford, *The Women's Suffrage Movement: A Reference Guide, 1866–1928* (London: UCL Press, 1999), pp. 567–74.

26. See *Times,* 5 October 1909.

27. "Against the 'Cat and Mouse' Act," *Vote,* 18 July 1913, p. 199.

28. "To Repeal the Cat and Mouse Act," issued by the Repeal the Act Committee, in E. Sylvia Pankhurst papers, reel 24, no. 202.

29. WFL, "Is Political Agitation a Crime?" (London: WFL, 1909).

30. Historians critical of militancy read her feminist autocritique as an act of betrayal, a case where a suffragette realized the error of her ways and renounced militancy (Brian Harrison, *Prudent Revolutionaries: Portraits of British Feminists Between the Wars* [Oxford: Clarendon Press, 1987], pp. 52–59). Feminist historians sympathetic to the Pankhursts see Billington Greig's critique as breaking with the true faith, as an indication of her less-than-authentic feminist credentials (see Mary Jean Corbett, *Representing Femininity: Middle-Class Subjectivity in Victorian and Edwardian Women's Autobiographies* [New York: Oxford University Press, 1992], pp. 171–73).

31. Teresa Billington Greig, *The Militant Suffrage Movement: Emancipation in a Hurry* (London: Frank Palmer, 1911); reprinted in *The Non-violent Militant: Selected Writings of Teresa Billington-Greig,* ed. Carol McPhee and Ann FitzGerald (London: Routledge and Kegan Paul, 1987), p. 147.

32. Homer Lawrence Morris, *Parliamentary Franchise Reform in England from 1885 to 1918* (New York: Columbia University Press, 1921; reprint, New York: AMS Press, 1969), pp. 62–68.

33. Teresa Billington Greig, "A Bombshell in the Camp of the Suffragists," *Nash's Magazine,* March 1911, p. 664.

34. See, for example, Charlotte Despard to Mrs. Solomon, 27 November 1910, Fawcett Autograph Collection, Militants (20D).

35. New Constitutional Society for Women's Suffrage, *First Annual Report, for the Year Ended 6 January 1910,* p. 1.

36. Morris, *Parliamentary Franchise Reform,* pp. 70–78.

37. Lloyd George used the term at a meeting of the National Liberal Federation at Bath, 24 November 1911; see Constance Rover, *Women's Suffrage and Party Politics in Britain, 1866–1914* (London: Routledge and Kegan Paul, 1967), p. 130.

38. Rosen, *"Rise Up, Women!"* pp. 146–55.

39. Charlotte Despard diary, 21 February 1913, D2479/1/1, Despard 1913, Public Record Office of Northern Ireland.

40. Eunice Guthrie Murray journals (held privately), vol. 2, June 1912, p. 107 (pagination not in original).

41. Ibid., April 1912, p. 164.

42. Alison Neilans, "Parliamentary Results of Militant Methods," *Vote,* 23 March 1912, p. 258.

43. Millicent Fawcett, "Broken Windows—and After," *Daily News,* 9 March 1912.

44. Huntly Carter, ed., *Women's Suffrage and Militancy* (London: Frank Palmer, 1912), pp. 60–61.

45. NUWSS leaflet, July 1914, "A Manifesto of Protest Against Militancy"; see also

NUWSS, "Militant Outrages," June 1914, both in NUWSS leaflets to 1914, the Women's Library.

46. Alison Neilans, "The Militancy of Conviction," *Vote,* 12 February 1910, p. 181.

47. "Notes of the Week," *Freewoman,* 30 November 1911, p. 23, and 7 December 1911, p. 44.

48. Dora Marsden, "Views and Comments," *Egoist,* 15 June 1914.

49. Teresa Billington-Greig, correspondence, *Vote,* 21 January 1911, p. 159.

50. Rowland Kenney, "Women's Suffrage: The Militant Movement in Ruins," *English Review* 13, no. 49 (1912): 101–2.

51. Ibid., p. 106.

52. "A Logical Protest," *Vote,* 11 February 1911, p. 195.

53. Charlotte Despard, "Lloyd George's Pronouncement," *Vote,* 2 December 1911, p. 66.

54. Circular letter, dated April 1912, signed by Edith How Martyn, Bessie Drysdale, Emma Sproson, Eileen Mitchell, Katherine Vuillamy, Alison Neilans, and Constance Tite, Suffragette Fellowship Archive, reel 2, group D, vol. III, Z6070, p. 80.

55. Edith How Martyn, letter resigning as Head of Political and Militant Department and from NEC of WFL, 17 April 1912, Suffragette Fellowship Archive, reel 2, group D, vol. III, Z6070, pp. 84–86.

56. Transcript of "WFL Special Conference Held the 27th and 28th April 1912," vol. I, p. 77.

57. Transcript of "WFL Special Conference," vol. II, pp. 27–28.

58. For details of these events, see Rosen, *"Rise Up Women!"* pp. 122–26, 171, 235; E. Sylvia Pankhurst, *The Suffragette Movement: An Intimate Account of Persons and Ideals* (London: Longman, 1931; reprint, London, Virago, 1977), pp. 296–97, 314, 328, 345. See also "Deeds, Not Words!" *Suffragette,* 1 November 1913, p. 84, and *Woman's Dreadnought,* 21 March 1914, p. 4.

59. Jorgensen-Earp, *The Transfiguring Sword;* also Christabel Pankhurst, "Shall Women Fight?" *Suffragette,* 1 November 1912, p. 36; Christabel Pankhurst, "Mr. Lloyd George on Militancy. A Reply," *Suffragette,* 27 June 1913, p. 615.

60. Christabel Pankhurst, "Militancy a Virtue," *Suffragette,* 10 January 1913, p. 186; see also "Verbatim Report of Mrs. Pankhurst's Speech, delivered Nov. 13, 1913 at Parson's Theatre, Hartford, Conn." (Hartford, Conn.: Connecticut Woman Suffrage Association, 1913), pp. 7, 16.

61. Christabel Pankhurst, "Standards of Morality," *Suffragette,* 14 April 1913, p. 404.

62. Rosen, *"Rise Up, Women!"* pp. 189–202.

63. Ibid., pp. 242–43.

64. Percy Cohen, letter to the editor, *Jewish World,* 14 May 1913, in Franklin/Duval papers, box 226, folder 2, the Women's Library.

65. "Clamour," *Vote,* 23 January 1914, p. 209.

66. For Rose Lamartine Yates, see Liz Stanley and Ann Morley, *The Life and Death of Emily Wilding Davison* (London: Virago, 1988); for Elinor Penn Gaskell, see Rosen, *"Rise Up, Women!"* p. 255. Stanley and Morley have argued that "as a single static entity 'the WSPU' did not exist." It was a "shifting alliance of different interests, motivations, and philosophies" (p. 175). Be that as it may, individuals maintained membership in the organization and, more important, retained conviction that the use of violence was an integral part of their militancy.

67. Krista Cowman, "'A Party Between Revolution and Peaceful Persuasion': A Fresh Look at the United Suffragists," in *The Women's Suffrage Movement: New Feminist*

Perspectives, ed. Maroula Joannou and June Purvis (Manchester: Manchester University Press, 1998), p. 80.

68. Crawford, *Women's Suffrage Movement,* p. 252.

69. East London Federation of Suffragettes, Minute Book, 27 January 1914, in E. Sylvia Pankhurst papers, reel 24, no. 206.

70. E. Sylvia Pankhurst, "Our Paper," *Woman's Dreadnought,* 8 March 1914, p. 2; see also "Join the People's Army," a circular letter signed by Sylvia Pankhurst, in E. Sylvia Pankhurst papers, reel 24, no. 202.

71. Caption under cover illustration, *Votes for Women,* 22 March 1912, p. 385.

72. Emmeline Pethick Lawrence, "Militancy for Non-Militants," *Votes for Women,* 7 February 1913, p. 273.

73. Jane E. Brailsford, "A Prisoner's Protest in 1843," *Votes for Women,* 10 May 1912, p. 499; "Wilks and Liberty," *Votes for Women,* 4 October 1912, p. 845.

74. On the break, see *Votes for Women,* 18 October 1912, p. 34; "Great Meeting in the Albert Hall," *Suffragette,* 18 October 1912, p. 16.

75. Historian June Balshaw argues that Emmeline Pethick Lawrence saw the role of the paper as that of interpreting militancy to the public; see "Sharing the Burden: The Pethick Lawrences and Women's Suffrage," in *The Men's Share? Masculinities, Male Support and Women's Suffrage in Britain, 1890–1920,* ed. Angela V. John and Claire Eustance (London: Routledge, 1997), p. 149.

76. "A 'Votes for Women' Fellowship," *Votes for Women,* 1 November 1912, p. 68; "A 'Votes for Women' Fellowship," *Votes for Women,* 8 November 1912, p. 82; "The Fellowship Reunion," *Votes for Women,* 11 July 1913, p. 606.

77. "The Movement as a Whole," *Votes for Women,* 1 August 1913, p. 642.

78. "The 'Votes for Women' Fellowship," *Votes for Women,* 21 February 1913, p. 294.

79. "A New Suffragist Federated Council," *Votes for Women,* 17 January 1913, p. 228.

80. Charlotte Despard noted that she had met with Emmeline Pethick Lawrence on 4 December 1913 to discuss formation of a Suffrage First Committee, in Charlotte Despard, diary, D2479/1/1, Despard 1913, Public Record Office of Northern Ireland; see also *Votes for Women,* 13 March 1914.

81. See, for example, Emmeline Pethick Lawrence, "Political Militancy: In Reply to the Women's Freedom League," *Votes for Women,* 21 February 1913, p. 295.

82. "Education and Citizenship," *Vote,* 9 May 1913, p. 34.

83. C. N. Boyle, "The Political Outlook," *Vote,* 2 January 1914, p. 156.

84. See *Suffragette,* 25 October 1912, p. 24; 11 April 1913, p. 435.

85. "Russian Methods in Victoria Park," *Woman's Dreadnought,* 30 May 1914, p. 41.

86. "The Deputation to King George," *Woman's Dreadnought,* 30 May 1914, p. 42.

87. Mrs. Despard and Constance Tite to Mrs. Garrett Badley, 13 March 1912, Fawcett Autograph Collection, Militants (20D).

88. WFL National Executive Committee Manifesto, 4 March 1912, in Suffragette Fellowship Archive, 50.82/556.

89. See Sandra Stanley Holton, "Manliness and Militancy: The Political Protest of Male Suffragists and the Gendering of the 'Suffragette' Identity," in John and Eustance, *The Men's Share?* p. 129.

90. The "Votes for Women" Fellowship called for "complete equality and perfect comradeship of men and women"; *Votes for Women,* 15 November 1912, p. 98; see also "In Hyde Park," *Woman's Dreadnought,* 11 April 1914, p. 2. The issue had been debated for years within the WFL; see Transcript 1909, II, pp. 23–25.

91. On heckling of local government officials, see "Silenced!" *Suffragette*, 7 November 1913, p. 83; on heckling of cabinet ministers, see "Cabinet Ministers' Statements," *Votes for Women*, 20 January 1912, p. 263; "Cabinet Ministers Confronted by Woman Suffragists," *Votes for Women*, 2 February 1912, p. 279; "The Rout of the Home Secretary," *Votes for Women*, 8 November 1912, pp. 91–92; on WFL divergence on political interruptions and violence, see *Votes for Women*, 21 February 1913, pp. 295, 301. On petitions to Parliament and the king, see *Votes for Women*, 25 April 1913, p. 423; 11 July 1913, p. 610; 14 March 1913, p. 336.

92. WFL, "National Insurance Bill and Votes for Women," a handbill protesting "Legislation for Women Without their Consent," in Suffragette Fellowship Archive, 50.82/488.

93. WFL, Middlesbrough Branch Minute Book, 29 May 1911, 59A, the Women's Library.

94. WFL National Executive Committee, 54C, June 29, 1912, p. 127; 20 and 21 September 1912, p. 156; 19 October 1912, p. 165. See also "Souvenir Programme of the Insurance Act Persecution," 13 September 1913, Teresa Billington Greig papers, box 375, the Women's Library.

95. WFL, "National Insurance Bill and Votes for Women"; Charlotte Despard, diary, 21 July 1913, Despard 1913, Public Record Office of Northern Ireland.

96. "The Government Moves Against Us," *Vote*, 8 May, 1914, p. 35.

97. The WFL discussed collaboration with the ELFS on this protest; see C. Nina Boyle to E. Sylvia Pankhurst, 15 January 1913, in E. Sylvia Pankhurst papers, reel 23, no. 179. See also ELFS minute book, 27 January 1914, reel 24, no. 206, and the *Woman's Dreadnought*, 8 March 1914, p. 8.

98. "War Against Law," *Vote*, 7 February 1913, p. 243.

99. C. Nina Boyle, "Our New Crusade," *Vote*, 14 February 1913, pp. 259–60; C. Nina Boyle, "The National Dilemma," *Vote*, 28 February 1913, p. 292.

100. In 1912, the WFL initiated correspondence with the lord chancellor, recorder, and judges of the King's Bench regarding the refusal of certain magistrates to allow women into Recorder's Courts. The issue was taken up by the Home Office, with the result that some women were admitted to suffrage trials; AR1912, p. 18.

101. Ibid., p. 19.

102. Boyle, "Our New Crusade," p. 259.

103. "The Prison Van Scandal," *Vote*, 30 May 1913, p. 71; "Political and Militant Work," *Vote*, 11 July 1913, p. 176. See also WFL correspondence, 24 May 1913 through July 1914, in MEPO 2/1557; HO45/11057/234294/5, /13, /23, /24, PRO.

104. "Deputation to Mr. McKenna," *Vote*, 14 February 1913, p. 258.

105. "A Women's Freedom League Militant Protest," *Vote*, 17 July 1914, p. 207; *Times*, 14 July 1914.

106. C. Nina Boyle, "Stop the Traffic," *Vote*, 24 July 1914, p. 224.

107. Emmeline Pethick Lawrence, "Our Policy," *Votes for Women*, 25 October 1912, p. 56.

108. Charlotte Despard, "Without Fear," *Vote*, 30 January 1914, p. 230.

109. Emmeline Pethick Lawrence, "Political Militancy," *Votes for Women*, 21 February 1913, p. 295.

110. Alexia B. Jack, correspondence to *Forward*, 15 December 1913.

111. "Militancy for Non-Militants," *Votes for Women*, 21 February 1913, p. 301; "Spiritual Militancy League for the Women's Charter of Rights and Liberties," *Vote*, 2 May 1913, p. 15.

112. Christabel Pankhurst, "Why the Union Is Strong," *Suffragette,* 20 December 1912, p. 160.

113. *Times,* 7 April 1913.

114. Ibid.

115. *Times,* 8 April 1913.

116. *Times,* 14 April 1913.

117. *Times,* 16 April 1913. This was an ongoing issue between April and June of 1913; see *Votes for Women,* 16 April 1913, p. 408; 25 April 1913, p. 424; 2 May 1913, pp. 440, 446; 9 May 1913, p. 456; 16 May 1913, p. 478; 23 May 1913, p. 496; and 6 June 1913, p. 520. On extension of the ban to WFL, see *Vote,* 9 May 1913, p. 24.

118. "'Free Speech' in Trafalgar Square," *Vote,* 2 May 1913, p. 4.

119. *Times,* 5 May 1913.

120. Pankhurst, *Suffragette Movement,* p. 457; Charlotte Despard, diary, 3 and 4 May 1913, D2479/1/1, Despard 1913, Public Record Office of Northern Ireland; *WFL Annual Report 1913* (London: WFL, 1914), pp. 17–18.

121. Charlotte Despard, "Inferno—Up-to-Date," *Vote,* 9 May 1913, p. 28.

122. "Welcome to Free Speech Prisoners," *Vote,* 23 May 1913, p. 56.

123. Rosen, *"Rise Up, Women!"* pp. 156–70, 183–90, 196–200; Pugh, *The March of the Women,* pp. 202–10.

CHAPTER 7

1. See Nicoletta Gullace, *"The Blood of Our Sons": Men, Women, and the Renegotiation of British Citizenship During the Great War* (New York: Palgrave Macmillan, 2002); Susan R. Grayzel, *Women's Identities at War: Gender, Motherhood, and Politics in Britain and France During the First World War* (Chapel Hill: University of North Carolina Press, 1999), pp. 157–89; E. Sylvia Pankhurst, *The Home Front* (London: Hutchinson, 1932; reprint, London: Cresset Library, 1987), pp. 364–70.

2. *Times,* 15 August 1914.

3. NUWSS, Executive Committee Minutes, 3 August 1914, cited in David Rubinstein, *Different World for Women: The Life of Millicent Garrett Fawcett* (Columbus: Ohio State University Press, 1991), p. 214.

4. Emmeline Pankhurst to WSPU members, circular letter, 13 August 1914, Suffragette Fellowship Archive, reel 2, group D, vol. II, Z6078, p. 63.

5. C. Nina Boyle, "The Crimes of Statecraft," *Vote,* 7 August 1914, p. 268; see also E. Sylvia Pankhurst, "Our Equal Birthright," *Woman's Dreadnought,* 14 August 1915, p. 298.

6. "Women and the War" (Manchester: Manchester Men's League for Women's Suffrage, 1914).

7. Suffragettes of the WSPU regrouped around Rose Lamartine Yates; see *Suffragette News Sheet,* published December 1915, and monthly from April 1916 to November 1918; see also "Caxton Hall Meeting," *Irish Citizen,* 6 November 1915, pp. 152–53. The Independent WSPU formed around Elinor Penn Gaskell; see *Independent Suffragette,* September 1916, p. 8.

8. Frederick Pethick Lawrence, *Fate Has Been Kind* (London: Hutchinson, 1943), pp. 103–4.

9. Liz Stanley and Ann Morley note personal connections during the war between members of the WFL, the SWSPU, US, Women's International League for Peace and

Freedom, and ELFS; see *Life and Death of Emily Wilding Davison* (London: Virago, 1988), pp. 181–83.

10. Such as the WFL's 5 December 1915 suffrage rally at the Bijou Theater, London; see *Vote,* 10 December 1915, p. 846.

11. On Sunday meetings in London parks, see "Headquarter Notes," *Vote,* 9 July 1915, p. 670; on special campaigns, see "Letchworth Campaign," *Vote,* 12 May 1916, p. 1033, and "WFL Activities," *Vote,* 7 July 1916, p. 1094; "WFL Coast Campaigns. North-East Coast," *Vote,* 24 August 1917, p. 335. On the United Suffragists, see "Suffragists and the P.M.," *Votes for Women,* 3 December 1915, p. 78. For notice of IWSPU meetings, see *Independent Suffragette,* September 1916, p. 8. For the SWSPU, see *Suffragette News Sheet,* April 1916, p. 6. For the ELFS, see "Suffrage Societies in Great Britain," *Woman's Dreadnought,* 22 January 1916, pp. 409–12. This last article provided brief histories of a number of suffrage organizations, with emphasis on their activities during the war. The *Woman's Dreadnought,* however, stopped carrying news of other women's suffrage organizations after it declared support for adult suffrage in March 1916.

12. "Wear Your Badge!" *Vote,* 1 September 1916, p. 1158.

13. See Elizabeth Crawford, *The Women's Suffrage Movement: A Reference Guide, 1866–1928* (London: UCL Press, 1999), p. 232.

14. Francis M. Mason, "The Newer Eve: The Catholic Women's Suffrage Society in England, 1911–1923," *Catholic Historical Review* 72, no. 4 (1986): 620–38.

15. Barbara Winslow, "Sylvia Pankhurst and the Great War," in *Sylvia Pankhurst: from Artist to Anti-Fascist,* ed. Ian Bullock and Richard Pankhurst (New York: St. Martin's Press, 1992), p. 91.

16. Evelyn Sharp to Ada Flatman, 9 November 1915 and 13 May 1916, in Flatman papers, Suffragette Fellowship Archive.

17. Florence Underwood, "A 'Vote' Seller in Lambeth Police Court," *Vote,* 14 September 1917, p. 358; "The Case of Miss Davison," *Vote,* 12 October 1917, p. 3.

18. See "The New Suffrage Demand," *Votes for Women,* July 1916, p. 180.

19. Discussion began with "Removal of the Sex Disability or Adult Suffrage," *Vote,* 7 July 1916, p. 1097, and concluded with correspondence in the "Open Column," *Vote,* 6 October 1916, p. 1202.

20. C. Nina Boyle, "The Downing Street Discord," *Vote,* 28 July 1916, p. 1117. See also "Branch Notes," *Vote,* 22 September 1916, p. 1187; Charlotte Despard, "The New Menace," *Vote,* 9 June 1916, p. 1064.

21. Winslow, "Sylvia Pankhurst and the Great War," p. 88. See also E. Sylvia Pankhurst, "Human Suffrage," *Woman's Dreadnought,* 11 December 1915, p. 384; Eleanor Barton, "Human Suffrage: The Motto of the Future," *Woman's Dreadnought,* 22 January 1916, p. 409.

22. "Meeting at Headquarters," *Vote,* 4 September 1914, p. 303.

23. "Our 'Wednesdays,'" *Vote,* 28 May 1915, p. 623.

24. Helen Fraser, *Women and War Work* (London: G. Arnold Shaw, 1918), pp. 26–27.

25. E. Sylvia Pankhurst, "Going to War," *Woman's Dreadnought,* 8 August 1914, p. 82.

26. Christabel Pankhurst, "The War," *Suffragette,* 7 August 1914, p. 301.

27. C. Despard and Annie A. Smith, "To Our Readers," *Vote,* 14 August 1914, p. 278.

28. Sybil Oldfield, "England's Cassandras in World War One," in *This Working-Day World: Women's Lives and Culture(s) in Britain, 1914–1945,* ed. Sybil Oldfield (London: Taylor and Francis, 1994), pp. 89–100; Jo Vellacott, "Feminist Consciousness and the First World War," *History Workshop Journal,* no. 23 (1987): 81–101; Harriet Hyman

Alonso, "Suffragists for Peace During the Interwar Years, 1919–1941," *Peace and Change* 14, no. 3 (1989): 243–62; Anne Wiltsher, *Most Dangerous Women: Feminist Peace Campaigners of the Great War* (London: Pandora Press, 1985); Jill Liddington, "The Women's Peace Crusade: The History of a Forgotten Campaign," in *Over Our Dead Bodies: Women Against the Bomb*, ed. Dorothy Thompson (London: Virago, 1983), pp. 180–98.

29. Margaret Mulvihill, *Charlotte Despard: A Biography* (London: Pandora Press, 1989), pp. 115–21.

30. Winslow, "Sylvia Pankhurst and the Great War," p. 92.

31. See ibid., pp. 93–100.

32. Some explain the shift as a miscalculation by the WSPU leadership of suffragette opposition to the war (Stanley and Morley, *Life and Death of Emily Wilding Davison*, p. 95); a continuation of Pankhursts' work for the nation (Susan Kingsley Kent, *Making Peace: The Reconstruction of Gender in Interwar Britain* [Princeton, N.J.: Princeton University Press, 1993], p. 20); consistent with their prewar opposition to masculine government (Andrew Rosen, *"Rise Up, Women!": The Militant Campaign of the Women's Social and Political Union, 1903–1914* [London: Routledge and Kegan Paul, 1974], p. 251); of a piece with their prewar rhetoric of just war (Cheryl Jorgensen-Earp, *The Transfiguring Sword: The Just War of the Women's Social and Political Union* [Tuscaloosa: University of Alabama Press, 1997], pp. 149–50).

33. Jacqueline de Vries, "Gendering Patriotism: Emmeline and Christabel Pankhurst and World War One," in Oldfield, *This Working-Day World*, p. 80.

34. See, for example, C. Nina Boyle, "We Present Our Bill," *Vote*, 19 February 1915, p. 504. On her resignation, see WFL National Executive Committee minutes, 54F, 23 March 1918, p. 80.

35. Martin Pugh, *The March of the Women: A Revisionist Analysis of the Campaign for Women's Suffrage, 1866–1914* (Oxford: Oxford University Press, 2000), p. 284.

36. Emmeline Pankhurst to WSPU members, 13 August 1914.

37. "Vive *La Suffragette!* Congratulations from Readers," *Suffragette*, 7 May 1915, p. 60.

38. Margaret R. Higonnet and Patrice L.-R. Higonnet, "The Double Helix," in their *Behind the Lines: Gender and the Two World Wars* (New Haven, Conn.: Yale University Press, 1987), pp. 7.

39. Charlotte Despard, "Our President's Message," *Vote*, 7 August 1914, p. 263.

40. Edith Shackleton, "Women in War: Mrs. Pankhurst's Plan," *Daily Sketch*, 27 January 1915.

41. Harriot Stanton Blatch to Adelaide Johnson, 4 January 1915, in Adelaide Johnson papers, Library of Congress, Washington, D.C.; see also "Speech Delivered by Miss Christabel Pankhurst, at Washington, U.S.A., January 24th, 1915" (London: WSPU, 1915).

42. See announcements in *Suffragette*, 7 May 1915, p. 63; *Suffragette*, 14 May 1915, p. 68.

43. Stamfordham, of Buckingham Palace, to David Lloyd George, Minister of Munitions, 28 June 1915, suggesting Mrs. Pankhurst help with recruitment of women, D/17/5/2, David Lloyd George papers, House of Lords Record Office.

44. Grace Roe to Miss Duval, 9 June 1915, in Hugh Arthur Franklin and Elsie Duval papers (hereafter Franklin/Duval papers), box 226, folder 5, the Women's Library; see also "Universal, Obligatory War Service Demanded," *Suffragette*, 11 June 1915, pp. 136–37.

45. This procession was financed by the government; see Christabel Pankhurst, *Unshackled: The Story of How We Won the Vote* (London: Hutchinson, 1959; reprint, London: Cresset Library, 1987), pp. 289–90; Pankhurst, *Home Front,* p. 198. See also Women's War Service, circular letter, 9 July 1915, in Franklin/Duval papers, box 226, folder 5; *Times,* 19 January 1915.

46. Grace Roe, circular letter, 13 July 1916, Franklin/Duval papers, box 226, folder 5; *Times,* 24 July 1916.

47. Christabel Pankhurst, "Industrial Unrest" (London: WSPU, n.d.); Annie Kenney, Hon. Sec., the Women's Party, appealing for funds to fight "the dangerous activities of the Bolshevists, Pacifists and Pro-Germans in our midst"; circular letter, 11 April 1918, in Franklin Duval papers, box 226, folder 5.

48. Christabel Pankhurst, "The Union of 'Democratic' Control," *Suffragette,* 30 April 1915, p. 38; Emmeline Pankhurst to David Lloyd George, 14 October 1915, on the "pernicious influence of the U.D.C." D/11/2/24, David Lloyd George papers.

49. Correspondence between Emmeline Pankhurst and David Lloyd George, 14 and 15 October 1915, D/11/2/24 and /25, David Lloyd George papers.

50. Burton Chadwick, Ministry of Munitions, to Sutherland at No. 10 Downing Street, 10 April 1917, F/93/2/4, David Lloyd George papers.

51. Jessie Kenney, "The Price of Freedom" (typescript, the Women's Library), p. 139.

52. *Times,* 13 June 1917.

53. Christabel Pankhurst, "Keeping the Flag Flying," *Suffragette,* 21 May 1915, p. 86.

54. *Britannia,* 18 August 1916, cited in Rosen, *"Rise Up, Women!"* p. 260.

55. Women's Party flyer, IND/EWD/C7/3, box 554, Emily Wilding Davison papers, the Women's Library.

56. Grace Roe, circular letter, 5 April 1916, Franklin/Duval papers, box 226, folder 5.

57. Emmeline Pankhurst to Mr. Franklin, 23 January 1917, Franklin/Duval papers, box 226, folder 5.

58. WSNAC leaflet, in "Women at Work," Imperial War Museum, Microfilm (hereafter "Women at Work"), SUF 9/7. See also "Victims of War," *Woman's Dreadnought,* 5 September 1914, p. 99.

59. Jo Vellacott Newberry, "Anti-war Suffragists," *History* 62, no. 206 (1977): 418.

60. Sandra Stanley Holton, *Feminism and Democracy: Women's Suffrage and Reform Politics in Britain, 1900–1918* (Cambridge: Cambridge University Press, 1986), p. 131.

61. WFL, Middlesbrough Branch Minute Book, 6 September 1915, 59B, the Women's Library.

62. Margaret Hodge, "Wake up, Suffragists," *Vote,* 26 May 1916, p. 1046.

63. On the WFL, see "Under the Suffrage Flag," *Vote,* 1 October 1915, p. 768, and WFL flyer, February 1916, in "Women at Work," SUF 9/4. On ELFS, see "We Are Keeping the Votes for Women Flag Flying," *Woman's Dreadnought,* 22 August 1914, p. 89, and "The Declaration of War," *Woman's Dreadnought,* 2 January 1915, p. 171. On United Suffragists, see "Keep the Suffrage Flag Flying," *Votes for Women,* 21 August 1914, p. 705. On the Catholic Women's Suffrage Society, see Francis M. Mason, "The Newer Eve: The Catholic Women's Suffrage Society in England, 1911–1923," *Catholic Historical Review* 72, no. 4 (1986), p. 624.

64. "The Women's Freedom League and the National Crisis," *Vote,* 4 September 1914, pp. 302–3; "WSNAC," *Vote,* 4 September 1914, p. 322; "The WSNAC," *Vote,* 18 December 1914, p. 433.

65. E. OE. Somerville and Martin Ross, "'With Thanks for Kind Enquiries': A Brief Review of the War Work of Suffragists" (London: CUWFA, 1915), pp. 7–8, in "Women at Work," SUF 6/4.

66. WSNAC, established in August 1914, was "in abeyance" by June 1916; see WFL National Executive Committee minutes, 54e, June 17, 1916, p. 119, the Women's Library.

67. "The WFL Settlement" (1918) and "The Children's Corner," in "Women at Work," SUF 9/8 and SUF 9/2.

68. "Report of the WFL Settlement" (1916), in "Women at Work," SUF 9/5; "Women's Freedom League Work in War- and Peace-Time," *Vote*, 16 March 1917, p. 151.

69. Workers' Suffrage Federation, "Report of Social Work in 1915" (London: WSF, 1916), pp. 3–5, in "Women at Work," SUF 8/1. See also "Relief Committees," *Woman's Dreadnought;* 15 August 1914, p. 85; and ELFS flyer, "Work to cope with the unemployment and distress caused by the War," in Franklin/Duval papers, misc. papers, box 226.

70. "Our Employment Bureau," *Woman's Dreadnought,* 15 August 1914, p. 87; for the ELFS's agenda during the war, see *Woman's Dreadnought,* 12 September 1914, p. 108.

71. See Charlotte Despard, diary, 28 August 1914, D2479/1/2, Despard 1914, Public Record Office of Northern Ireland.

72. Lena Ashwell, Women's Emergency Corps, to Miss Flatman, 10 October 1914, Suffragette Fellowship Archive, reel 2, Flatman papers.

73. Hilary Frances, "'Pay the Piper, Call the Tune!': The Women's Tax Resistance League," in *The Women's Suffrage Movement: New Feminist Perspectives,* ed. Maroula Joannou and June Purvis (Manchester: Manchester University Press, 1998), p. 74; see also "Tax Resistance," *Vote,* 11 September 1914, p. 311.

74. See *Vote,* 30 October 1914, p. 369; "Branch Notes," *Vote,* 18 December 1914, p. 436; "The Writ Against Our Secretary," *Vote,* 8 January 1915, p. 455. Charlotte Despard continued her tax resistance; see transcript of "Report of the Tenth Annual Conference of the Women's Freedom League, Held on Saturday, 16th October, 1915" (hereafter Transcript 1915), p. 33. Some members chose not to continue their tax resistance during the war; see Margaret Wynne Nevinson, *Life's Fitful Fever: A Volume of Memories* (London: A. and C. Black, 1926), p. 211; and Marie Lawson, "Our Open Column," *Vote,* November 19, 1915, p. 825.

75. Notes of WFL Political and Militant Department, 56Q, January 1, 1917, Women's Library; see also "Tax Resistance. Statement by Dr. Winifred S. Patch," *Vote,* 12 January 1917, p. 77; and *Report of the Women's Freedom League from October, 1915 to April, 1918,* p. 8, the Women's Library.

76. "Tax Resistance," *Vote,* 11 September 1914, p. 311.

77. Grayzel, *Women's Identities at War,* p. 152.

78. On the involvement of the ELFS on this issue, see E. Sylvia Pankhurst, "Beware the C.D. Acts!" *Woman's Dreadnought,* 17 October 1914, p. 122; and E. Sylvia Pankhurst, "Josephine Butler," *Woman's Dreadnought,* 24 October 1914, p. 127. On the CWSS, see Mason, "The Newer Eve," pp. 620–638; on the British Dominions Woman Suffrage Union, see notice in *Jus Suffragii,* 1 November 1914, in "Women at Work," SUF 10/2.

79. "Proposed Revival of the CD Acts," *Vote,* 16 October 1914, p. 349.

80. "The Danger to Women Averted!" *Vote,* 23 October 1914, pp. 357–58.

81. C. Nina Boyle, "The Prime Minister and a 'Scrap of Paper,'" *Vote,* 4 December 1914, pp. 409–10.

82. Pankhurst, *Home Front,* p. 104. Members of the Church League for Women's Suffrage joined this protest as well; see "An Infamous Proposal," *Church League for Women's Suffrage Monthly Paper,* November 1914, p. 196.

83. Anne E. Corner, "Political Notes," *Vote,* February 23, 1917, p. 125; "Criminal Law Amendment Bill," *Vote,* March 2, 1917, p. 133.

84. "Venereal Diseases," *Vote,* 10 November 1916, p. 6. See also "The Manifesto of Organised Women," *Suffragette News Sheet,* December 1916, p. 3.

85. "Deputation to Home Secretary," *Vote,* December 8, 1916, p. 34; "Deputation to Home Secretary," *Suffragette News Sheet,* January 1917, p. 2; "Venereal Diseases," *Suffragette News Sheet,* February 1917, p. 4.

86. The Catholic Women's Suffrage Society was involved as well; see Mason, "The Newer Eve," p. 626.

87. Grayzel, *Women's Identities at War,* pp. 149–51.

88. The WFL worked with the Women's International League (WIL) and the Independent WSPU; see "The 'Cayeux' Policy and '40D,'" Women's International League, *Third Yearly Report, 1917–1918,* pp. 22–23, in "Women at Work," SUF 12/3.

89. "Maisons Tolérées," *Vote,* 29 March 1918, p. 199.

90. See ticket for admission to 10 July 1918 meeting in Fawcett Autograph Collection, Militants (20D); for the September meeting, see Mason, "The Newer Eve," p. 626.

91. Susan Pedersen, "Gender, Welfare and Citizenship in Britain During the Great War," *American Historical Review* 95, no. 4 (1990): 985.

92. *Times,* 7 October 1914. For the class dimension of this legislation, see Bernard Waites, *A Class Society at War, England 1914–1918* (Leamington Spa: Berg, 1987), pp. 161–62.

93. "The Situation at Plymouth," *Vote,* 30 October 1914, p. 365.

94. Emily Juson Kerr, letter to the *Times,* 6 October 1914; *Times,* 28 October 1914.

95. Tipperary Rooms were slated to open in London, in North Kensington, St. Pancras, Chelsea, Marylebone, and Shepherd's Bush, and in Norwich, Birmingham, and Ireland, within the year; *Times,* 28 and 29 October 1914.

96. "Women's 'Tipperary' Rooms," *Vote,* 6 November 1914, p. 378.

97. See, for example, WFL, Middlesbrough Branch Minute Book, 59B, 11 January 1915; "Branch Notes," *Vote,* 23 June 1916, p. 1084; "Branch Notes," *Vote,* 4 August 1916, p. 1132.

98. Charlotte Despard, "Public House," *Vote,* 13 November 1914, pp. 386–87; "Mrs. Despard on the Public House," *Vote,* 19 March 1915, p. 537.

99. *Times,* 5 November 1914.

100. "Our Present Duty," *Suffragette,* 21 May 1915, p. 85.

101. E. Sylvia Pankhurst, "Insults to Soldiers' Wives and Mothers," *Woman's Dreadnought,* 14 November 1914, p. 138; C. Nina Boyle, "Woman—The Whipping Boy," *Vote,* 6 November 1914, p. 376; "Freedom and Franchise," *Church League for Women's Suffrage Monthly Paper,* December 1914, p. 214.

102. Florence Underwood, "Mothers Don't Count," *Vote,* 25 September 1914, p. 328.

103. See *Vote,* 22 January 1915, p. 469; *Times,* 25 January 1915.

104. *Times,* 26 January 1915; "Deputation to the War Office," *Vote,* 29 January 1915, p. 478; "Suffragist Demonstration to the Home Office," *Woman's Dreadnought,* 30 January 1915, p. 185.

105. Nevinson, *Life's Fitful Fever,* p. 247.

106. "The Girls of England," *Vote,* 11 September 1914, pp. 309–10.

107. WFL, Sheffield Branch Minute Book, 22 February 1917, the Women's Library.

108. See the *Woman's Dreadnought,* 22 January 1916, p. 407, and 4 March 1916, p. 435.

109. WFL letter to Walter Runciman, President of the Board of Trade, dated 20 March 1915, in "The Women's Freedom League and the Government," *Vote,* 26 March 1915, p. 542.

110. Charlotte Despard, Florence Underwood, and Elizabeth Knight, "The Government's Appeal to Women for War Service. Our Manifesto," *Vote,* 26 March 1915, pp. 541–42; see also Pankhurst, *Home Front,* p. 157. The *Woman's Dreadnought* published manifestos of the US, WFL, NUWSS, IWFL, and WWSL, 27 March 1915, pp. 217, 219.

111. Arthur Marwick, *The Deluge: British Society and the First World War* (London: Norton, 1970), p. 58.

112. *Times,* 14 and 15 April 1915; "Report of Board of Trade Conference," *Woman's Dreadnought,* 17 April 1915, pp. 229–31; Pankhurst, *Home Front,* pp. 160–61.

113. Margaret Hodge, "Our NSO: In Great Things Unity," *Vote,* 8 October 1915, p. 775.

114. WFL National Executive Committee Minutes, 22 January 1916, 54e, p. 37, Women's Library; Transcript 1915, pp. 104–18.

115. Marwick, *The Deluge,* p. 61.

116. "East London Federation of Suffragettes," *Vote,* 13 August 1915, p. 715; "Resolutions," *Woman's Dreadnought,* 14 August 1915, p. 297.

117. "National Register Day," *Vote,* 30 July 1915, p. 700; "Branch Notes," *Vote,* 20 August 1915, p. 723; "Registration Sunday," *Woman's Dreadnought,* 21 August 1915, pp. 301–3.

118. "National Registration," *Vote,* 10 September 1915, p. 748.

119. "No Vote. No Register," *Suffragette News Sheet,* March 1916, p. 3.

120. "Women Police Volunteers," personal account, handwritten, n.d., in "Women at Work," EMP 41/2.

121. C. Nina Boyle, "The Women's Freedom League and the National Crisis," *Vote,* 21 August 1914, pp. 286–87.

122. Joan Lock, *The British Policewoman: Her Story* (London: Robert Hale, 1979), p. 19; John Carrier, *The Campaign for the Employment of Women as Police Officers* (Avebury: Gower, 1988), pp. 9–10; Mary S. Allen, *The Pioneer Policewoman* (London: Chatto and Windus, 1925), p. vii.

123. "Women Police Volunteers," EMP 41/2.

124. Sir Edward Henry, Commissioner of Police for the Metropolis, labeled Boyle "'an intransigeante [*sic*] and in opposition to constituted authority'"; quoted in Lock, *British Policewoman,* pp. 20–21.

125. Lock, *British Policewoman,* pp. 24–29; Carrier, *Campaign for Employment of Women as Police Officers,* p. 10; Allen, *Pioneer Policewoman,* pp. 29–37.

126. "Women Police Volunteers," *Vote,* 19 February 1915, p. 506.

127. C. Nina Boyle, "The Hidden Scourge," *Vote,* 1 September 1916, p. 1162.

128. As late as February 1916, the WPV was active in London; see "WPV," *Vote,* 4 Feb-

ruary 1916, p. 914. The WPV was "wound up" in June 1916; Minutes of the National Executive Committee, 17 June 1916, 54e, p. 117, the Women's Library.

129. Homer Lawrence Morris, *Parliamentary Franchise Reform in England from 1885 to 1918* (New York: Columbia University Press, 1921; reprint, New York: AMS Press, 1969), p. 106.

130. On interactions of women's suffrage organizations and the parliamentary campaign, see Holton, *Feminism and Democracy*, pp. 116–50; Kent, *Making Peace*, pp. 74–96; Martin Pugh, *Electoral Reform in War and Peace, 1906–1918* (London: Routledge and Kegan Paul, 1978), pp. 136–54.

131. Morris, *Parliamentary Franchise Reform*, pp. 131–35.

132. "Deputation to the Right Hon. David Lloyd George at No. 10, Downing Street, S.W., on Thursday, March 29th, 1917," Suffragette Fellowship Archive, Z6065, reel 2, group D, vol. I, pp. 124–36.

CONCLUSION

1. Joan Scott, *Only Paradoxes to Offer: French Feminists and the Rights of Man* (Cambridge, Mass.: Harvard University Press, 1996), p. 49.

2. Adela Pankhurst to Helen Fraser Moyes, quoted in Helen Moyes, *A Woman in a Man's World* (Sydney: Alpha Books, 1961), p. 37.

3. Laura E. Nym Mayhall, "Creating the 'Suffragette Spirit': British Feminism and the Historical Imagination," *Women's History Review* 4, no. 3 (1995): 319–44.

4. Jay Winter, *Sites of Memory, Sites of Mourning: The Great War in European Cultural History* (Cambridge: Cambridge University Press, 1995).

5. Brian Harrison, *Prudent Revolutionaries: Portraits of British Feminists Between the Wars* (Oxford: Clarendon Press, 1987).

6. Suffragette Fellowship, *Second News Letter*, December 1936.

7. Mayhall, "Creating the 'Suffragette Spirit,'" p. 329.

8. See correspondence between former WSPU member Helen Archdale and staff at the BBC on the occasion of the Woman Suffrage Silver Jubilee, October 1942 through August 1943; in "Talks. Women's Suffrage, 1942–43," R51/647, BBC Written Archives Center, Caversham; see also Laura E. Nym Mayhall, "Domesticating Emmeline: Representing the Suffragette, 1930–1993," *National Women's Studies Association Journal* 11, no. 2 (1999): 1–24.

9. Emmeline Pethick Lawrence to E. Sylvia Pankhurst, 17 December 1929, in E. Sylvia Pankhurst papers, reel 1.

10. See Jean Metcalfe's introductory comments to her interview with Monica Whately, 12 July 1951, BBC, WAC, Caversham.

11. Stella Newsome to Teresa Billington Greig, 28 August 1959, in Teresa Billington Greig, box 404, folder "corr suffragist and writing," the Women's Library.

12. Marian Reeves, correspondence, *Women's Freedom League Bulletin*, 5 December 1958, p. 2.

13. Theresa Garnett, correspondence, *Women's Freedom League Bulletin*, 30 January 1959, p. 3.

14. "Suffragette Memories," *Westminster Gazette*, 6 February 1928.

15. *Daily News*, 6 February 1928.

16. "'Suffragettes' Descend on London Again," *Evening Standard*, 2 April 1928.

17. For the contemporary view, see R. M. Wilson, *Wife, Mother, Voter. Her Vote. What Will She Do with It?* (London: Hodder and Stoughton, 1918), p. 13. A consensus has

emerged among historians that women's war work had little to do with the provisions of the bill that became law in 1918; see especially Susan R. Grayzel, *Women's Identities at War: Gender, Motherhood, and Politics in Britain and France During the First World War* (Chapel Hill: University of North Carolina Press, 1999); and Martin Pugh, *Women and the Women's Movement in Britain* (New York: Paragon House, 1993). For a challenge to this interpretation, see Nicoletta Gullace, *"The Blood of Our Sons": Men, Women, and the Renegotiation of British Citizenship during the Great War* (New York: Palgrave Macmillan, 2002).

18. *Manchester Guardian,* 6 February 1928.

19. E. Katharine Willoughby Marshall, "Suffragette Escapes and Adventures" (1947), Suffragette Fellowship Archive, reel 1, group B, 50.82/1132, p. 96.

20. See, for example, Annie Kenney, *Memories of a Militant* (London: Edward Arnold, 1924); Mary Richardson, *Laugh a Defiance* (London: George Weidenfeld and Nicolson, 1953); and Christabel Pankhurst, *Unshackled: The Story of How We Won the Vote* (London: Hutchinson, 1959). For an exception to this rule, see Evelyn Sharp, *Unfinished Adventure* (London: John Lane, 1933).

21. Angela Woollacott, *On Her Their Lives Depend: Munition Workers in the Great War* (Berkeley: University of California Press, 1994); Pugh, *Women and the Women's Movement,* pp. 41–42.

22. Shaw Desmond, "Do Women Care?" *Evening Standard,* 18 January 1928.

23. "They Need Not Fear Us," *Manchester Guardian,* 8 March 1928.

24. Nancy Stewart Parnell, "Equal Franchise," *Manchester Guardian,* 9 February 1928.

25. Ralph Rooper, "Women Enfranchised," in *The Making of Women: Oxford Essays in Feminism,* ed. Victor Gollancz, ed. (London: George Allen and Unwin, 1918), p. 85.

26. Harrison, *Prudent Revolutionaries.*

27. "The Modern World. BBC Radio for Schools (1965)," vol. xcvii, pamphlets, spring 1965, BBC, WAC, Caversham.

28. E. Sylvia Pankhurst, "Women's Citizenship" (unpublished manuscript, ca. 1934), in E. Sylvia Pankhurst papers, reel 18, no.231.

29. Bill Schwarz, "The Language of Constitutionalism: Baldwinite Conservatism," in *Formations of Nation and People,* ed. Formations Editorial Collective (London: Routledge and Kegan Paul, 1984), p. 2.

30. "Votes for Women," *Evening Standard,* 4 February 1928.

31. "Scene as Former Suffragists Saw It," *Manchester Guardian,* 30 March 1928.

32. Jurgen Habermas, *The Structural Transformation of the Public Sphere: An Inquiry into a Category of Bourgeois Society,* trans. Thomas Burger (1962; Cambridge, Mass.: MIT Press, 1989); James Vernon, *Politics and the People: A Study in English Political Culture, c. 1815–1867* (Cambridge: Cambridge University Press, 1993); Martin Pugh, *Electoral Reform in War and Peace, 1906–1918* (London: Routledge and Kegan Paul, 1978), pp. 183–84.

33. Cicely Hamilton, *Life Errant* (London: J. M. Dent and Sons, 1935), pp. 73–76.

34. Hilda Kean, "Some Problems of Constructing and Reconstructing a Suffragette's Life: Mary Richardson, Suffragette, Socialist and Fascist," *Women's History Review* 7, no. 4 (1998): 475–93; Julie Gottlieb, "Suffragette Experience Through the Filter of Fascism," in *A Suffrage Reader: Charting Directions in British Suffrage History,* ed. Claire Eustance, Joan Ryan, and Laura Ugolini (Leicester: Leicester University Press, 2000), pp. 105–25.

35. Cartoon, "News Psycho-Analysed," *Evening News,* 15 May 1929.

36. Rev. W. R. Inge, "Votes for Girls: Does Universal Suffrage Mean the Death of Parliamentary Government?" *Evening Standard,* 13 April 1927.

37. Rev. W. R. Inge, "The He-Woman, the She-Woman, and the Girl Voter of 25," *Evening Standard,* 25 April 1928.

38. F. J. C. Hearnshaw, "King Edward VII," in *Edwardian England, A.D. 1901–1910: A Series of Lectures Delivered at King's College, University of London, During the Session 1932–3,* ed. F. J. C. Hearnshaw (London: Ernest Benn, 1933; reprint, New York: Books for Libraries Press, 1968), pp. 56–58.

39. George Dangerfield, *The Strange Death of Liberal England* (London, 1935; reprint, London: Granada, 1983), p. 75.

40. Roger Fulford, *Votes for Women: The Story of a Struggle* (London: Faber and Faber, 1957); Martin Pugh, *The March of the Women: A Revisionist Analysis of the Campaign for Women's Suffrage, 1866–1914* (Oxford: Oxford University Press, 2000).

Bibliography

ARCHIVAL SOURCES
(LOCATED IN LONDON UNLESS OTHERWISE NOTED)

Maude Arncliffe Sennett Papers, British Library
Stanley Baldwin Papers, University Library, Cambridge
BBC Written Archives, Caversham
Teresa Billington Greig Papers, Women's Library
Josephine Butler Papers, Women's Library
Cavendish Bentinck Pamphlet Collection, Women's Library
Collected Pamphlets, Women's Suffrage, Women's Library
Emily Wilding Davison Papers, Women's Library
Charlotte Despard Papers, Public Record Office Northern Ireland, Belfast
Elsie Duval Papers, Women's Library
Elizabeth Wolstenholme Elmy Papers, British Library
Fawcett Autograph Collection, Women's Library
Ada Flatman Papers, Suffragette Fellowship Archive, Museum of London
Hugh Franklin Papers, Women's Library
David Lloyd George Papers, House of Lords Record Office
Gerritsen Collection of Women's History. Glen Rock, N.J.: Microfilming Corporation
      of America, 1975.
Herbert Gladstone Papers, British Library
Vida Goldstein Papers, Women's Library
Adelaide Johnson Papers, Library of Congress, Washington, D.C.
Jessie Kenney, "The Price of Freedom" (typescript), Women's Library
London Society for Women's Suffrage, Women's Library
Manchester Central Library, Women's Suffrage Collection, Manchester
E. Katherine Willoughby Marshall, "Suffragette Escapes and Adventures" (1947 type-
      script), Suffragette Fellowship Archive, Museum of London
Edith How Martyn Papers, Women's Library
Eunice Murray Papers, privately held
National Union of Women's Suffrage Societies, Women's Library
Helena Normanton Papers, Women's Library

E. Sylvia Pankhurst Papers, Instituut voor Sociale Geschiedenis, Amsterdam
Muriel Pierotti Papers, Women's Library
Six Point Group, Women's Library
Suffragette Fellowship, Museum of London
Women at Work, Imperial War Museum
Women's Freedom League, Women's Library
Women's Tax Resistance League, Women's Library

GOVERNMENTAL PAPERS

Central Criminal Court Papers, Public Record Office, London
Great Britain. House of Commons Debates. 5th series, 1909–19
Great Britain. Parliamentary Debates. 4th series, 1905–8
Home Office, Public Record Office, London
Metropolitan Police, Public Record Office, London
Public Works, Public Records Office, London
Report from the Select Committee (1908), on House of Commons (Admission of Strangers), PP1908 (HC371)
Treasury, Public Records Office, London

DIRECTORIES, REFERENCE BOOKS, ANNUAL REPORTS, AND YEARBOOKS

Banks, Olive. *Biographical Dictionary of British Feminists. Vol. 1, 1800–1930.* Brighton, Sussex: Wheatsheaf Books, 1985.
———. *Biographical Dictionary of British Feminists. Vol. 2, Supplement. 1900–1945.* New York: New York University Press, 1990.
Bellamy, Joyce, and John Saville, eds. *The Dictionary of Labour Biography.* London: Macmillan, 1972–93.
Crawford, Elizabeth. *The Women's Suffrage Movement: A Reference Guide, 1866–1928.* London: UCL Press, 1999.
Doughan, David, and Denis Sanchez. *Feminist Periodicals, 1885–1984: An Annotated Bibliography.* Hassocks, Sussex: Harvester Press, 1984.
Englishwoman's Year Book and Directory. London: A. and C. Black, 1884–1915.
Gates, Evelyn. *The Woman's Year Book, 1923–24.* London: Women Publishers, 1924.
Men's League for Women's Suffrage. *Annual Reports,* 1910–14.
———. *Handbook on Women's Suffrage.* London, 1912.
New Constitutional Society. *Annual Reports,* 1910–11.
Normanton, Helena, and Millicent Garrett Fawcett. "Women." In *Encyclopedia Britannica.* 13th ed. London and Chicago, 1926.
North of England Society for Women's Suffrage. *Annual Reports,* 1899–1902.
Reformers' Year Book (formerly the *Labour Annual*), ed. F. W. Pethick Lawrence and Joseph Edwards. London: Taylor, Garnett, and Evans, 1903–9.
Suffrage Annual and Women's Who's Who., ed. A. J. R. London: Stanley Paul, 1913.
Sullivan, Alvin, ed. *British Literary Magazines: The Victorian and Edwardian Age.* 3 vols. Westport, Conn.: Greenwood Press, 1983.
United Suffragists. *Annual Report,* 1915.
Women's Emancipation Union. *Annual Reports,* 1892, 1894, 1896.

Women's Freedom League. *Annual Reports,* 1907–29.
Women's Social and Political Union. *Annual Reports,* 1907–14.

CONTEMPORARY PERIODICALS
(PUBLISHED IN LONDON UNLESS OTHERWISE NOTED)

Britannia
Calling All Women
Church League for Women's Suffrage Monthly Paper
Common Cause
Contemporary Review
Daily Chronicle
Daily Telegraph
Echo
Edinburgh Evening Dispatch (Edinburgh)
Egoist
Englishwoman
Englishwoman's Review
Ethical World
Evening Standard
Forward (Glasgow)
Freewoman
Independent Suffragette
Manchester Guardian (Manchester)
New Age
New Freewoman
Shafts
Standard
Suffragette
Suffragette News Sheet
Vote
Times
Votes for Women
Westminster Review
Woman's Dreadnought
Woman's Herald
Woman's Signal
Women's Franchise
Women's Freedom League Bulletin

CONTEMPORARY BOOKS, ESSAYS, MEMOIRS, AND LETTERS

Abadam, Alice. "The Feminist Vote: Enfranchised or Emancipated?" London: WFL, 1920.
Allen, Mary S. *The Pioneer Policewoman.* London: Chatto and Windus, 1925.
Anon. "Woman's Position Under Laws Made by Man." London: Women's National Anti-Suffrage League, 1908.
Bax, Ernest Belfort. *The Fraud of Feminism.* London: Grant Richards, 1913.

Billington Greig, Teresa. "A Bombshell in the Camp of the Suffragists." *Nash's Magazine,* March 1911.

———. *The Militant Suffrage Movement: Emancipation in a Hurry.* London: Frank Palmer, 1911; reprinted in *The Non-Violent Militant: Selected Writings of Teresa Billington-Greig,* ed. Carol McPhee and Ann FitzGerald. London: Routledge and Kegan Paul, 1987.

———. *The Non-Violent Militant: Selected Writings of Teresa Billington Greig.* Ed. Carol McPhee and Ann Fitzgerald. London: Routledge and Kegan Paul, 1987.

———. "Suffragist Tactics: Past and Present." London: WFL, 1909.

———. "Towards Women's Liberty." London: WFL, 1908.

Billington Greig, Teresa, and Maude FitzHerbert, eds. *The Hour and the Woman.* Nos. 1–3. London: WFL, 1909.

Blackburn, Helen. *Women's Suffrage: A Record of the Women's Movement in the British Isles with Biographical Sketches of Miss Becker.* London: Williams and Norgate, 1902.

Blease, Walter Lyon. "Against Prejudice: A Reply to Professor Dicey." London: WFL, 1913.

———. "Concerning the Status of Political Prisoners." London: National Political Reform League, 1910.

———. *The Emancipation of English Women.* London: Constable, 1910.

Bondfield, Margaret. *A Life's Work.* London: Hutchinson, 1949.

Boyle, C. Nina. "Principle—Not Party." London: WFL, 1918.

Brailsford, H. N. "The Conciliation Bill: An Explanation and Defence." London: Women's Press, 1910.

Bryce, James. *The Hindrances to Good Citizenship.* Oxford: Oxford University Press, 1909.

Butler, Josephine. *Native Races and the War.* London: Gay and Bird, 1900.

———, ed. *Women's Work and Women's Culture: A Series of Essays.* London: Macmillan, 1869.

Buxton, C. R., ed. *Towards a Lasting Settlement.* London: George Allen and Unwin, 1915.

Carter, Huntly, ed. *Women's Suffrage and Militancy.* London: Frank Palmer, 1912.

Challoner, Phyllis. *Towards Citizenship: A Handbook of Women's Emancipation.* London: P. S. King and Son, 1928.

Chapman, Annie, and Mary Wallis Chapman. *The Status of Women Under the English Law.* London: G. Routledge, 1909.

Cholmeley, R. F. "Women's Suffrage: The Demand and Its Meaning." London: Woman Citizen Society, 1909.

Cleveland, Arthur Rackham. *Woman Under the English Law: From the Landing of the Saxons to the Present Time.* London: Hurst and Blackett, 1896.

Cobb, W. F. "Women and Brute Force." London: Woman's Press, 1912.

Cobbe, Frances Power. "Criminals, Idiots, Women, and Minors. Is the Classification Sound? A Discussion on the Laws Concerning the Property of Married Women." Manchester: A. Ireland, 1869.

Cobden Sanderson, Thomas James. *The Journals of Thomas James Cobden Sanderson.* 2 vols. London: Richard Cobden Sanderson, 1926.

Cousins, James, and Margaret Cousins. *We Two Together.* Madras: Ganesh, 1950.

Dangerfield, George. *The Strange Death of Liberal England.* London, 1935. Reprint, London: Granada, 1983.

Davies, Emily. *Thoughts on Some Questions Relating to Women, 1860–1908.* Cambridge: Bowes and Bowes, 1910. Reprint, New York: AMS Press, 1973.

Despard, Charlotte. "Woman in the Nation." London: WFL, 1910.

———. "Woman in the New Era." London: Suffrage Shop, 1910.

———. "Woman's Franchise and Industry." London: WFL, 1913.

Dicey, A. V. "Woman Suffrage." *Quarterly Review,* January 1909, pp. 276–304.

Donaldson, Rev. F. Lewis. "The Religion of Women's Suffrage." London: Central Society for Women's Suffrage, 1905.

Earengey, W. G. "Woman Under the Insurance Act." London: WFL, 1913.

———. "Woman Under the Law." London: WFL, 1909.

Elmy, Elizabeth C. Wolstenholme. "Women's Franchise: The Need of the Hour." London: ILP, 1907.

Fawcett, Millicent Garrett. *Five Famous French Women.* London: Cassell, 1905.

———. "Home and Politics: An Address Delivered at Toynbee Hall and Elsewhere." London: Women's Printing Society, 1889.

———. "Report on the Concentration Camps in South Africa by the Committee of Ladies Appointed by the Secretary of State for War Containing Reports on the Camps in Natal, the Orange River Colony, and the Transvaal." London: HMSO, 1902.

———. *What I Remember.* London: T. Fisher Unwin, 1925.

———. *Women's Suffrage: A Short History of a Great Movement.* London: T. C. and E. C. Jack, 1912. Reprint, New York: Source Book Press, 1970.

———. *The Women's Victory and After: Reminiscences, 1911–1918.* London: Sidgwick and Jackson, 1920.

Ford, Isabella O. "Women and Socialism." London: ILP Press, 1904.

Fraser, Helen. *Women and War Work.* London: G. Arnold Shaw, 1918.

Gawthorpe, Mary. *Uphill to Holloway.* Penobscot, Me.: Traversity Press, 1962.

Gollancz, Victor, ed. *The Making of Women: Oxford Essays in Feminism.* London: George Allen and Unwin, 1918.

Gower, Lord Ronald. *Joan of Arc.* London: John C. Nimmo, 1893.

Green, T. H. *Lectures on the Principles of Political Obligation.* London, 1882. Reprint, Ann Arbor: University of Michigan, 1976.

Grey, Mrs. William. "Is the Exercise of the Franchise Unfeminine?" London: London National Society for Women's Suffrage, 1870.

Hamilton, Cicely. *Life Errant.* London: J. M. Dent and Sons, 1935.

———. *Marriage as a Trade.* London: Chapman and Hall, 1909.

———. "Women in the Great State." In *The Great State: Essays in Reconstruction,* ed. H. G. Wells, 219–47. London: Harper and Bros., 1912.

Hand, J. E., ed. *Good Citizenship.* London: G. Allen, 1899.

Hardie, J. Keir. "The Citizenship of Women." London: ILP, 1906.

———. "The Labour Party and Women's Suffrage." London: Central Society for Women's Suffrage, 1912.

———. "Radicals and Reform." Manchester: National Labour Press, 1912.

Harrison, Mrs. Darent. "John Hampden." London: WTRL, 1913.

———. "The Right to Resist." London: WTRL, 1913.

Hart, Heber. "Woman Suffrage: A National Danger." London: P. S. King and Son, 1912.

Healy, T. M. "Defence at Bow Street Police Court." London: WFL, 1909.

Hearnshaw, F. J. C., ed. *Edwardian England, A.D. 1901–1910: A Series of Lectures Delivered at King's College, University of London, During the Session 1932–3.* London: Ernest Benn, 1933. Reprint, New York: Books for Libraries Press, 1968.

Helsinger, Elizabeth K., Robin Lauterbach Sheets, and William Veeder. *The Woman Question: Society and Literature in Britain and America*. New York: Garland, 1983.

Hill, Ethel, and Olga Fenton Shafer. *Great Suffragists — and Why: Modern Makers of History*. London: H. J. Drane, 1909.

Hobson, J. A. *The War in South Africa: Its Causes and Effects*. London: Macmillan, 1900.

Holmes, Marion. "The A.B.C. of Votes for Women." London: WFL, 1910.

———. *Elizabeth Fry: A Cameo-Life Sketch*. London: WFL, 1913.

———. *Florence Nightingale: A Cameo-Life Sketch*. London: WFL, 1911.

———. *Frances Mary Buss: A Cameo-Life Sketch*. London: WFL, 1913.

———. *Josephine Butler: A Cameo-Life Sketch*. London: WFL, 1911.

———. *Lydia Becker: A Cameo-Life Sketch*. London: WFL, 1912.

Housman, Laurence. "Be Law-Abiding." London: WFL, 1913.

———. "The Census: News from No-Man's Land." London: WFL, 1911.

———. "The Physical Force Fallacy." London: Women's Press, 1912.

———. *The Unexpected Years*. London: Jonathan Cape, 1937.

———. "What Is Womanly?" London: WFL, 1913.

Howe, Stephen, ed. *Lines of Dissent: Writing from the New Statesman, 1913–1988*. London: Verso, 1988.

Jacques, J. W. F. "Women: And the Unfair Position They Occupy at the Present Time from a Legal Point of View." London: NUWSS, 1912.

Jeffreys, Sheila, ed. *The Sexuality Debates*. London: Routledge and Kegan Paul, 1987.

Jorgensen-Earp, Cheryl, ed. *Speeches of the Militant Suffragettes*. Cranbury, N.J.: Associated University Presses, 1999.

Joshi, Pushpa, comp. *Gandhi on Women*. Ahmedabad: Navajivan Publishing House, 1988.

Kamester, Margaret, and Jo Vellacott, ed. *Militarism Versus Feminism: Writings on Women and War*. London: Virago, 1987.

Kenney, Annie. *Memories of a Militant*. London: Edward Arnold, 1924.

Kenney, Rowland. "Women's Suffrage: The Militant Movement in Ruins." *English Review* 13, no. 49 (1912): 98–108.

Kidd, Ronald H. "For Freedom's Cause: An Appeal to Working Men." London: Woman's Press, 1912.

Koss, Stephen, ed. *The Pro-Boers: The Anatomy of an Antiwar Movement*. Chicago: University of Chicago Press, 1973.

Lacey, Candida Ann, ed. *Barbara Leigh Smith Bodichon and the Langham Place Group*. London: Routledge and Kegan Paul, 1987.

Leeds, Hester. "Origin and Growth of the Union." London: Union of Practical Suffragists, 1898.

Lewis, Jane, ed. *Before the Vote Was Won: Arguments for and Against Women's Suffrage*. London: Routledge and Kegan Paul, 1987.

Lytton, Constance. *Prisons and Prisoners: Some Personal Experiences*. London: William Heinemann, 1914. Reprint, London: Virago, 1988.

Maccunn, John. *Six Radical Thinkers*. London: Edward Arnold, 1910.

MacMillan, Chrystal. "The Struggle for Political Liberty." London: Woman's Press, 1909.

Manchester Men's League for Women's Suffrage. "Women and the War." Manchester: Manchester Men's League for Women's Suffrage, 1914.

Marcus, Jane, ed. *Suffrage and the Pankhursts*. London: Routledge and Kegan Paul, 1987.

————. *The Young Rebecca: Writings of Rebecca West, 1911–1917.* New York: Viking, 1982.

Mason, Bertha. *The Story of the Women's Suffrage Movement.* London: Sherratt and Hughes, 1912.

Maurois, Andre. *The Edwardian Era.* Trans. Hamish Miles. New York: D. Appleton-Century, 1933.

Mazzini, Giuseppe. *The Duties of Man.* Trans. Emilie A. Venturi. London: Chapman and Hall, 1862.

McIlquham, Harriet. "The Enfranchisement of Women: An Ancient Right, a Modern Need." Congleton, England: WEU, 1891.

McLaren, W. S. B. "The Political Emancipation of Women." London: Woman's Printing Society, ca. 1888.

Mellone, Sydney Herbert. "The Position and Claims of Women: A Historical Survey with Reference to Present Conditions." London: Woman's Press, 1909.

Mill, John Stuart. *Considerations on Representative Government.* New York: Henry Holt, 1874.

————. *The Subjection of Women.* Edited, with introduction, by Susan Moller Okin. London, 1869. Reprint, Indianapolis: Hackett, 1988.

Miller, Florence Fenwick. "Real Representative Government." London: WSPU, 1907.

Miller, Irene. "From Holloway to Hyde Park: The Coming of True Chivalry." *Referee,* 21 June 1908.

Mitchell, Hannah. *The Hard Way Up.* London: Faber and Faber, 1968. Reprint, London: Virago, 1977.

Montefiore, Dora. *From a Victorian to a Modern.* London: E. Archer, 1927.

————. *Serf Life in Russia.* London: W. Heinemann, 1906.

Morris, Homer Lawrence. *Parliamentary Franchise Reform in England from 1885 to 1918.* New York: Columbia University Press, 1921. Reprint, New York: AMS Press, 1969.

Moyes, Helen Fraser. *A Woman in a Man's World.* Sydney: Alpha Books, 1971.

Murray, Eunice Guthrie. "The Illogical Sex?" Edinburgh: Scottish Council of the WFL, 1914.

————. "Prejudices Old and New." Edinburgh: Scottish Council of the WFL, 1913.

————. "Women's Value in Wartime." London: WFL, 1917.

Neilans, Alison. "Ballot Box Protest: Defence at Old Bailey." London: WFL, 1910.

Nevinson, Henry W. *Essays in Freedom.* London: Duckworth, 1909.

————. *Essays in Freedom and Rebellion.* New Haven, Conn.: Yale University Press, 1921.

————. *Essays in Rebellion.* London: James Nisbet, 1913.

————. *Fire of Life.* London: Camelot Press, 1935.

————. *A Modern Slavery.* London: Harper, 1906.

————. *More Changes, More Chances.* London: J. Nisbet, 1925.

Nevinson, Margaret Wynne. "Ancient Suffragettes." London: WFL, 1909.

————. *Life's Fitful Fever: A Volume of Memories.* London: A. and C. Black, 1926.

Norquay, Glenda, ed. *Voices and Votes: A Literary Anthology of the Women's Suffrage Campaign.* Manchester: Manchester University Press, 1995.

Ostrogorski, Moisei. *The Rights of Women: A Comparative Study in History and Legislation.* 2d ed. London: George Allen and Unwin, 1908.

Pankhurst, Christabel. *The Great Scourge and How to End It.* London: E. Pankhurst, 1913.

————. *Unshackled: The Story of How We Won the Vote.* Ed. F. W. Pethick Lawrence. London: Hutchinson, 1959.

Pankhurst, Emmeline. *My Own Story.* London: Eveleigh Nash, 1914.

———. "Verbatim Report of Mrs. Pankhurst's Speech. Delivered Nov. 13, 1913 at Parson's Theatre, Hartford, Conn." Hartford, CT: Connecticut Woman Suffrage Association, 1913.

Pankhurst, E. Sylvia. *The Home Front.* London: Hutchinson, 1932. Reprint, London: Cresset Library, 1987.

———. *The Life of Emmeline Pankhurst.* London: T. W. Laurie, 1935.

———. *The Suffragette: The History of the Women's Militant Suffrage Movement, 1905–1910.* London: Gray and Hancock, 1911.

———. *The Suffragette Movement: An Intimate Account of Persons and Ideals.* London: Longman, 1931. Reprint, with new introduction by Dr. Richard Pankhurst, London: Virago, 1977.

Parkes, Margaret Kineton. "Why We Resist Our Taxes." London: WTRL, 1911.

Pethick Lawrence, Emmeline. "The Faith That Is in Us." London: Woman's Press, 1908.

———. "The Meaning of the Woman's Movement." London: Woman's Press, 1907.

———. *My Part in a Changing World.* London: Victor Gollancz, 1938.

———. "The New Crusade." London: NWSPU, 1907.

———. "Women's Fight for the Vote." London: Woman's Press, 1910.

Pethick Lawrence, Frederick. *Fate Has Been Kind.* London: Hutchinson, 1943.

———. "Is the English Law Unjust to Women?" London: Woman's Press, 1909.

———. "Women and Physical Force." London: Woman's Press, n.d.

Phillips, Marion, ed. *Women and the Labour Party.* New York: B. W. Huebsch, 1920.

Priestman, Miss. "Women and Votes." London: Union of Practical Suffragists, 1897.

Rathbone, Eleanor. *Milestones: Presidential Addresses at the Annual Council Meetings of the NUSEC.* Liverpool: NUSEC, 1929.

Richardson, Mary. *Laugh a Defiance.* London: George Weidenfeld and Nicolson, 1953.

Roberts, Marie Mulvey, and Tamae Mizuta. *Sources of British Feminism.* 6 vols. London: Routledge/Thoemmes Reprints, 1993.

Robins, Elizabeth. *Ancilla's Share: An Indictment of Sex Antagonism.* London: Hutchinson, 1924.

Royden, A. Maude. "The True End of Government." London: NUWSS, 1912.

Schloesser, Henry H. "The Legal Status of Women in England." London: Woman's Press, 1907.

Scott, A. MacCallum. "The Physical Force Argument Against Woman Suffrage." London: National League for Opposing Woman Suffrage, 1912.

Scottish Women Graduates Committee. "Report of the Scottish Women Graduates Appeal in the House of Lords." London: Woman Citizen Publishing Society, 1908.

Sennett, Maud Arncliffe. *The Child.* London: C. W. Daniel, 1938.

Sharp, Evelyn. *Unfinished Adventure.* London: John Lane, 1933.

Smyth, Ethel Mary. *Female Pipings in Eden.* London: P. Davies, 1934.

Snowden, Ethel. *The Feminist Movement.* London: Collins, 1913.

Stanton, Theodore, ed. *The Woman Question in Europe: A Series of Original Essays.* London, 1884. Reprint, New York: Source Book Press, 1974.

Stopes, Charlotte Carmichael. *British Freewomen: Their Historical Privilege.* London: Swann Sonnenschein, 1894.

———. "The Constitutional Basis of Women's Suffrage." Edinburgh: Darien Press, 1908.

―――. *The Sphere of "Man" in Relation to That of "Woman" in the Constitution.* London: T. Fisher Unwin, 1907.

―――. "The Women's Protest." Paper read at the WEU's London Conference, 15 October 1892.

Strachey, Ray. *"The Cause": A Short History of the Women's Movement in Great Britain.* London, G. Bell and Sons, 1928. Reprint, London: Virago, 1978.

―――. *Millicent Garrett Fawcett.* London: John Murray, 1931.

Swanwick, Helen. *I Have Been Young.* London: Victor Gollancz, 1935.

Thompson, Tierl, ed. *Dear Girl: The Diaries and Letters of Two Working Women, 1897–1917.* London: Women's Press, 1987.

Thurston, Herbert. "Blessed Joan of Arc in English Opinion." *The Month* 113 (May 1909): 449–64.

Villiers, Brougham, ed. [Frederick John Shaw]. *The Case for Women's Suffrage.* London: T. Fisher Unwin, 1907.

―――. *The Socialist Movement in England.* London: T. Fisher Unwin, 1908.

Women's Freedom League. "Is Political Agitation a Crime?" London: WFL, 1909.

―――. "The Protection of Criminals by the Government and the Law Courts: A Scandalous Case." London: WFL, 1914.

―――. "Some Social Problems and Votes for Women." London: 1908.

―――. "Why the Lords Threw Out the Budget." London: WFL, 1909.

―――. "Why We Petition the King." London: WFL, 1909.

―――. "Women and the Law Courts." London: WFL, 1907.

Women's Social and Political Union. *Suffrage Speeches from the Dock (Conspiracy Trial, Old Bailey, May 15th–22nd, 1912).* London: WSPU, 1912.

Wells, H. G. *The New Machiavelli.* London: John Lane, 1911.

Wilson, R. M. *Wife, Mother, Voter. Her Vote. What Will She Do with It?* London: Hodder and Stoughton, 1918.

Wright, Almoth E. *The Unexpurgated Case Against Woman Suffrage.* London: Constable, 1913.

Zangwill, Israel. "One and One Are Two." London: WFL, 1907.

―――. "Talked Out!" London: WFL, 1907.

SECONDARY SOURCES

Adelman, Paul. *Victorian Radicalism: The Middle-Class Experience, 1830–1914.* London: Longman, 1984.

Alberti, Johanna. *Beyond Suffrage: Feminists in War and Peace, 1914–1929.* London: Macmillan, 1994.

―――. *Eleanor Rathbone.* London: Sage, 1996.

Allen, Judith A. *Rose Scott: Vision and Revision in Feminism.* Melbourne: Oxford University Press, 1994.

Alonso, Harriet. "Suffragists for Peace During the Interwar Years, 1919–1941." *Peace and Change* 14, no. 3 (1989): 243–62.

Ardis, Ann L. *New Women, New Novels: Feminism and Early Modernism.* New Brunswick, N.J.: Rutgers University Press, 1990.

Auld, John W. "The Liberal Pro-Boers." *Journal of British Studies* 14, no. 2 (1975): 78–101.

Auslander, Leora. "Feminist Theory and Social History: Explorations in the Politics of Identity." *Radical History Review* 54 (1992): 158–76.

Banks, Olive. *Becoming a Feminist: The Social Origins of "First Wave" Feminism.* Athens: University of Georgia Press, 1986.

Barker, Rodney. *Political Ideas in Modern Britain.* London: Methuen, 1978.

Barrow, Logie, and Ian Bullock. *Democratic Ideas and the British Labour Movement, 1880– 1914.* Cambridge: Cambridge University Press, 1996.

Barstow, Susan Torrey. "Acting Like a Feminist: The Theatrical Origins of the Suffragette Movement." Ph.D. diss., University of Virginia, 1994.

Beckett, Jane, and Deborah Cherry, eds. *The Edwardian Era.* London: Phaidon Press and Barbican Art Gallery, 1987.

Beiner, Ronald, ed. *Theorizing Citizenship.* Albany: State University of New York Press, 1995.

Belchem, John. *Class, Party and the Political System in Britain, 1867–1914.* Oxford: Basil Blackwell, 1990.

Bellamy, Richard, ed. *Victorian Liberalism: Nineteenth-Century Political Thought and Practice.* London: Routledge, 1990.

Benhabib, Seyla, ed. *Democracy and Difference: Contesting the Boundaries of the Political.* Princeton, N.J.: Princeton University Press, 1996.

Bentley, Michael. *The Climax of Liberal Politics: British Liberalism in Theory and Practice, 1868–1918.* London: Edward Arnold, 1987.

Bentley, Michael, and John Stevenson, eds. *High and Low Politics in Modern Britain: Ten Studies.* Oxford: Clarendon Press, 1983.

Biagini, Eugenio F., ed. *Citizenship and Community: Liberals, Radicals, and Collective Identities in the British Isles, 1865– 1931.* Cambridge: Cambridge University Press, 1996.

Biagini, Eugenio F., and Alistair J. Reid. *Currents of Radicalism: Popular Radicalism, Organised Labour, and Party Politics in Britain, 1850–1914.* Cambridge: Cambridge University Press, 1991.

Blewett, Neal. "The Franchise in the United Kingdom, 1885–1918." *Past and Present* 32 (1965): 27–56.

Blom, Ida, Karen Hagemann, and Catherine Hall, eds. *Gendered Nations: Nationalisms and Gender Order in the Long Nineteenth Century.* Oxford: Berg, 2000.

Bock, Gisela, and Susan James, eds. *Beyond Equality and Difference: Citizenship, Feminist Politics and Female Subjectivity.* London: Routledge, 1992.

Bottomley, Anne, and Joanne Conaghan. "Feminist Theory and Legal Strategy." In *Feminist Theory and Legal Strategy.* Oxford: Basil Blackwell, 1993.

Bradley, Ian. *The Strange Rebirth of Liberal Britain.* With a foreword by the Rt. Hon. David Steel, M.P. London: Chatto and Windus/Hogarth Press, 1985.

Brooks, David. *The Age of Upheaval: Edwardian Politics, 1899–1914.* Manchester: Manchester University Press, 1995.

Brophy, Julia, and Carol Smart, eds. *Women-in-Law: Explorations in Law, Family and Sexuality.* London: Routledge and Kegan Paul, 1985.

Bullock, Ian, and Richard Pankhurst, eds. *Sylvia Pankhurst: From Artist to Anti-Fascist.* New York: St. Martin's Press, 1992.

Burton, Antoinette. *Burdens of History: British Feminists, Indian Women, and Imperial Culture, 1865–1915.* Chapel Hill: University of North Carolina Press, 1994.

———. "The Feminist Quest for Identity: British Imperial Suffragism and 'Global Sisterhood,' 1900–1915." *Journal of Women's History* 3, no. 2 (1991): 46–81.

———. "History Is Now: Feminist Theory and the Production of Historical Feminisms." *Women's History Review* 1, no. 1 (1992): 25–38.

Butler, Judith, and Joan W. Scott, eds. *Feminists Theorize the Political*. London: Routledge, 1992.

Byrt, George William. *John Clifford: A Fighting Free Churchman*. London: Kingsgate Press, 1947.

Caine, Barbara. *English Feminism, 1780–1980*. New York: Oxford University Press, 1997.

———. "Feminism, Suffrage and the Nineteenth-Century English Women's Movement." *Women's Studies International Forum* 5, no. 6 (1982): 537–50.

———. "Feminism and Political Economy in Victorian England—or John Stuart Mill, Henry Fawcett and Henry Sidgwick Ponder the 'Woman Question.'" In *Feminism and Political Economy in Victorian England*, ed. Peter Groenewegen, 25–45. Aldershot, England: Edward Elgar, 1994.

———. *Victorian Feminists*. Oxford: Oxford University Press, 1992.

Canning, Kathleen. "Feminist History After the Linguistic Turn: Historicizing Discourse and Experience." *Signs* 19, no. 21 (1994): 368–404.

Carrier, John. *The Campaign for the Employment of Women as Police Officers*. Avebury: Gower, 1988.

Centre for Contemporary Cultural Studies. *Making Histories: Studies in History-Writing and Politics*. London: Hutchinson, 1982.

Chadwick, Andrew. *Augmenting Democracy: Political Movements and Constitutional Reform During the Rise of Labour, 1900–1924*. Aldershot, Hampshire, England: Ashgate, 1999.

Clark, Anna. *The Struggle for the Breeches: Gender and the Making of the British Working Class*. Berkeley: University of California Press, 1995.

Clarke, Peter. *Liberals and Social Democrats*. Cambridge: Cambridge University Press, 1978.

Close, David H. "The Collapse of Resistance to Democracy: Conservatives, Adult Suffrage, and Second Chamber Reform, 1911–1928." *Historical Journal* 20, no. 4 (1977): 893–918.

Cockin, Katharine. *Women and Theatre in the Age of Suffrage: The Pioneer Players, 1911–1925*. Houndsmills, Basingstoke, Hampshire: Palgrave, 2001.

Collini, Stefan. *Public Moralists: Political Thought and Intellectual Life in Britain 1850–1930*. Oxford: Clarendon Press, 1991.

Cook, Kay, and Neil Evans. "'The Petty Antics of the Bell-Ringing Boisterous Band'? The Women's Suffrage Movement in Wales, 1890–1918." In *Our Mothers' Land: Chapters in Welsh Women's History, 1830–1939*, ed. Angela V. John, 159–88. Cardiff: University of Wales Press, 1991.

Corbett, Mary Jean. *Representing Femininity: Middle-Class Subjectivity in Victorian and Edwardian Women's Autobiographies*. New York: Oxford University Press, 1992.

Cowman, Krista. "'Incipient Toryism'? The Women's Social and Political Union and the Independent Labour Party, 1903–14." *History Workshop Journal* 53 (2002): 129–48.

———. "'The Stone-Throwing Has Been Forced upon Us': The Function of Militancy Within the Liverpool WSPU, 1906–1914." *Transactions of the Historic Society of Lancashire and Cheshire* 145 (1996): 171–92.

Cunningham, Hugh. *The Challenge of Democracy: Britain, 1832–1918*. London: Longman, 2001.

Daley, Caroline, and Melanie Nolan, eds. *Suffrage and Beyond: International Feminist Perspectives*. New York: New York University Press, 1994.

Davis, David Brion. *The Problem of Slavery in the Age of Revolution, 1770–1823.* Ithaca, N.Y.: Cornell University Press, 1966.

Diamond, Irene, ed. *Families, Politics, and Public Policy: A Feminist Dialogue on Women and the State.* New York: Longman, 1983.

Dietz, Mary. "Context Is All: Feminism and Theories of Citizenship." *Daedalus* 116, no. 4 (1987): 1–24.

Dixon, Joy. *Divine Feminine: Theosophy and Feminism in England.* Baltimore: Johns Hopkins University Press, 2001.

Dodd, Kathryn. "Cultural Politics and Women's Historical Writing: The Case of Ray Strachey's *The Cause.*" *Women's Studies International Forum* 13 (1990): 127–37.

Dubois, Ellen Carol. "Working Women, Class Relations, and Suffrage Militance: H. S. Blatch and the New York Woman Suffrage Movement, 1894–1909." In *History of Women in the United States: Historical Articles on Women's Lives and Activities,* ed. Nancy Cott, 19: 147–71. Munich: K. G. Saur, 1994.

Dubow, Saul. "Colonial Nationalism, the Milner Kindergarten and the Rise of 'South Africanism,' 1902–10." *History Workshop Journal* 43 (1997): 53–85.

Edelman, Murray. *The Symbolic Uses of Politics.* Urbana: University of Illinois Press, 1967.

Ellman, Maud. *The Hunger Artists: Starving, Writing, and Imprisonment.* Cambridge, Mass.: Harvard University Press, 1993.

Eltis, David, and James Walvin, eds. *The Abolition of the Atlantic Slave Trade: Origins and Effects in Europe, Africa, and the Americas.* Madison: University of Wisconsin Press, 1981.

Epstein, James A. *Radical Expression: Political Language, Ritual, and Symbol in England, 1790–1850.* New York: Oxford University Press, 1994.

Eustance, Claire. "'Daring to Be Free': The Evolution of Women's Political Identities in the Women's Freedom League, 1907–1930." Ph.D. diss., York University, 1993.

———. "Protests from Behind the Grille: Gender and the Transformation of Parliament, 1867–1918." *Parliamentary History* 16, no. 1 (1997): 107–26.

Eustance, Claire, Joan Ryan, and Laura Ugolini, eds. *A Suffrage Reader: Charting Directions in British Suffrage History.* London: Leicester University Press, 2000.

Farwell, Byron. *The Great Anglo-Boer War.* New York: Norton, 1990.

Ferguson, Moira. *Subject to Others: British Women Writers and Colonial Slavery, 1670–1834.* New York: Routledge, 1992.

Finn, Margot. *After Chartism: Class and Nation in English Radical Politics, 1848–1874.* Cambridge: Cambridge University Press, 1993.

Fletcher, Ian Christopher. "Liberalism and the Rule of Law: Protest Movements, Public Order, and the Liberal Government, 1905–14." Ph.D. diss., Johns Hopkins University, 1990.

———. "'Prosecutions . . . Are Always Risky Business': Labor, Liberals, and the 1912 'Don't Shoot' Prosecutions." *Albion* 28, no. 2 (1996): 251–78.

———. "'A Star Chamber of the Twentieth Century': Suffragettes, Liberals, and the 1908 'Rush the Commons' Case." *Journal of British Studies* 35, no. 4 (1996): 504–30.

———. "'This Zeal for Lawlessness': A. V. Dicey, *The Law of the Constitution,* and the Challenge of Popular Politics, 1885–1915." *Parliamentary History* 16, no. 3 (1997): 309–29.

Fletcher, Ian Christopher, Laura E. Nym Mayhall, and Philippa Levine, eds. *Women's Suffrage in the British Empire: Citizenship, Nation, and Race.* London: Routledge, 2000.

Flint, Kate. *The Woman Reader, 1837–1914.* Oxford: Clarendon Press, 1993.

Formations Editorial Collective. *Formations of Nation and People*. London: Routledge and Kegan Paul, 1984.

Fowler, Rowena. "Why Did Suffragettes Attack Works of Art?" *Journal of Women's History* 2, no. 3 (1991): 109–25.

Frader, Laura L., and Sonya O. Rose, eds. *Gender and Class in Modern Europe*. Ithaca, N.Y.: Cornell University Press, 1996.

Fraser, Nancy. *Unruly Practices: Power, Discourse and Gender in Contemporary Social Theory*. Minneapolis: University of Minnesota Press, 1989.

Freeden, Michael. *The New Liberalism: An Ideology of Social Reform*. Oxford: Clarendon Press, 1978.

Fulford, Roger. *Votes for Women: The Story of a Struggle*. London: Faber and Faber, 1957.

Garner, Les. *A Brave and Beautiful Spirit: Dora Marsden, 1882–1960*. Brookfield, Vt.: Gower, 1990.

―――. *Stepping Stones to Liberty: Feminist Ideas in the Women's Suffrage Movement*. Rutherford, N.J.: Fairleigh Dickinson University Press, 1988.

Gies, Frances. *Joan of Arc: The Legend and the Reality*. New York: Harper and Row, 1981.

Gleadle, Kathryn. *The Early Feminists: Radical Unitarians and the Emergence of the Women's Rights Movement, 1831–51*. New York: St. Martin's Press, 1995.

Gleadle, Kathryn, and Sarah Richardson, eds. *Women in British Politics, 1760–1860: The Power of the Petticoat*. New York: St. Martin's Press, 2000.

Grayzel, Susan R. *Women's Identities at War: Gender, Motherhood, and Politics in Britain and France During the First World War*. Chapel Hill: University of North Carolina Press, 1999.

Green, Barbara. *Spectacular Confessions: Autobiography, Performative Activism, and the Sites of Suffrage, 1905–1938*. New York: St. Martin's Press, 1997.

Green, S. J. D., and R. C. Whiting, eds. *The Boundaries of the State in Modern Britain*. Cambridge: Cambridge University Press, 1996.

Greenleaf, W. H. *The British Political Tradition*. 2 vols. London: Methuen, 1983.

Gullace, Nicoletta. *"The Blood of Our Sons": Men, Women, and the Renegotiation of British Citizenship During the Great War*. New York: Palgrave Macmillan, 2002.

Habermas, Jurgen. *The Structural Transformation of the Public Sphere: An Inquiry into a Category of Bourgeois Society*. Trans. Thomas Burger. 1962; reprint, Cambridge, Mass.: MIT Press, 1989.

Hall, Catherine. "Histories, Empires and the Post-Colonial Moment." In *The Post-Colonial Question: Common Skies, Divided Horizons,* ed. Iain Chambers and Lidia Curti, 65–77. London: Routledge, 1996.

―――. "Rethinking Imperial Histories: The Reform Act of 1867." *New Left Review* 208 (1994): 3–29.

Hall, Catherine, Keith McClelland, and Jane Rendall. *Defining the Victorian Nation: Class, Race, Gender and the Reform Act of 1867*. Cambridge: Cambridge University Press, 2000.

Hannam, June. *Isabella Ford*. Oxford: Basil Blackwell, 1989.

Hannam, June, and Karen Hunt. *Socialist Women: Britain, 1880s to 1920s*. London: Routledge, 2002.

Harrison, Brian. "The Act of Militancy: Violence and the Suffragettes, 1904–1914." In *Peaceable Kingdom: Stability and Change in Modern Britain*. Oxford: Clarendon Press, 1982.

―――. *Prudent Revolutionaries: Portraits of British Feminists Between the Wars*. Oxford: Clarendon Press, 1987.

————. *Separate Spheres: The Opposition to Women's Suffrage*. London: Croom Helm, 1978.

Hayward, Jack, ed. *Out of Slavery: Abolition and After*. London: Frank Cass, 1985.

Herstein, Sheila R. *A Mid-Victorian Feminist, Barbara Leigh Smith Bodichon*. New Haven, Conn.: Yale University Press, 1985.

Hewitt, Nancy A., and Suzanne Lebsock, eds. *Visible Women: New Essays on American Activism*. Urbana: University of Illinois Press, 1993.

Higonnet, Margaret R., and Patrice L.-R. Higonnet. "Introduction." In *Behind the Lines: Gender and the Two World Wars*. New Haven, Conn.: Yale University Press, 1987.

Hirsch, Susan F., and Mindie Lazarus-Black. *Contested States: Law, Hegemony, and Resistance*. New York: Routledge, 1994.

Hirshfield, Claire. "The Actresses' Franchise League and the Campaign for Women's Suffrage, 1908–1914." *Theatre Research International* 10, no. 2 (1985): 129–53.

————. "Fractured Faith: Liberal Party Women and the Suffrage Issue in Britain, 1892–1914." *Gender and History* 2 (1990): 173–97.

Holcombe, Lee. *Wives and Property: Reform of the Married Women's Property Law in Nineteenth-Century England*. Toronto: University of Toronto Press, 1983.

Holledge, Julie. *Innocent Flowers: Women in the Edwardian Theatre*. London: Virago, 1981.

Hollis, Patricia. *Ladies Elect: Women in English Local Government, 1865–1914*. Oxford: Clarendon Press, 1987.

Holt, Thomas. *The Problem of Freedom: Race, Labor, and Politics in Jamaica and Britain, 1832–1938*. Baltimore: Johns Hopkins University Press, 1992.

Holton, Sandra Stanley. *Feminism and Democracy: Women's Suffrage and Reform Politics in Britain, 1900–1918*. Cambridge: Cambridge University Press, 1986.

————. *Suffrage Days: Stories from the Women's Suffrage Movement*. London: Routledge, 1996.

————. "The Suffragist and the 'Average' Woman." *Women's History Review* 1, no. 1 (1992): 9–24.

————. "'To Educate Women into Rebellion': Elizabeth Cady Stanton and the Creation of a Transatlantic Network of Radical Suffragists." *American Historical Review* 99, no. 4 (1994): 1112–36.

Howlett, Caroline. "Writing on the Body? Representation and Resistance in British Suffragette Accounts of Forcible Feeding." *Genders* 23 (1996): 3–41.

Hume, Lesley Parker. *The National Union of Women's Suffrage Societies, 1897–1914*. New York: Garland Press, 1982.

Hunt, James. *Gandhi and the Nonconformists: Encounters in South Africa*. New Delhi: Promilla, 1986.

————. *Gandhi in London*. Rev. ed. Springfield, Va.: Nataraj Books, 1993.

Hunt, Karen. *Equivocal Feminists: The Social Democratic Federation and the Woman Question, 1884–1911*. Cambridge: Cambridge University Press, 1996.

Hynes, Samuel. *The Edwardian Turn of Mind*. Princeton, N.J.: Princeton University Press, 1968.

Jenkins, T. A. *The Liberal Ascendancy, 1830–1886*. New York: St. Martin's Press, 1994.

Joannou, Maroula. "She Who Would Be Free Herself Must Strike the Blow: Suffragette Autobiography and Suffragette Militancy." In *The Uses of Autobiography*, ed. Julia Swindells, 31–44. London: Taylor and Francis, 1995.

Joannou, Maroula, and June Purvis, eds. *The Women's Suffrage Movement: New Feminist Perspectives*. Manchester: Manchester University Press, 1998.

John, Angela V., and Claire Eustance, eds. *The Men's Share? Masculinities, Male Support and Women's Suffrage in Britain, 1890–1920.* London: Routledge, 1997.

Jones, Gareth Stedman. *Languages of Class: Studies in English Working-Class History, 1832–1982.* Cambridge: Cambridge University Press, 1983.

Jorgensen-Earp, Cheryl. *The Transfiguring Sword: The Just War of the Women's Social and Political Union.* Tuscaloosa: University of Alabama Press, 1997.

Joyce, Patrick. *Democratic Subjects: The Self and the Social in Nineteenth-Century England.* Cambridge: Cambridge University Press, 1994.

———. *Visions of the People: Industrial England and the Question of Class, 1848–1914.* Cambridge: Cambridge University Press, 1994.

Kaplan, Joel H., and Sheila Stowell. *Theatre and Fashion: Oscar Wilde to the Suffragettes.* Cambridge: Cambridge University Press, 1994.

Kean, Hilda. *Deeds Not Words: The Lives of Suffragette Teachers.* London: Pluto Press, 1990.

———. "Searching for the Past in Present Defeat: The Construction of Historical and Political Identity in British Feminism in the 1920s and 1930s." *Women's History Review* 3, no. 1 (1994): 57–80.

———. "Some Problems of Constructing and Reconstructing a Suffragette's Life: Mary Richardson, Suffragette, Socialist and Fascist." *Women's History Review* 7, no. 4 (1998): 475–93.

Kent, Susan Kingsley. *Making Peace: The Reconstruction of Gender in Interwar Britain.* Princeton, N.J.: Princeton University Press, 1993.

———. *Sex and Suffrage in Britain, 1860–1914.* Princeton, N.J.: Princeton University Press, 1987.

Kinzer, Bruce L., Ann P. Robson, and John M. Robson. *A Moralist in and out of Parliament: John Stuart Mill at Westminster, 1865–1868.* Toronto: University of Toronto Press, 1992.

Koven, Seth, and Sonya Michel, eds. *Mothers of a New World: Maternalist Politics and the Origins of Welfare States.* New York: Routledge, 1993.

Kranidis, Rita S. *Subversive Discourse: The Cultural Production of Late Victorian Feminist Novels.* New York: St. Martin's Press, 1995.

Langan, Mary, and Bill Schwarz, eds. *Crises in the British State, 1880–1930.* London: Hutchinson, 1985.

Law, Cheryl. *Suffrage and Power: The Women's Movement, 1918–1928.* London: I. B. Tauris, 1997.

Lawrence, Jon. *Speaking for the People: Party, Language and Popular Politics in England, 1867–1914.* Cambridge: Cambridge University Press, 1998.

Lawrence, Jon, and Miles Taylor, eds. *Party, State and Society: Electoral Behavior in Britain Since 1820.* Aldershot, Hants, England: Scolar Press, 1997.

Ledger, Sally. "The New Woman and the Crisis of Victorianism." In *Cultural Politics at the Fin de Siècle,* ed. Sally Ledger and Scott McCracken, 22–44. Cambridge: Cambridge University Press, 1995.

Leneman, Leah. *A Guid Cause: The Women's Movement in Scotland.* Aberdeen: Aberdeen University Press, 1991.

Levine, Philippa. *Feminist Lives in Victorian England.* Oxford: Basil Blackwell, 1990.

———. "'The Humanising Influences of Five o'Clock Tea': Victorian Feminist Periodicals." *Victorian Studies* 33 (1990): 293–306.

———. "'So Few Prizes and So Many Blanks': Marriage and Feminism in Later Nineteenth-Century England." *Journal of British Studies* 28 (1989): 150–74.

———. *Victorian Feminism, 1850–1900.* London: Hutchinson, 1987.

Lewis, Jane. *Women and Social Action in Victorian and Edwardian England*. Stanford, Calif.: Stanford University Press, 2000.

Liddington, Jill, and Jill Norris. *One Hand Tied Behind Us: The Rise of the Women's Suffrage Movement*. London: Virago, 1978.

Lightbody, Charles Wayland. *The Judgements of Joan*. Cambridge, Mass.: Harvard University Press, 1961.

Linklater, Andro. *An Unhusbanded Life. Charlotte Despard: Suffragette, Socialist, and Sinn Feiner*. London: Hutchinson, 1980.

Lister, Ruth. *Citizenship: Feminist Perspectives*. New York: New York University Press, 1997.

Lock, Joan. *The British Policewoman: Her Story*. London: Robert Hale, 1979.

Lyon, Janet. "Militant Allies, Strange Bedfellows: Suffragettes and Vorticists Before the War." *differences* 4 (1992): 100–133.

———. "Women Demonstrating Modernism." *Discourse* 17, no. 2 (1994–95): 6–25.

Machin, Ian. *The Rise of Democracy in Britain, 1830–1918*. Hampshire: Macmillan, 2001.

MacKillop, I. D. *The British Ethical Societies*. Cambridge: Cambridge University Press, 1986.

Margolis, Nadia. *Joan of Arc in History, Literature, and Film*. New York: Garland, 1990.

Marks, Shula, and Stanley Trapido, eds. *The Politics of Race, Class, and Nationalism in Twentieth-Century South Africa*. London: Longman, 1987.

Marwick, Arthur. *The Deluge: British Society and the First World War*. London: Norton, 1970.

Mason, Francis M. "The Newer Eve: The Catholic Women's Suffrage Society in England, 1911–1923." *Catholic Historical Review* 72, no. 4 (1986): 620–38.

Mayhall, Laura E. Nym. "Creating the 'Suffragette Spirit': British Feminism and the Historical Imagination." *Women's History Review* 4, no. 3 (1995): 319–44.

———. "'Dare to Be Free': The Women's Freedom League, 1907–1928." Ph.D. dissertation, Stanford University, 1993.

———. "Domesticating Emmeline: Representing the Suffragette, 1930–1993." *National Women's Studies Association Journal* 11, no. 2 (1999): 1–24.

———. "The Making of a Suffragette: The Legacy of Radicalism and the Uses of Reading, 1890–1918." In *Singular Continuities: Tradition, Nostalgia, and Identity in Modern British Culture,* ed. George Behlmer and Fred Leventhal, 75– 88. Stanford, Calif.: Stanford University Press, 2000.

———. "The Rhetorics of Slavery and Citizenship: Suffragist Discourse and Canonical Texts in Britain, 1880–1914." *Gender and History* 13, no. 3 (2001): 481–97.

McClintock, Anne. *Imperial Leather: Race, Gender and Sexuality in the Colonial Context*. New York: Routledge, 1994.

Meadowcroft, James. *Conceptualizing the State: Innovation and Dispute in British Political Thought, 1880–1914*. Oxford: Clarendon Press, 1995.

———, ed. *The Liberal Political Tradition: Contemporary Reappraisals*. Cheltenham, U.K.: Edward Elgar, 1996.

Melman, Billie, ed. *Borderlines: Genders and Identities in War and Peace, 1870–1930*. New York: Routledge, 1998.

Melzer, Sara E., and Leslie W. Rabine, eds. *Rebel Daughters: Women and the French Revolution*. New York: Oxford University Press, 1992.

Midgley, Clare. *Women Against Slavery: The British Campaigns, 1780–1870*. London: Routledge, 1992.

Miller, Jane Eldridge. *Rebel Women: Feminism, Modernism and the Edwardian Novel*. London: Virago, 1994.

Mitchell, David. *The Fighting Pankhursts: A Study in Tenacity.* London: Jonathan Cape, 1967.

———. *Queen Christabel: A Biography of Christabel Pankhurst.* London: Macdonald and Jane's, 1977.

Moore, Lindy. "Feminists and Femininity: A Case-Study of WSPU Propaganda and Local Response at a Scottish By-Election." *Women's Studies International Forum* 5, no. 6 (1982): 675–84.

Morgan, David. *Suffragists and Liberals: The Politics of Woman Suffrage in England.* Totowa, N.J.: Rowman and Littlefield, 1975.

Morrell, Caroline. *"Black Friday" and Violence Against Women in the Suffrage Movement.* London: Women's Research and Resources Centre, 1981.

Morris, A. J. A., ed. *Edwardian Radicalism, 1900–1914: Some Aspects of British Radicalism.* London: Routledge and Kegan Paul, 1974.

Mouffe, Chantal, ed. *Dimensions of Democracy: Pluralism, Citizenship, Community.* London: Verso, 1992.

Mulvihill, Margaret. *Charlotte Despard: A Biography.* London: Pandora Press, 1989.

Murphy, Cliona. *The Women's Suffrage Movement and Irish Society in the Twentieth Century.* London: Harvester Wheatsheaf, 1984.

Murray, Simone. "Deeds and Words: The Woman's Press and the Politics of Print." *Women: A Cultural Review* 11, no. 3 (2000): 197–222.

Okin, Susan Moller. *Women in Western Political Thought.* Princeton, N.J.: Princeton University Press, 1979.

Oldfield, Adrian. *Citizenship and Community: Civic Republicanism and the Modern World.* London: Routledge, 1990.

Oldfield, Sybil, ed. *This Working-Day World: Women's Lives and Culture(s) in Britain, 1914–1945.* London: Taylor and Francis, 1994.

Oliver, Dawn, and Derek Heater. *The Foundations of Citizenship.* London: Harvester/Wheatsheaf, 1994.

Parkins, Wendy. "Protesting Like a Girl: Embodiment, Dissent and Feminist Agency." *Feminist Theory* 1, no. 1 (2000): 59–78.

Parry, Jonathan. *The Rise and Fall of Liberal Government in Victorian Britain.* New Haven, Conn.: Yale University Press, 1993.

Pateman, Carol. *The Disorder of Women: Democracy, Feminism and Political Theory.* Stanford, Calif.: Stanford University Press, 1989.

———. *The Sexual Contract.* Stanford, Calif.: Stanford University Press, 1988.

———. "Women, Nature, and the Suffrage." *Ethics* 90 (1980): 564–70.

Pedersen, Susan. "Gender, Welfare and Citizenship in Britain During the Great War." *American Historical Review* 95, no. 4 (1990): 983–1006.

Phillips, Anne. *Democracy and Difference.* University Park: Pennsylvania State University Press, 1993.

Plasa, Carl, and Betty J. Ring. *The Discourse of Slavery: Aphra Behn to Toni Morrison.* London: Routledge, 1994.

Poovey, Mary. *Making a Social Body: British Cultural Formation, 1830–1864.* Chicago: University of Chicago Press, 1995.

———. *Uneven Developments: The Ideological Work of Gender in Mid-Victorian England.* Chicago: University of Chicago Press, 1988.

Porter, Bernard. *Critics of Empire: British Radical Attitudes to Colonialism in Africa, 1895–1914.* London: Macmillan, 1968.

Price, Richard. *An Imperial War and the British Working Class: Working-Class Attitudes and*

Reactions to the Boer War, 1899–1902. London: Routledge and Kegan Paul, 1974.

Pugh, Martin. *Electoral Reform in War and Peace, 1906–1918.* London: Routledge and Kegan Paul, 1978.

———. *The Making of Modern British Politics, 1867–1939.* 2d ed. Oxford: Basil Blackwell, 1993.

———. *The March of the Women: A Revisionist Analysis of the Campaign for Women's Suffrage, 1866–1914.* Oxford: Oxford University Press, 2000.

———. *Women and the Women's Movement in Britain.* New York: Paragon House, 1993.

———. *Women's Suffrage in Britain.* London: Historical Association, 1980.

Purvis, June. *Emmeline Pankhurst: A Biography.* London: Routledge, 2002.

———. "'A Pair of . . . Infernal Queens'? A Reassessment of the Dominant Representations of Emmeline and Christabel Pankhurst, First Wave Feminists in Edwardian Britain." *Women's History Review* 5, no. 2 (1996): 259–80.

———, ed. *Women's History: Britain, 1850–1914.* New York: St. Martin's Press, 1995.

Purvis, June, and Sandra Stanley Holton, eds. *Votes for Women.* London: Routledge, 2000.

Rappaport, Erica Diane. *Shopping for Pleasure: Women in the Making of London's West End.* Princeton, N.J.: Princeton University Press, 2000.

Read, Donald, ed. *Edwardian England.* New Brunswick, N.J.: Rutgers University Press, 1990.

Rendall, Jane. *The Origins of Modern Feminism: Women in Britain, France and the United States, 1760–1860.* London: Macmillan, 1985.

———, ed. *Equal or Different: Women's Politics, 1800–1914.* Oxford: Basil Blackwell, 1987.

Riley, Denise. *"Am I That Name?": Feminism and the Category of "Women" in History.* London: Macmillan, 1988.

Roberts, M. J. D. "Feminism and the State in Later Victorian England." *Historical Journal* 38, no. 1 (1995): 85–110.

Rogers, Helen. *Women and the People: Authority, Authorship, and the Radical Tradition in Nineteenth-Century England.* Aldershot, Hampshire, England: Ashgate, 2000.

Rolley, Katrina. "Fashion, Femininity, and the Fight for the Vote." *Art History* 13, no. 1 (1990): 48–70.

Ronning, Anne Holden. *Hidden and Visible Suffrage: Emancipation and the Edwardian Woman in Galsworthy, Wells and Forster.* Bern: Peter Lang, 1995.

Rosen, Andrew. *"Rise Up, Women!": The Militant Campaign of the Women's Social and Political Union, 1903–1914.* London: Routledge and Kegan Paul, 1974.

Rover, Constance. *Women's Suffrage and Party Politics in Britain, 1866–1914.* London: Routledge and Kegan Paul, 1967.

Rubinstein, David. *Before the Suffragettes: Women's Emancipation in the 1890s.* New York: St. Martin's Press, 1986.

———. *A Different World for Women: The Life of Millicent Garrett Fawcett.* Columbus: Ohio State University Press, 1991.

Sawer, Marian. "Gender, Metaphor and the State." *Feminist Review,* no. 52 (1996): 118–34.

Schneer, Jonathan. "The Politics of Feminism in 'Outcast London': George Lansbury and Jane Cobden's Campaign for the First London County Council." *Journal of British Studies* 30 (1991): 63–82.

Scott, Joan W. *Only Paradoxes to Offer: French Feminists and the Rights of Man.* Cambridge, Mass.: Harvard University Press, 1996.

Scott, W. S. *Jeanne d'Arc.* London: Harrup, 1974.

Semmel, Bernard. *John Stuart Mill and the Pursuit of Virtue.* New Haven, Conn.: Yale University Press, 1984.

Shanley, Mary Lyndon. *Feminism, Marriage, and the Law in Victorian England.* Princeton, N.J.: Princeton University Press, 1989.

Smart, Carol, ed. *Regulating Womanhood: Historical Essays on Marriage, Motherhood and Sexuality.* London: Routledge, 1992.

Smith, Harold L., ed. *British Feminism in the Twentieth Century.* Amherst: University of Massachusetts Press, 1991.

Smith, Iain R. *The Origins of the South African War, 1899–1902.* London: Longman, 1996.

Stanley, Liz, and Ann Morley. *The Life and Death of Emily Wilding Davison.* London: Virago, 1988.

Stowell, Sheila. "Dame Joan, Saint Christabel." *Modern Drama* 37, no. 3 (1994): 421–36.

———. "Drama as a Trade: Cicely Hamilton's *Diana of Dobson's.*" In *The New Woman and Her Sisters: Feminism and Theatre, 1850–1914,* ed. Vivien Gardner and Susan Rutherford, 11–22. Ann Arbor: University of Michigan Press, 1992.

———. *A Stage of Their Own: Feminist Playwrights of the Suffrage Era.* Ann Arbor: University of Michigan Press, 1992.

———. "Suffrage Critics and Political Action: A Feminist Agenda." In *The Edwardian Theatre: Essays on Performance and the Stage,* ed. Michael R. Booth and Joel H. Kaplan, 166–84. Cambridge: Cambridge University Press, 1996.

Sypher, Eileen. *Wisps of Violence: Producing Public and Private Politics in the Turn-of-the-Century British Novel.* London: Verso, 1993.

Tanner, Duncan. *Political Change and the Labour Party, 1900–1918.* Cambridge: Cambridge University Press, 1990.

Taylor, Barbara. *Eve and the New Jerusalem: Socialism and Feminism in the Nineteenth Century.* London: Virago, 1983.

Thompson, Dorothy, ed. *Over Our Dead Bodies: Women Against the Bomb.* London: Virago, 1983.

Thompson, F. M. L., ed. *The Cambridge Social History of Britain, 1750–1950.* 3 vols. Cambridge: Cambridge University Press, 1990.

Thompson, Leonard. *A History of South Africa.* Rev. ed. New Haven, Conn.: Yale University Press, 1995.

Tickner, Lisa. *The Spectacle of Women: Imagery of the Suffrage Campaign, 1907–1914.* London: Chatto and Windus, 1987.

Turner, Bryan S., and Peter Hamilton. *Citizenship: Critical Concepts.* London: Routledge, 1994.

Turner, Bryan S., ed. *Citizenship and Social Theory.* London: Sage, 1993.

van Wingerden, Sophia A. *The Women's Suffrage Movement in Britain, 1866–1928.* Hampshire: Macmillan, 1999.

Veeser, H. Aram, ed. *The New Historicism.* New York: Routledge, 1989.

Vellacott, Jo. "Feminist Consciousness and the First World War." *History Workshop Journal,* no. 23 (1987): 81–101.

———. *From Liberal to Labour with Women's Suffrage: The Story of Catherine Marshall.* Montreal and Kingston: McGill-Queen's University Press, 1993.

BIBLIOGRAPHY

Vellacott Newberry, Jo. "Anti-War Suffragists." *History* 62, no. 206 (1977): 411–425.

Vernon, James. *Politics and the People: A Study in English Political Culture, c. 1815–1867.* Cambridge: Cambridge University Press, 1993.

———, ed. *Re-Reading the Constitution: New Narratives in the Political History of England's Long Nineteenth Century.* Cambridge: Cambridge University Press, 1996.

Vicinus, Martha. *Independent Women: Work and Community for Single Women, 1850–1920.* Chicago: University of Chicago Press, 1985.

Vickery, Amanda, ed. *Women, Privilege, and Power: British Politics, 1750 to the Present.* Stanford, Calif.: Stanford University Press, 2001.

Vincent, Andrew, and Raymond Plant. *Philosophy, Politics and Citizenship: The Life and Thought of the British Idealists.* Oxford: Basil Blackwell, 1984.

Vogel, Ursula, and Michael Moran, eds. *The Frontiers of Citizenship.* New York: St. Martin's Press, 1991.

Waites, Bernard. *A Class Society at War, England, 1914–1918.* Leamington Spa: Berg, 1987.

Walkowitz, Judith R. *City of Dreadful Delight: Narratives of Sexual Danger in Late-Victorian London.* Chicago: University of Chicago Press, 1992.

———. "Going Public: Shopping, Street Harassment, and Streetwalking in Late-Victorian London." *Representations,* no. 62 (spring 1998): 1–30.

Walsh, Margaret, ed. *Working Out Gender: Perspectives from Labour History.* Aldershot, Hants, England: Ashgate, 1999.

Ward, Paul. *Red Flag and Union Jack: Englishness, Patriotism, and the British Left, 1881–1924.* Bury St. Edmunds, Suffolk: Boydell Press, 1998.

Ware, Vron. *Beyond the Pale: White Women, Racism and History.* London: Verso, 1992.

Warner, Marina. *Joan of Arc: The Image of Female Heroism.* New York: Knopf, 1981.

Warwick, Peter, ed. *The South African War: The Anglo-Boer War, 1899–1902.* London: Longman, 1980.

Weiler, Peter. *The New Liberalism: Liberal Social Theory in Great Britain, 1889–1914.* New York: Garland, 1982.

West, Robin. *Narrative, Authority, and Law.* Ann Arbor: University of Michigan Press, 1993.

Wheeler, Bonnie, and Charles T. Wood, eds. *Fresh Verdicts on Joan of Arc.* New York: Garland, 1996.

Whittick, Arnold. *Woman into Citizen.* London: Athenaeum, 1979.

Williams, Joan. "Domesticity as the Dangerous Supplement of Liberalism." *Journal of Women's History* 2, no. 3 (1991): 69–88.

Willis, Michael. *Democracy and the State, 1830–1945.* Cambridge: Cambridge University Press, 2001.

Wiltsher, Anne. *Most Dangerous Women: Feminist Peace Campaigners of the Great War.* London: Pandora Press, 1985.

Winter, Jay. *Sites of Memory, Sites of Mourning: The Great War in European Cultural History.* Cambridge: Cambridge University Press, 1995.

Woodward, Kenneth L. *Making Saints.* New York: Simon and Schuster, 1990.

Woollacott, Angela. *On Her Their Lives Depend: Munitions Workers in the Great War.* Berkeley: University of California Press, 1994.

———. *To Try Her Fortune in London: Australian Women, Colonialism, and Modernity.* New York: Oxford University Press, 2001.

Yeo, Eileen Janes, ed. *Radical Femininity: Women's Self-Representation in the Public Sphere.* Manchester: Manchester University Press, 1998.

Index

Fawcett, Millicent Garrett
  on embodiment of citizenship,
    87–89
  on militancy, 70, 105
  on the relationship of home to
    politics, 20
  on the relationship of property to
    citizenship, 15–16
  during South African War, 25, 26,
    28–29, 30, 31
  during World War I, 118
Feminism
  as critique, 20, 22, 70–71
  liberal, 14, 16–17, 26, 30, 31, 69–70,
    93–95
  socialist, 14, 22
  unitarian, 14, 92
femininity, 10, 56–57, 84–91. *See also*
  womanliness
Flatman, Ada, 127
Forcible feeding, 83–84, 89, 102
Fortnightly Review, 17
Fox, Helen, 49
Fraser, Helen, 119
Fraser, Nancy, 7
Free Church League for Women's
  Suffrage, 60, 111, 119, 128, 129
Free Church Suffrage Times (later the
  Coming Day), 119
Free Speech Defence Committee, 115
Freedom
  as absence of restraint, 92–95
  organic conception of, 95–97
  suffragette rhetoric of, 10, 92–97,
    114–15
Freewoman, 105
French Revolution, 83

Gandhi, Mohandas, 37, 89, 95
Garnett, Theresa, 137
Gaskell, Elinor Penn, 108, 175n66
Gladstone, Herbert, 55, 47, 75, 84
Gould, Barbara Ayrton, 109
Green, Barbara, 7
Grey, Sir Edward, 38

Hall, Stuart, 15
Hamilton, Cicely, 72, 85, 141
Harburn, Ellen, 133

Harrison, Mrs. Darent, 60
Hart, Heber, 100
Hastings and St. Leonard's Women's
  Suffrage Propaganda League, 128
Haverfield, Evelina, 54, 56
Healy, T. M., 58–59, 79, 80
Hearnshaw, F. J. C., 142
Henderson, Arthur, 131
Hendon Women's Franchise Society, 128
Henlé, Mr., 54
Henry, Sir Edward, 53, 114, 133
Heyrick, Elizabeth, 29
Higonnet, Margaret and Patrice, 121
Hobhouse, Emily, 29–30, 153n24
Hobson, J. A., 34
Hodge, Margaret, 124
Holmes, Marion, 96
Holmes, Vera, 53
Holton, Sandra Stanley, 7, 24, 124
Housman, Laurence, 45, 60, 99, 100
Hunger strike
  and embodiment of citizenship, 87
  and forcible feeding, 101–102
  as militancy, 3, 51, 83–84, 87, 105

Independent Labour Party, 26, 37, 38
Independent Women's Social and
  Political Union (IWSPU), 40,
  118, 128, 129
Inge, Rev. W. R., 142
Ireland, and parliamentary franchise,
  14, 19, 26
Irish Women's Franchise League, 111,
  131
Irishwomen's Suffrage Federation, 128
Isaacs, Sir Rufus, 80, 81

Jamaica, 13–14, 26
James, Susan, 9
Jarvis, Inspector, 53, 54
Joan of Arc, 10, 84–89, 170n35
Johnson, Alderman Edward (London),
  130
Jones, Gareth Stedman, 7
Jorgensen-Earp, Cheryl, 99
Joyce, Patrick, 7
Judiciary
  challenges to, 72–74, 113
  criticism of, 10, 63, 64, 66, 69, 70